D1552471

WORKSPACE

WORKSPACE
Creating Environments in Organizations

Franklin D. Becker

PRAEGER

PRAEGER SPECIAL STUDIES • PRAEGER SCIENTIFIC

Library of Congress Cataloging in Publication Data

Becker, Franklin D.
  Workspace: Creating environments in organizations.

  Bibliography: p.
  Includes index.
  1. Work environment.   I. Title.
HD7261.B36   658.2   81-10671
ISBN 0-03-059137-6   AACR2

Published in 1981 by Praeger Publishers
CBS Educational and Professional Publishing
A Division of CBS, Inc.
521 Fifth Avenue, New York, New York 10175 U.S.A.

© 1981 by Praeger Publishers

123456789   145   987654321

Printed in the United States of America

PREFACE

After more than three-quarters of a century of formal studies of organizations, we still know relatively little about the role physical settings play in them. This book is intended as an initial step toward filling this gap.

Rather than assessing the relationship between the effects of selected environmental variables like noise, lighting, temperature, and density on measures of productivity, satisfaction, and motivation, *Workspace* takes a broader view. While it presents evidence on the relationship between the effects of selected environmental variables, such as spatial position, privacy, and territory, on behaviors like commitment, motivation, and participation, this is not the main emphasis. Underlying these kinds of concerns is a more basic question, from an organizational-development perspective: the nature of the processes through which physical settings are created in organizations. Who makes what kinds of decisions regarding environmental form and use, on what basis, and for what (and whose) ends? These processes are social and they occur in a political context. They are directly concerned with the allocation of scarce resources among individuals and groups with diverse and often competing values, goals, and expectations.

I view the physical setting as a socially constructed environmental-support system and communication medium. Its form and management are shaped by conceptions of the environment, of work and workers, and of productivity. I have tried to suggest alternative ways of thinking about the design, management, and evaluation of physical settings in complex organizations that are in keeping with trends toward increased democratization of the workplace. There is no doubt that changes, radical changes, are going to occur in the American workplace. They will be stimulated by our desire to remain competitive in world markets, as well as at home. As the Japanese are showing us, productivity is not only a function of sophisticated technology. It is driven, to a large extent, as American companies are beginning to acknowledge, by how we organize work and workers. If productivity is the lock, they key is likely to be employee involvement.

Personnel functions have generally taken a back-seat role in comparison to marketing, production, and finance functions, but they are likely to become more important as awareness grows, among top management, that the individual employee's experience at work is critical to economic success. Organizations will spend hundreds of thousands of dollars on new personnel training programs in the process of genuinely attempting to restructure the way in which work is organized. Employees will be asked to participate, and their voices heard, at all levels of the organization. Yet, if past experience is any guide, the potential for the most pervasive resource in the work environment, the physical setting, to contribute to these efforts will be largely overlooked.

The fundamental premise of this book is that the nature of the physical settings of organizations, and the processes through which they are created, can have a significant impact on the quality of work life and on the effectiveness of these new programs.

A word about my intent: This book advances a particular point of view. But one of the many things I learned from my friend, Bob Sommer, is that advocacy need not, and indeed should not, ignore facts. Nor should facts and figures be presented as though they have a life of their own. I have drawn on research evidence where it was available and I thought it appropriate. I have also felt free to speculate about the role of physical settings in organizations. I did not restrict myself to presenting a body of well-documented facts. I could not, for they do not exist. The intent, rather, is to generate discussion and research, about the role of physical settings in organizations, among students of business and public administration, of environmental psychology and design, and of organizational behavior. The book is also intended for practitioners, despite its academic cast. The intent is an important, but modest one: to stimulate reassessment of working assumptions and operating procedures, and to explore how some of these might be improved and altered to meet the challenge of continually evolving worker expectations.

I have benefited greatly from discussions with architects, facility planners, and colleagues and students in psychology, planning, and organizational behavior. There is an increasing awareness that the physical setting contributes in significant ways to our behavior and to our satisfaction with what we do and who we do it with, not only at home, but in the workplace. Many of the people I have talked with are committed to creating outstanding facilities that work for all who use them. I hope that this book contributes to their efforts, if in no other way than by raising answerable questions.

Much of my thinking was influenced by Bob Sommer. Linda Gostanian, Jackie Landau, and Maddie Holzer read the original manuscript and made many useful comments. As usual, Eva Pantos typed rewrite after rewrite without complaint. Her efforts were indispensable. Harriet Becker did the Figures.

CONTENTS

LIST OF FIGURES

WORKSPACE

1

HUMAN/ENVIRONMENT RELATIONS
IN PERSPECTIVE

We usually take the obvious for granted. We store it in the back of our minds until its existence is threatened or its use impaired. Then we pluck, from the back shelf of our consciousness, our awareness of its value, often its essential contribution to some activity: broken legs reveal the gift of walking; earthquakes, our unquestioning faith in the stability of our surroundings. With the exception of a few professionals whose identity is defined by an interest in the nature, quality, and creation of our physical surroundings— people like architects, industrial designers, product engineers, operations researchers, geographers—the very pervasiveness of our physical surroundings typically masks its importance.

SOCIAL SCIENCES AND DESIGN

Yet over the last two decades, an increasing number of psychologists, sociologists, urban planners, and architects have been systematically exploring the relationships between people and their physical surroundings (Sommer, 1969; Proshansky et al., 1970; Michelson, 1970; Lynch, 1960; Altman, 1975). Knowledge gained from studies of the relationships between people and their physical surroundings provides a basis for planning environments that are responsive to and supportive of intended social and programmatic functions: schools that promote learning, hospitals that facilitate the delivery of quality health care, offices that are pleasant to work in and that promote desired and appropriate forms of interaction and activities. What distinguishes this work from research begun in the 1920s by the Chicago school of human ecologists (Theodorson, 1961), and having its roots in English demographic studies of crime and delinquency done in the

1

last quarter of the 19th century, is the desire to go beyond describing the ways in which social behaviors are geographically distributed. Environmental psychologists and sociologists have been explicit about wanting to influence the nature of experience and behavior by creating physical settings congruent with and supportive of specified individual, organizational, and community goals. Their intent, when working at the facility level, has been organizational development, though it is seldom labeled as such (Steele, 1973). The premise has been that research which clarified human/environment relations would provide a solid empirical basis, for making design decisions, to those most responsible for determining the nature and quality of the built environment.

As a result of the fragile bridge still being built between the social sciences and the design professions, changes in design practice have occurred. There is greater concern today, than there was 15 years ago, for designing buildings that are sensitive to human requirements and preferences. There is little doubt that what Carol Weiss (1977) calls the "enlightenment function" of policy research, in which concepts, ideas, and information are filtered more or less unconsciously into policymakers' decisions, has occurred. Yet environments are not created solely by architects or other specially trained design professionals.

The orientation toward the design professions that has characterized much of the work and many publications in the field of environmental psychology and sociology has tended to obscure the role managers and administrators play in day-to-day environmental-design decisions. They decide who will use what space and equipment, in what ways, when, and with whom. They decide when to renovate, or when to build a new facility. These kinds of organizational decisions constitute a form of environmental design.

DEFINING DESIGN

Part of the reason managers and administrators have been overlookded as principal players in the creation of physical settings stems from a failure to distinguish between environmental planning and design stimulated by the decision to construct a new building or do a major renovation, and the kind of planning and design required on an ongoing basis over the entire life of a building (Boutourline, 1970). As one person has quipped (Propst, 1978), "There is life after installation." The primary liaison with architects tended to put this distinction aside.

Architects have little or no direct control or responsibility over a building or renovation once it is legally completed. Their role focuses their attention on a particular stage in the design process. Their professional self-interest tends to discourage design determined by decisions about use of existing facilities. Designers often view such involvement as a form of interference because these decisions may modify or undermine the uses they envisioned. Most students of organizations have rather uncritically accepted the designer's profession-bound ground rules for defining space as that form-shaping activity which precedes occupancy. By doing so, they have excised from consideration important questions concerning the ways in which facilities can continuously be created by various users over time. They have also obscured the effects that organizing space, facilities, activities, and people, in alternative ways, may have on behavior.

The planning and design of new buildings or major renovations has received considerable attention (Preiser, 1978; Sanoff, 1977). Ongoing environmental-space management, as a form of environmental design involving day-to-day decisions about the use of facilities (Boutourline, 1970) is recognized, but it has not been institutionalized in a meaningful way. The belief that it is institutionalized in organizations is one of the assumptions I hope this book will dispel.

FACILITY PLANNING AND MANAGEMENT

Facility planning and management is the process of organizing the internal proximate environment of facilities, such as schools, hospitals, offices, and factories, in relation to people, technology, and activities. Within large facilities with multiple components, it involves determining the location and arrangement of these component parts in relation to each other. Organizing occurs along a continuum. It ranges from the planning and design of the basic form of the facilities (including selection of furniture, equipment, and technical systems) to managing these environmental elements once they have been selected and are in use. The distinction between planning and management as organizing activities is useful since it highlights the fact that organizing facilities is a continuous process that involves both physical elements and rules and regulations (formal and informal) governing their use. Together, they comprise a "sociotechnical" system (Cooper and Foster, 1971) that is created and maintained by all users of the facility, not only those with formal design training.

Facility planning is thus concerned with the decision to make, as well as deciding the form of, major additions or renovations. Facility management is concerned with decisions about the use of an existing environment or facility on an ongoing basis: decisions about which group can use the conference room; where the file cabinets should be located; how often the office landscape should be changed, by whom, and on what basis; when the corridor needs to be repainted, and in what colors; whether secretaries should be allowed in staff dining rooms, or the dining room should be separated into areas used by specific groups. And it deals with how these decisions are reached.

The purpose of facility planning and management is to shape the form of the proximate environment of facilities such that individuals and groups are able to comfortably, efficiently, safely, and with enjoyment, carry out the kinds of activities, and have the kinds of experiences, which they desire and for which an organization or institution exists. The orientation takes into consideration all users of the system. Its basic premise is that no organization or institution can become outstanding or remain so over long periods of time unless there is a good fit between the environmental-support structure, organizational structure, and a full range of user requirements.

Those attributes of the facility setting which may be organized to support or constrain individual or group action and to communicate meaning and value, and with which the facility planner and manager must be concerned are:

- The spatial form of settings: the size, shape, and character of bounding surfaces; and the internal organization of objects withing a setting and their connection to ther settings. Circulation paths that bring some employees into more frequent contact than others; the height and opacity of partitions between offices; or the location of offices in relation to conference rooms, libraries, and windows reflect decisions about the spatial form of settings.
- Patterns of activity: the location, intensity, type, flow, and scheduling of activities within and between settings. Decisions about what time employees should arrive and depart from work; scheduling of lunch, breaks, meetings, and use of facilities like shops and laboratories; and the number of people who can use a facility are the kinds of factors that determine activity patterns.
- Communications: implicit and explicit signals, signs, or symbols communicate information to users. These range from explicit memos and signs, detailing formal rules and regulations, to decisions about the type of material that lines one's walls (wood versus drywall) and indicates one's standing in the organizational hierarchy.
- Ambience: the microclimate, light, sounds, texture, and smells of a setting create its ambience. Selection of overhead fluorescent lights rather than task-ambient lighting, the type and effectiveness of sound-absorbant materials, and the use of colors, as well as the degree to which these environmental characteristics are responsive to individual control, are some of the factors that influence the setting's ambience.

The facility planner and/or manager must also be concerned with how these characteristics are affected by, and in turn affect, the social and organizational system. To what extent do decisions about degree of enclosure, or the arrangement of offices or circulation paths, for example, influence the opportunity for working and social relationships to develop? To what extent do they place special burdens on supervisors in insuring effective performance of those working under them? To what extent do such decisions take into account differences in authority and status, individual work style, or an organization's implicit and explicit views of work and workers? One must also be able to view the operation of the facility as a whole within the broad social, political, and economic contexts of a city, region, state, or country. A facility located in San Francisco exists in a different social and political context than one located in a small midwestern city. Organizations need to be sensitive to the difference between being located in the heart of the financial district of a major city and in being in a suburban location. Some of the facility planner's and manager's responsibilities are outlined in Figure 1.1.

Environmentally related decisions are routinely made in organizations, usually without much attention to their ramifications for organizational behavior. The phrases "environmental-space management," "facility management," and "facility planning" contribute to the problem. (In Chapter 8, the terms "ecosystem planning" and "milieu management" are suggested as ways of conceptualizing the breadth of the facility planner's or manager's role as conceived here.) The language is misleading. This is an acute problem because the way in which one defines the concept will largely determine whether or not one perceives the function being fulfilled. The words "environmental" and "space" are associated with architects, designers, or planners. Although "management" is associated with administrators, managers, and executives, the overall impression of the phrase "environmental-space management" is that it refers to activities falling within the domain of the design and engineering professions. Management concerns about authority structure, supervision patterns, motivation, alienation, and communication appear to fall outside the domain of "space management." This separation of functions is supported by the kinds of persons found in departments which have an explicit responsibility for environmental or design matters within the organization.

In smaller organizations, persons without any special training are made responsible for space allocation, often as a subsidiary aspect of other responsibilities. Most of their energy is spent trying to resolve crises resulting from fluctuating staffing and programmatic requirements. Success is finding a place, any place, for new or displaced persons and programs. In larger organizations, staff members of in-house facility-planning departments are generally trained as architects, interior designers, or engineers. Most of their work centers on plant reorganizations and on coordinating major additions or new buildings in response to new product lines, new technologies, or expansion of production. Increasingly, with the introduction of modular furniture systems, facility planners are also responsible for rearranging in response to directives from changes in staffing patterns, new technologies, and changes in market conditions.

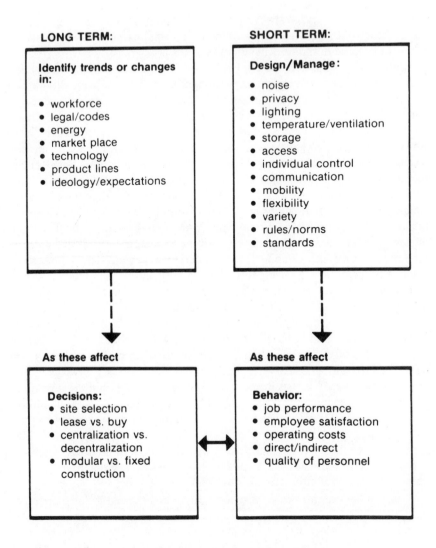

LONG TERM:

Identify trends or changes in:

- workforce
- legal/codes
- energy
- market place
- technology
- product lines
- ideology/expectations

SHORT TERM:

Design/Manage:

- noise
- privacy
- lighting
- temperature/ventilation
- storage
- access
- individual control
- communication
- mobility
- flexibility
- variety
- rules/norms
- standards

As these affect

Decisions:
- site selection
- lease vs. buy
- centralization vs. decentralization
- modular vs. fixed construction

As these affect

Behavior:
- job performance
- employee satisfaction
- operating costs
- direct/indirect
- quality of personnel

FIGURE 1.1 Environmental-Space Management: Responsibilities

A MULTISKILLED ACTIVITY

Facility planning and management is not a separate profession, although it may be practiced or studied as a speciality. It is a problem-solving activity that lies on the boundaries between architecture, interior-space planning and product design, organizational behavior, planning, and environmental psychology. It is an issue that is confronted and responded to by professionals from all these groups. It is however, a problem-solving activity of such complexity as to require training beyond that which is ordinarily a part of the education of these professions.

The facility planner and/or manager must be able to develop solutions to problems utilizing existing environmental, organizational, and personnel resources, and to develop performance specifications and design requirements (programming) when necessary. Many large firms have their own in-house design department to implement the kinds of programs developed by a facility planner. In the case of smaller firms or situations where major renovation or design is required, the facility planner will develop detailed programs, act as liaison between the organization and the outside architects, and review preliminary and final plans to insure they meet the specified design requirements.

These kinds of responsibilities require a broad range of capacities. While no single facility planner is likely to be equally proficient or interested in all areas, he or she should at least be familiar with most of the following types of capacities and be skillful in several of them:

- Assessing environmental performance: This involves being able to project economic, population, energy, technological, and social trends; being able to identify appropriate environmental supports for given activity and interaction patterns; helping identify and rank objectives, programs, and facilities that should be eliminated, preserved, or modified.
- Assessing organizational impact: This includes the ability to predict and evaluate the effects that various ways of organizing space and facilities have on individuals, small groups, the organization as a whole, and the community within which it is located.
- Designing support systems: These support systems include the physical design of the facility, and the design and selection of equipment and technology. They also include coordinated sets of actions and policies aimed at complementing the physical design and determining use patterns.
- Evaluating support systems: This involves reassessing, following implementation and use, the level of effective performance the changes in the environment have produced.

In addition to these capacities, facility planners often find themselves involved with a number of other activities (Schlitt, 1980) and should be familiar with them. These include financial accounting, contract and lease negotiation, construction management, furniture and equipment purchase, land acquisition, and use of technical systems. Given this spectrum of concerns and responsibilities, the need for special training, beyond what the traditional disciplines like architecture, engineering, and organizational behavior provide, becomes clear.

Architects are, by training and inclination, more often interested in the way the environment looks than how it functions programmatically (Becker, 1978; Sommer, 1969; Perin, 1970; Preiser, 1978). When explicitly considered, its function is generally defined as accommodating a specified number of employees in specified spaces within a cost framework provided by the client (Steele, 1973). Even when designers are concerned with the programmatic implications of a design, or want a more behaviorally based rationale for design decisions, neither their own training, nor their staff's, nor that of staff in departments like organizational development or management is of much help.

Concern with the environment is structurally separated from concern with program, with personnel, and with management. By the time designers become involved in the design process, the problem has already been defined and a solution related to some kind of physical modification identified. Design is essentially a reactive profession. Operations engineers and human-factor specialists, who are also responsible for decisions about the physical setting, are primarily concerned with production technology and the design of equipment and work procedures. The performance of tasks is analyzed in terms of human capabilities (perception, dexterity, memory, fatigue, attention), largely outside the social context within which the tasks are routinely performed in the everyday world of work.

In contrast, organizational-development and personnel specialists are typically concerned primarily about the social context of work. Their interest is in group processes, norms, and expectations; authority structures; incentive plans; personnel testing and screening; organizational size; and the organizational environment, including economic conditions, the nature of the labor force, and the nature and diversity of the market, and its predictability. A basic concern with the relation of these kinds of social behaviors to characteristics of the physical setting and its management rarely occurs. The role the physical setting plays as a medium of communication, as well as how it structures interaction and communication patterns, remains largely overlooked.

Exceptions prove the rule. There are architectural and planning firms that take into consideration issues other than aesthetics, including the social and behavioral aspects of design. But they are not typical of architectural practice, and they have little to do with issues of organizational design and planning. Almost never are they involved in the operation of a facility after it is legally turned over to the client. Similarly, there are some organizational-development experts who are sensitive to and concerned about the role of the physical setting in the organization (Steele, 1973; Pfeffer, 1980). Yet organizational theory as a whole continues to study behavior as though the physical context within which it occurs is irrelevant. Operations reserachers and human-factors specialists typically ignore the ways in which users invest the equipment and processes they design with meaning, and how the environment thus created affects patterns of work activity, interpersonal relations, motivation, and other behaviors central to the study of behavior in organizations. Part of this orientation stems from a focus on the environment as direct support system.

ENVIRONMENT AS SUPPORT:
FIRST-ORDER EFFECTS

The obvious role of the physical setting is to provide one the requisite support to engage in one's job or carry out an activity effectively, comfortably, and with dignity. Ranging from prosthetic devices life artificial limbs that enable persons to walk who otherwise could not, to a telephone that becomes an extension of the voice, allowing people to communicate directly who otherwise could not, to a private conference room that allows a small number of persons to interact without interruption, the physical setting, and its equipment and furnishings, are generally analyzed in terms of their first-order, or direct, effects on behavior. These effects are critical. Failure to construe the physical setting as a basic programmatic support system is like designing a magnificent train and trying to operate it on a dirt path. It may run, but at a far lower level of performance than that for which it was designed. A program without an appropriate environmental-support system is as useful as a law without enabling legislation. Both serve mainly as symbols of actions while diverting attention from inaction (Edelman, 1971). Yet viewing the physical setting as teacher's "aide," or work "assistant," focuses on only one level of environmental meaning: the instrumental, or the physical setting as direct activity-support system. It is this aspect of the physical setting's influence on human behavior that operations researchers, human-factor specialists, and others interested in work or performance take as their special province.

The environment operates at several levels simultaneously, however. Our physical surroundings serve symbolic and expressive purposes as well as instrumental ones (Gibson, 1950; Sommer, 1972; Ruesch and Kees, 1964). The role of the physical setting as it serves these functions, as well as in serving the instrumental, can also be analyzed in terms of second-order, or indirect, effects on behavior. With this pair of lenses attached, the focus may be on the environment as catalyst. These effects are typically masked and difficult to trace, but important because they are the link to the kinds of behavior and activity patterns that are of direct interest to administrators, managers, and organization theorists: commitment, involvement, conflict, misunderstanding, resistance.

ENVIRONMENT AS CATALYST: SECOND-ORDER EFFECTS

The idea of environment as prosthesis, or support, is reasonably easy to understand and document. Environment as catalyst is more difficult to comprehend, and much harder to investigate. As a catalyst, some aspect of the physical setting sets in motion a series of linked events or behavioral reactions. These reactions may be positive or negative. Adequate space, comfortable furniture, acceptable humidity, temperature, and lighting levels, and the opportunity for movement, for example, will directly increase user satisfaction. In addition to the importance of the satisfaction per se, such environmental factors may also stimulate types of social interaction and communication that, in turn, provide the opportunity for building trust, demonstrating concern, or providing timely feedback. These factors are related to various measures of organizational effectiveness (see Figure 1.2).

The importance of the catalyst by itself may be negligible. Its value lies in its capacity to set in motion new events or processes. These events or processes, in turn, may, in combination, act as a catalyst for additional reactions. The direct value, for an individual employee, of being able to take home a computer terminal, for example, is that one can work at home, presumably at one's leisure. The seemingly obvious first-order effect may set in motion, however, a series of other unexpected events, processes, and reactions. Working at home means one avoids the interruptions that frequently occur in the office. Avoiding these interruptions allows one to become more productive. Become more productive (writing more papers, for instance), in turn, may be associated with professional recognition and advancement. This behavior is reinforcing, so one begins to spend more and more time at home, now not only working at the terminal, but writing, reading, corresponding. These may be positive, and not entirely expected outcomes of relocating the terminal.

At the same time productivity is increasing because of the relocation, one might find that much less time is made available for students, colleagues, and for general department affairs. Spontaneous discussions that used to occur in and around the office now may not. Feedback on ideas, efforts to keep up with new developments and to develop working relationships with colleagues and students may decline, and with it the quality of the work. At

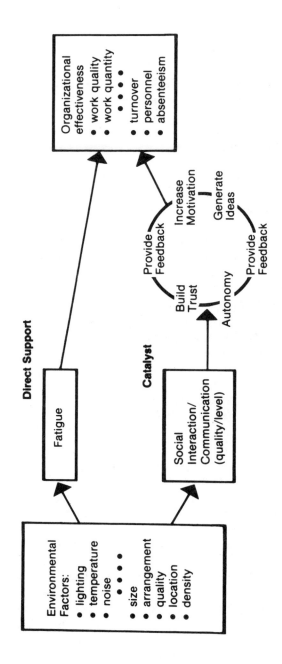

FIGURE 1.2 Environment as Support and Catalyst

11

home, if there are children, the nature and lcoation of their play, and the quality and extent of their interaction with the parent, may be altered as a result of more time being spent in the home. Family tension may be exacerbated, or reduced.

Construing the physical environment as catalyst requires anyone planning, designing, or managing a facility to think of it as a series of linked, interdependent settings. Any physical setting, from a psychiatric ward to a landscaped office or an individual work cubicle, exists as part of the larger and more encompassing physical and social setting it influences and is influenced by. Administrative decisions or physical design changes made in one part of a system will affect behavior in other parts. Decisions concerning the number of persons that share an office, the size of the office, the times when a conference room can be used, or the necessary procedures for reserving the room alter the nature of the physical setting and the behavior that occurs in it, or in spaces related to it.

These kinds of administrative decisions set in motion a variety of adaptation strategies by individuals, and these behaviors, not only the intended or expected behaviors, are the ones most in need of study and least likely to be studied. These are second-order, or "inconspicuous," effects (Steele, 1973). We will only find them if we hunt for them. They are potentially very important because they begin to justify an interest in the environmental setting, on the part of organizational theorists as well as administrators, that has not been piqued by the focus on the more direct, instrumental effects of the physical setting on behavior.

THE PHYSICAL SETTING AND ORGANIZATIONAL DEVELOPMENT

Organizational theorists are very sensitive to the fact that work in organizations is typically carried out in a social situation. They need to become equally sensitive to the fact that work in organizations is also always carried out in a physical setting. One of the traps theorists fall into is making distinctions, for analytical or methodological purposes, that unintentionally distort their understanding of a system. The physical environment is separated from social behavior; job design is separated from social context. A cake can be described in terms of its separate elements: flour, butter, sugar, eggs; but to know anything about cake, one needs to know how these elements interact, especially under different environmental conditions.

Concern about productivity and worker motivation are permanent fixtures of the organizational world, as are the costs of rapid staff turnover, poor-quality work, absenteeism, lack of employee commitment to the organization, and in some instances, damage to or theft of plant facilities, supplies, and equipment. These problems are due in part to many workers' intense dislike of the specific, often simple and repetitive, tasks they are required to perform. Their dissatisfaction derives, as well, from what are perceived as (and often are) capricious and nonspecific performance evaluations, arbitrary work procedures, and loud, dangerous, and unpleasant work environments.

These issues have been addressed in a number of different ways by human-relations programs, job enlargement, development of new incentive plans, more specific feedback, more elaborate screening, increased worker involvement. For the most part, systematic studies of these programs show mixed results. It is not my intention here to review the extensive research literature on organizational behavior (see Dunnette [1976]; Porter et al. [1975]). Rather, I would like to suggest that almost all organizational theory fails to take sufficiently into account the physical setting of work. Since this is as permanent a fixture of organizational life as authority structures, incentive plans, and supervisory practices, and there is research evidence that links these concerns to environmental factors (see Chapter 6), the reasons the physical setting has received little attention by organizational theorists are worth examining.

2

THE PHYSICAL SETTING AS
SOCIAL PROCESS

How the physical environment is construed, what our view of work and workers is, and the ways in which we define and study productivity and effectiveness—these have all contributed to the neglect of the role of the physical setting in organizational research. Organizational consultants are often sensitive to the role the physical setting plays in organizational processes, but they typically incorporate these observations into conversations as anecdotes that become part of folklore, rather than using them as a starting point for more systematic and empirical investigations. Without a conceptual scaffolding onto which they can be hung and organized, observations indeed become stories rather than studies.

Our conception of the physical environment is constrained by its concreteness, its apparent literalness. Because we can touch, smell, and see our physical surroundings in a way that we cannot apprehend social structure, we tend to construe the physical environment in narrower, more static, and less significant ways than we do the social environment. We focus on product in the former case, on process in the latter. One reason norms, for example, may seem so much more significant than furniture arrangement is that we simply have not spent as much effort looking at how physical settings develop, or at how they help structure and influence social relations or developmental processes, as we have with a social product like a norm. If we spend as much effort trying to understand how our physical surroundings are created, and how they influence social relations, as we have with similar aspects of norms, we might begin to develop a deeper understanding of the role of physical settings in social and organizational life. This chapter and the next one attempt to do this by treating design, in its broadest sense, as a process of organizing, to which general theories of organizing can be fruitfully applied. It is useful to begin by looking at the major influence a

14

single set of studies has had on organizational theorists' view of environment.

It is impossible to understand organizational theorists' view of what the environment is and what role it plays in organizations without mentioning what are probably the most famous and influential studies of organizational behavior ever done: the Hawthorne Studies (Roethlisberger and Dickson, 1939). These studies, done in the late 1930s at Western Electric, changed the attention in research on organizations to a focus that persists to this day.

Early management theorists focused on formal, prescribed aspects of organizations. Their concern was with how greater rationality and efficiency could be built into the design of organizations (Porter et al., 1975). This particular set of research spectacles was formed within the framework of scientific management, to be discussed in detail in Chapter 4. Organizational problems that developed were usually attributed to "recalcitrant workers." Solutions were sought in the development of more adequate designs for the formal organizational structure. Better employee-selection systems, dismantling of work into its constituent components, and the design of the workplace and equipment occupied the time of industrial psychologists, operations researchers, and human-factors specialists.

Concentration on the formal aspects of organizations began to weaken in the 1930s as it became apparent that the study of the formal organiztion by itself was insufficient to either understand behavior in organizations or change it. The Hawthorne studies explored how formal organizational factors and physical characteristics of the work environment, including varying light levels and the presence or absence of Musak, influenced employee performance. Contrary to expectations, the results demonstrated the existence and influence of the informal social structures which pervade organizations, and which are much less subject to formal organizational control than, for example, employee-selection procedures. No one interested in the behavior of employees could any longer consider them as isolated individuals. Individuals were now viewed as operating within a social context where group influences, social status, informal communication, roles, and norms influenced their behavior (Porter et al., 1975).

Unfortunately for the study of organizational ecology, the Hawthorne studies effectively exiled the role of the physical setting from its field of consideration, also, presumably, on the basis of solid empirical evidence. The possibility that informal communication patterns, roles, norms, and other social processes were influenced by aspects of the physical setting were not given much consideration in light of the interpretations given to other findings related to aspects of the physical setting specifically investigated.

With respect to the physical setting, the very general impression drawn from the Hawthorne studies has been that the physical environment of work (e.g., lighting level, presence or absence of Musak) had no effect. This impression is based on the fact that regardless of changes in lighting level, for example, productivity increased. Sommer (1968) has argued that all the Hawthorne studies demonstrated was that a simple deterministic model for environment-behavior effects is inadequate. The environment did make a difference, but its effect was a function of the ways in which individuals interpreted the changes. Changes in the physical environment were taken as very tangible evidence by employees that management was concerned about their work environment and welfare. The environmental changes operated as part of a nonverbal communication system (Becker, 1977). They were a form of paralanguage that supported other cues employees had that they were special, including being sequestered in a special room and having highly placed experts fuss over them. In effect, the employees created the environment they reacted to, not the researchers. We will develop this point in detail.

The same effects could not have been found had the employees' physical location in the plant not been altered. The development of informal norms the researchers chose to emphasize required physical separation from other employees. At the same time the researchers were denying the importance of the physical environment, and attributing their findings to the operation of social forces, they were demonstrating, by the way they designed the study (creating a special spatially segregated work environment), that these social forces were highly determined by a characteristic of the physical setting: namely, the physical arrangement of workers. The layout of the rooms allowed easy contact among workers and facilitated the formation and maintenance of group norms concerning behavior and output. Homans (1950, pp. 80–81) pointed out:

> The men were working in a room of a certain shape, with fixtures such as benches oriented in a certain way. They were working on materials with certain tools. These things formed the physical and technical environment in which the human relationships within the room developed, and they made these relationships more likely to develop in some ways than in others. For instance, the sheer geographical position of the men within the room had something to do with the organization of work and even with the appearance of cliques.

The premise that single cause-and-effect relationships characterize behavior, and can be identified and manipulated, made the interpretation of the physical-setting data as having no effect almost inevitable. It also prevented the researchers from looking for more complex ways in which the environment might relate to social phenomena. The Hawthorne studies demonstrate the power of scientific paradigms to control and limit the nature of scientific investigation and interpretation (Kuhn, 1962).

The Hawthorne studies suffered additional problems centering around the interpretation of the findings. In the sense that the Hawthorne studies created a novel and unfamiliar environment, they were more akin to a laboratory study than to a field study done under natural conditions. The problem with laboratory studies of performance done under novel or unfamiliar conditions is that the behavior observed is often a function of the special circumstances of the study (including its physical location and the characteristics of the physical surroundings), its temporary duration, and the lack of ego-involvement with the products produced during the study (this was not the case with the Hawthorne studies, since worker's wages were based on their productivity during the experiment). Sommer describes a study done in 1928 by Hovey that provides a dramatic example of some of these kinds of problems (and the difficulty in generalizing about the findings for the everyday world of work). Sommer (1968, p. 594) notes the experimenter

> administered two forms of an intelligence test to 171 people. The first form was filled out in a quiet room, the second in a room with seven bells, five buzzers, a 550-watt spotlight, a 90,000-volt rotary spark gap, a phonograph, two organ pipes of varying pitches, three metal whistles, a 55-pound circular saw mounted on a wooden frame, a well-known photographer taking pictures, and four students doing acrobatics. Sometimes there was quiet in the second room, but at other times a number of these distractors were operating simultaneously. In terms of outcome, the group did as well in the noisy room as in the quiet room.

In assessing this type of research, Sommer notes that such studies illustrate environmental events whose social import depends upon psychological factors. He (1968, p. 594) argues that people can tolerate minor and major nuisances and even threats to life and property if they believe their sacrifice is for a good cause:

> Morale can rise as a group's external situation deteriorates. Does this prove that external conditions have no effects on morale? Hardly—it would seem to establish the opposite. Environmental changes do not act directly upon human organisms. They are interpreted according to the individual's needs, set, and state of awareness. What has so disparagingly been called the Hawthorne or placebo effect is the very heart of the subject matter of psychology—need, motivation, perception, and psychophysics. If monetary reward affected output in a direct and unequivocal manner, industrial psychology could merge with economics.

The environment, when abstracted and considered in isolation from the social and historical context within which it is embedded, is, indeed, not terribly meaningful. But the problem lies in the senselessness of the researcher's conceptualization of the environment, not in the senselessness of the environment itself.

As Proshansky (1970, p. 28) argues, at the level of human interaction in any social setting, the individual responds not to a diffusion of proximal and distal light and sound waves, shapes, and structures, objects and spaces, but to another person, who is engaged in a specific activity in a specific place, for a specific purpose. Physical settings—simple or complex—evoke complex human responses in the form of feelings, attitudes, values, expectancies, and desires, and it is in this sense, as well as by their known physical properties, that their relationships to human experience and behavior must be understood. This is a phenomenological approach to the environment, one in which the object of study is not the environment as it is, but as it is experienced. It is what Koffka (1935) called the "behavioral environment."

The fact that the environment as experienced is the object of study is not inconsistent with the observation that human behavior, in relation to a physical setting, is enduring and consistent over time and situations. Common tasks, shared space and equipment, identical operating procedures, and similar education and socioeconomic backgrounds form the foundation of similar experience. Yet these differ among employees in the same organizations, leaving the problem of defining the environment, whether social or physical, unresolved.

DEFINING THE ORGANIZATIONAL ENVIRONMENT

Difficulty defining what constitutes the organizational environment, and where its boundaries lie, is a major conceptual issue in organizational theory (Starbuck, 1976; Weick, 1969). Most theorists view the individual as responding to environmental contingencies. These contingencies can occur inside or outside the organization, but the notion is that one responds to what one regards as a given. Karl Weick has persuasively challenged this prevailing viewpoint. In the discussion that follows, I will rely heavily on his work (1969), and in particular on the concept of the environment as being continually created through individual attention process. Weick's approach is similar to Proshansky's (1970). It is useful because it provides a framework for construing the physical environment dynamically as a social process amenable to the kinds of analyses appropriate to other types of social structure.

Attention

The environment, according to Weick, is a phenomenon tied to processes of attention. Unless something is attended to, it does not exist. Contrary to the notion that what we attend to is a function of enduring sets, or stable characteristics that are constituted on the basis of past experience and are carried from one situation to another, Weick argues that our perception helps us create as well as react to an environment. The fundamental question, for Weick, involves what is happening in the person's present situation that controls the nature of the attention one directs to one's past experience (1969, p. 39).

Meaning, according to Weick, involves the kind of attention directed to the past; that is, attention to actions we have already taken. One's current interest and concerns influence the events, processes, and behavior we choose to focus our attention on. Any action performed in the past may be subject to changing interpretations over time as a function of changing interests or concerns. And since any action carries surplus meaning (our attention is directed only to a portion of the total possible behaviors we have engaged in), portions of the stream of experience that went unnoticed at the moment of a reflective glance can still be noticed on some future occasion.

Weick's conception of organizing processes is useful in shifting the focus of attention from the physical setting as a product, which is viewed as something relatively permanent and unresponsive and largely existing outside of everyday ongoing social processes, to the physical setting as a dynamic ongoing process. As such, the physical setting can no longer be accepted as a given. The way in which it develops, its meaning, and the role it plays become open to question. The remainder of this chapter describes how the physical settings of organizations are created, and suggests some of the roles these settings play for individuals and organizations when they are created in particular ways.

To say that a physical setting is "created" does not imply that either the process of creation or the consequences of it are conscious and deliberate. The opposite is true in many cases. One of the reasons so little attention has been paid to the physical environment as it affects organizational behavior is that the unending concern, in all organizations, with space and equipment is taken as evidence that organizations are aware of the role of the physical setting, and are constantly operating on it to achieve certain desired goals. Yet our physical surroundings generally enter into our awareness only when they deviate from our expectations, and particularly when they deviate in a negative direction. It is much easier for us to identify the dysfunctional effects of environments than their role in facilitating or promoting desired behaviors. Most people are unaware of how their behavior is affected by characteristics of their physical surroundings, but this does not mean they are unmoved by these (Sommer, 1969; Proshansky et al., 1970; Hall, 1966). To learn what individuals attend to, we need to focus as much on their behavior, what they actually do, as on what they say they do or attend to.

The question is not whether or not organizations are concerned about space, or whether they create their physical settings. The question is how they are concerned, and how they create the physical setting. What considerations are taken into account in environmental decision making? Who makes these decisions? On what basis are decisions made, and with what attention not only to immediate but to long-term effects? And for which employees?

CREATING ENVIRONMENTS: DEEMPHASIZING FORMAL PROCESSES

The prevailing view is that environments are created at specially designated points in time, and by persons with formal responsibility for this activity. The special times typically have followed the decision to make a major renovation, or design a new building. The persons with formal responsibility are those in the design professions: architects and interior designers, and their associates, the engineers, lighting and temperature consultants, human-factor specialists, and operations researchers.

A new building or a renovation is completed and the facility occupied. Over time, beginning with initial occupancy, programmatic dysfunctions related to the environment will occur. These are usually ignored until the dysfunctions reach the point where they have been recognizable to everyone for years and are now such an overwhelming barrier to effective organizational functioning that a decision is made to return to the drawing boards. A major design project is undertaken, and the cycle begins anew (see Figure 2.1).

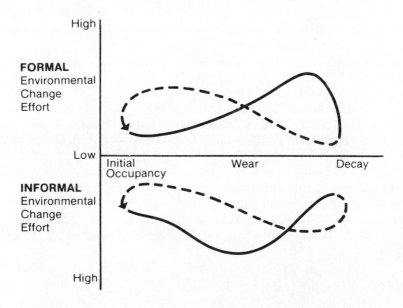

FIGURE 2.1 Formal and Informal Environmental-Change Effort

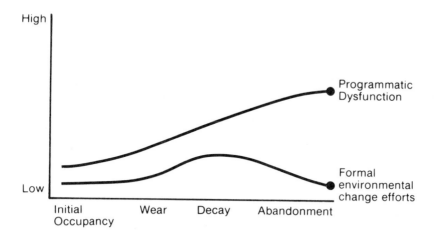

FIGURE 2.2 Programmatic Dysfunction in Relation to Environmental Change

Figure 2.2 describes the level of environmentally related programmatic dysfunction as a function of time spent in a building, from initial occupancy to final abandonment of the building altogether. It shows that there is always environmentally related programmatic dysfunction. Buildings are never perfect. It also shows that over time, one expects the level of programmatic dysfunction to increase as the building becomes outmoded. Parenthetically, this may not be the case. It is theoretically possible for a building to become less dysfunctional over time as the organizational program is modified to fit the enironmental constraints of the building. This follows Weick's notion of goals stemming from observations of behavior: In this case the functioning of the building is the behavior and the program the goal. The building determines the program, rather than the program determining the building. This happens, but more often through the occupancy of an entirely new organization rather than the radical transformation of the existing one. In any case, what Figure 2.1 and 2.2 suggest is that formal environmental-change efforts are required, or at least need to be monitored and considered, on a continuous basis. They also suggest that even when major formal environmental-change efforts are undertaken, they are unlikely to completely eliminate all programmatic dysfunctions. These may even be greater at this transition point because of conflicting, competing, and habitual ways of organizing people, space, and activities.

Landscape and modular office design, with its emphasis on flexibility, is slowly changing this pattern, but there are many reasons why buildings typically have not evolved over time as part of a continuous process of planned reassessment/redesign. These include the basic belief in many quarters that the environment is relatively unimportant, as well as beliefs toward new buildings and major design projects, and the processes through which these are created.

Altering a building after just having spent a large sum of money to create it seems like madness to most people. The tendency is to ignore problems that appear immediately because their recognition implies mistakes were made in initial planning. Neither the organization members responsible for overseeing the design project, nor the project architects, are eager to make such an admission. The operating premise is that it is possible to create a perfect building—one without mistakes—although all of the participants will readily admit this is not, in fact, possible. Accepting, from the beginning (regardless of the nature of the design process used), that mistakes will be made that are serious enough to require immediate rectification, and allocating funds expressly for this purpose, would go a long way toward making buildings more responsive to the organizational objectives they presumably are intended to support.

Such an approach to design represents a cybernetics model for planning (Bauer, 1966). The word "cybernetics" comes from the Greek "helmsman" and reflects the constant adjustments of course that characterize the way in which a sensitive helmsman controls a ship. When the wind changes direction, the helmsman changes the tack or misses the destination point. Winds are unpredictable and change all the time, as are the forces influencing behavior in any organization. The essence of this model is the assumption that one can achieve at best only some approximation of what one aims at, based on an initial course of action. As Bauer notes, salvation lies in rapid detection of error and adjustment to correct for that error. Bauer (1966, p. 25) says the value of this planning approach is that it removes the stigma of not attaining a goal in an anticipated manner:

> This cybernetic model also makes it natural to think of the second-order consequences of one's actions. "Error" is not a rare phenomenon that occurs because of bad planning and inept control. It is the natural and inevitable feature of all purposive action. Ironically, this technologically modern view of planning and control gives respectability to the once derogated British doctrine of "muddling through" [which]...might be described as deciding generally where one wants to go, taking a step in that direction, reassessing the consequences, reassessing one's goals and methods, taking another step, and so on.

Office-landscape design essentially legitimizes just such cybernetic behavior by providing an organizationally acceptable justification for frequent change; namely, that such design is specifically intended to respond to program goals and needs that are constantly in a state of flux, requiring different personnel with different communication requirements and work patterns. Changes to avoid dysfunction often do not occur, however (Dean, 1977), for the same reasons they have not occurred with conventional offices: inertia, complacency, anxiety about status change or potential conflict with colleagues, and reluctance to devote energy to an activity that may have little professional legitimacy.

When changes do occur, they often result in new, smaller space standards that are typically arbitrary in terms of meeting individual activity requirements. They often make sense, however, as a means of reducing direct operating expenses (*Contract* 1980a). Canty (1977) has shown that the amount of square footage per person in an office environment was reduced by 50 percent over a several-year period that spanned a change from a conventional redesigned office environment to a landscape design. A landscape-design office using top-of-the-line systems furniture may, however, cost more initially than a conventional office plan. Higher initial costs may be offset, over time, by significant reductions in time and effort to rearrange the work environment in response to changing conditions. For such change efforts to be successful, they must take into consideration the fact that our physical surroundings are constantly being created, informally, by all organizational members, not only those with formal responsibility for making design decisions.

CREATING PHYSICAL SETTINGS

The physical settings of organizations are created by several inter-dependent processes which occur continuously over time. These include the selection and organization of environmental elements; selection and organi-zation of time/use patterns; personal characteristics and circumstances; and the overall social context within which each of these processes occurs. Each of these processes creates physical settings by redirecting or altering aspects of the setting we attend to (Becker et al., 1978; Pfeffer 1980). As such, each reflects social-psychological processes of attention, and the individual and organizational values and intentions underlying them. These processes, and the issues surrounding their development and use in organizations, are central to the study of sociotechnical systems and organizational ecology: understanding how to organize people, technology, and activities to effec-tively produce goods, services, and information in ways that recognize and build upon human needs for recognition, control, and social integration.

All four of the above processes influencing the experienced environment are discussed below, but relatively more emphasis is placed on the first two, and particularly on the second process, selection and organization of time/use patterns. There are several reasons for this emphasis. The primary one is that, as noted in Chapter 1, the management of environmental-support systems on an ongoing basis over time has been relatively neglected in studies of both organizational behavior and environmental design. To the extent that there has been concern for the behavioral implications of physical design, most of the research energy has focused on first-use design or behavioral programming, rather than on the management of the space once it is in use. The opportunities for altering the nature of the physical setting, without altering its actual physical structure, have received much less attention. They are particularly important, practically, because developing time/use alternatives may be far less expensive than selecting and/or reorganizing physical elements. Secondly, more emphasis is placed on the first two processes because both personal characteristics and characteristics of the job, as these interact with and influence the role of the physical setting, are discussed in more depth in the next chapter.

Selection and Organization of Physical Elements

We physically design the physical setting by adding and subtracting, transforming, relocating, or recombining elements. Decisions about where to place walls, or about the size of the rooms and the location of windows and doors, are essentially projections by one group, the designers, about how they think another group will act in the environment when construction is completed. Designers assume that those using the environment will direct their attention to the same aspects of the environment they themselves focused their attention on when planning the environment. Designers design on the basis of how they imagine others behaving in the completed environment.

Particular design elements direct our attention to selected aspects of the overall environment. Indeed, the flamboyant entry, the skylight in the kitchen, and the deep pile carpet direct our attention because they fall outside our expectations, or our own experience in similar settings. These physical elements help us form a selected visual image of the setting that stands for the whole. In studies of housing (Becker et al., 1978), for example, we found that persons increased their satisfaction with their otherwise unsatisfactory house by concentrating on selected aspects of the total setting: a large deck, a quiet location, hardwood floors, a cathedral ceiling. The attentional changes in these cases were planned either by the resident, who personalized the environment after occupancy, or by the developer, who included several design features that, experience has taught him, people attend and respond to favorably: bay windows, brick facades, cedar shingles, stone, any type of column, shutters, hardwood floors, a fireplace.

The designed environment is an environment of possibilities. The created environment, or what Gans (1972) has referred to as the "effective" environment, is a set of possibilities to which individual user have attended. In almost any designed environment, some of the possibilities will not be attended to, while other possibilities the designers did not imagine will be attended to.

Architects and other official space planners within organizations often try to insure that the potential environment they create becomes the effective environment of the users. An effective way of insuring this control is to physically restrict the easy manipulation of the environment. Architects' fondness for built-ins, and master plans that indicate not only what each piece of equipment or furniture should be, but where it should be located, stem from the desire to prevent, as much as possible, users from creating their own environment. Individual diversity is sacrificed for the sense of order the master plan projects. But order for what? And for whom? Order becomes an aesthetic justification for administrative control of all decision processes. Social control, in terms of the maintenance of established patterns of influence among persons occupying different positions in the organizational hierarchy, irrespective of its actual effect on behavior, becomes a critical attribute and major form determinant of the environmental-support system.

Visual Order and Social Control

Visual order reduces ambiguity by masking individual differences among setting occupants. It is a form of social control. Environments that acknowledge differences in individual requirements for environmental support (e.g., different individuals may need different levels of privacy to perform at comparable levels) are often considered chaotic because all the offices or work stations do not have identical equipment or the same type of visual and acoustical barriers. Such an environment is ambiguous, and threatening, because it forces recognition of individual capabilities, preferences, and work habits that may be unrelated to hierarchical positions.

Using information theory's basic notion that information results when uncertainty is removed, Weick (1969, p. 29) argues that

> organizing is directed toward resolving the equivocality that exists in informational inputs judged to be relevant....Any item of information contains several possibilities or implications. It is more or less ambiguous and is subject to a variety of interpretations. If action is to be taken, the possibilities must be narrowed and the equivocal properties of the message made more unequivocal. Organizing is concerned with removing equivocality from information and structuring processes so that this removal is possible.

From this perspective, a major function of the physical setting of organizations can be seen as an attempt to visually and physically reduce the ambiguity of social position and power within the organization by marking distinctions among job classifications with clear signs of spatial privilege (size of office, quality of furnishings) and by minimizing distinctions within job classifications by rendering all environmental support identical. The physical design attempts to narrow possibilities and reduce ambiguity by ignoring the differences among individuals within job classifications.

If order, and control, are defined in terms of increasing the probability of a given outcome, rather than in terms of the extent to which they maintain a pattern of social influence, what is obtained by visual order is a reduction in control. Pseudoorder is attained. The appearance of order is based on the premise that the designed environment will also be the created environment of the user, and that all the users are, at least for the purposes of organizational design, more or less identical.

Control would be better achieved in many cases by the appearance of disorder on a visual level. The visual disorder or ambiguity would support individual differences among employees. The attempt to ignore individual differences through uniform design works on the assumption that excluding individual differences from the design eliminates them. This contradicts Ashby's Law of Requisite Variety (1956), which states that it takes variety to destroy variety. Social or task-oriented order is more likely to result when the variety of individuals is reflected in the variety of the environmental supports, except under one (the usual) set of conditions: standardized offices. The unambiguous visual order of such offices serves the employees as well as management as long as individual differences in environmental support and use occur within a context where decisions concerning such differences are viewed by employees as arbitrary and are, in fact, related almost entirely to marking status distinctions. Under these conditions, many persons find comfort in being treated identically. Equity, one of the major purposes of standards of all kinds, is insured. Looking around at others at the same job level, one can readily see that they are being treated to better (or worse) than oneself.

The fact that the equity of space and furniture allocations is visible to critical to its value. As Porter and Steers (1973) have argued, important organizational behaviors, such as turnover and absenteeism, have consistently been related to perceived equity: the sense that one is getting his or her fair share of the rewards in relation to others. In fact, the rewards may be quite unequal (such as salary increases), but satisfaction remains high as long as one perceives equity along a given dimension (the issue of equity is discussed in more detail in Chapter 7). Tension among staff is reduced, and staff can admire the pseudoorder for some of the same reasons management can. The attitude of persons in these conditions is typically one of resignation and getting by rather than of enthusiasm or involvement.

Not much is known about how these same individuals would react under conditions where environmental differences were related to differences in activities, individual capabilities, and experience. Sloan (1972) found that an office rearranged to provide varying levels of privacy for persons within the same job classification increased satisfaction and productivity in the office.

In another report of the same study, Sommer (1979, pp. 4–5), noted that allowing employees to select their own furniture from sample items of furniture, obtained from suppliers and assembled in a vacant warehouse, resulted in a layout that "was decentralized, modest, and personal, with the individual work station at its core. The office had an unplanned quality to it, as the total arrangement evolved from the sum of individual decisions." Different employees had different equipment and furnishings, and were more satisfied with their work setting than were those in a comparable sample of employees who worked in a setting furnished from a single furniture system prescribed by expert space planners. Of particular interest here is that the former building has been denied design awards while the latter has received several. One juror described his denial of the award on the basis of the plan's "residential quality" and "lack of discipline and control of the interiors" (Sommer, 1979, p. 5). In the former case, visual order and social control becomes the goal, not productivity or user satisfaction. The argument that employees want everyone treated in a visibly identical fashion does not hold up when employees participate in a procedure that allows them a genuine opportunity to make informed choices. Under these conditions, differences can be treated as a variation in preference and work style rather than as preferential or shoddy treatment by management.

Time/Use Patterns

The second way in which the physical settings of organizations are created is through the management of existing facilities, including decisions regarding the use of space and equipment made by members of the organization. The physical setting is created by changing the relationship of individuals to it. Decisions can be made, for example, that allow or encourage more or less freedom of movement among parts of the environment. We can change the speed with which one moves through the environment, or the means of locomotion or transportation; the time of day or season one experiences the environment; the number of people present; the vantage point of the experience; the nature of the activity performed in the space. These ways of creating the environment take advantage of existing possibilities in the physical setting. Nothing new is built, nor are existing furnishings or structure physically modified in any way. The possibility of designing a new environment without physically altering the existing one is dramatically illustrated by manned space flight.

In a space capsule, one has the unique opportunity to experience the environment from different perspectives because of the effects of zero gravity. Henry Cooper, Jr. (1976, p. 40) writing about the American astronauts, described some of the possibilities and feelings that occurred by changing one's relation to the space:

> There was a reason for the astronauts' keeping themselves upright. Although there is no gravity in space, the workshop was designed as if there were; that is, a definite sense of up and down, or what the astronauts called a "local vertical," was provided architecturally by a definite floor and ceiling, and the astronauts felt most comfortable when they and the room were the same way up. Getting out of kilter was both exhilarating and worrisome—as Garriott found out one day when he took a walk on the ceiling of the experiment room. "It gives a very strange sensation," he said later. "You just have no idea how cluttered up the ceiling, which is now the floor, has become. Wires and cables and everything else tumbling over. And it's really like a whole new room that you walk into. It's a fascinating new room. It's a pleasant psychological sensation just to see it with the lights underneath your feet, and it's just an amazing situation to find yourself in."

On earth, our ways of changing spatial relations are more prosaic. We often overlook even the simplest possibilities, however. Students often complain to me about the comfort of the chairs in our classroom. New chairs are seen as the solution. Since even the most naive student does not believe the administration is going to buy new chairs, the situation is treated as fixed and discomfort is inevitable. No student has ever asked if he or she might get up and stretch, or walk around the class for a minute. I, of course, do this all the time. It is not that I prevent students from moving around or stretching. They never seem to consider it a possibility. An instructor could encourage this kind of movement by interpreting it, for the group as a whole, as a means of maintaining attention over a relatively long period of time, and not as a form of basic disinterest or inattention. Movement is now considered inappropriate because it openly acknowledges that all individuals are not totally engrossed in the class discussion or lecture for every minute of the class period. Why are yawns and glassy eyes better than a few-seconds walk or stretch?

The Physical Setting and Time

Perhaps even less understood than our use and management of space is our awareness of how we manage time. In a stimulating book called *What Time Is This Place?*, Kevin Lynch (1972) explores how the rhythms of a place contribute to our experience of it and to our well-being. He radically departs from most conventional images of the design activity by suggesting that designers need to consider, as a design or creative activity, the form of time as much as they do the form of the space. He makes clear that packaging time in new ways is extraordinarily difficult because existing time forms are so thoroughly ingrained. Transgressions against culturally accepted patterns of time management are treated as egregious affronts to personal dignity, a reflection of laziness and indifference, aggressiveness, insensitivity, or of any number of other uncivilized behaviors (Hall, 1966).

Yet changes have occurred in the way we manage time in work settings, and will continue to do so at an increasing rate. The five-day workweek with a two-day weekend is a relatively recent invention, as is the notion that people should work on a fixed schedule from, say, eight in the morning until five at night. Flextime is less a new invention than a return to older craft-oriented ways of managing time. Many Latin American countries follow different time patterns than we do today. The advent of sophisticated electronic telecommunications opportunities, which make possible a much greater decentralization of work in a wider variety of settings, will also affect how we package time. The notion of flextime may be tremendously expanded. People might work from 9:00 P.M. until midnight or 2:00 A.M., or on weekends, depending on personal considerations that may range from weather conditions, personal health, whim, and childrearing practices, to spouses' and friends' work schedules (Vail, 1978).

Managing time, like managing space, is an organizing process. It is a social process that contributes as much to the nature and character of the physical setting, and our experience of it, as do the more tangible walls, desks, lights. By identifying many more dimensions along which time structure can vary than are typically considered, Lynch (1972) greatly expands the range of organizing options available to the administrator or organizational consultant seeking imaginative ways of restructuring work patterns and the work environment. The same activities restructured in time transform our experience of space. Three hours of meetings scheduled as two hour-and-a-half sessions, or three one-hour sessions, or one three-hour session will elicit different behaviors from participants and different evaluations of identical environmental supports. Chairs comfortable for an hour are hell for three. The same can be true for acoustics, lighting, colors, and almost any other environmental element. For the organizational theorist, consideration of time structure offers unexplored territory that lies close to our most basic living and working patterns.

The following dimensions along which time structure can vary are adapted from Lynch (1972). He was concerned with the structure of time at an urban design scale, but several possibilities for restructuring time in the office setting suggest themselves:

● Grain: the size and precision of the chunks into which time is divided. The length of the workday, for example, can (and often does) vary around the basic eight-hour module. The higher in the echelon one moves, in general, the more varied and less precise is the texture of one's time, including its grain. Executives may come in very early, have an early lunch, and stay late. They may work sometimes for a long period before lunch, sometimes for a short period. Clerical workers generally show a might tighter-grained time texture, with their work and break periods' duration, frequency, and periodicity more closely monitored.

- Period: the length of time within which events recur. On an assembly line, this might be every few seconds, as the welding of a hinge onto a door is endlessly repeated. For a secretary, a major manuscript may only appear every few weeks or months. Different persons in the organizational hierarchy will experience different time structures. Since time structures, particularly in the assembly-line sense of pace, are associated with work degradation and boredom (Blauner, 1964), it should come as no surprise that persons at different levels of the organizational hierarchy may have completely different experiences in and images of the organization. These different experiences can lead to misunderstanding and conflict in the same way that Hall (1966) describes cross-cultural conflict stemming from alternative norms about time and space usage.

- Amplitude: the degree of change within a cycle. Within a shift on an assembly line, there is essentially no change in activity. Within a shift for a secretary, a number of different activities may be performed: telephoning, receiving calls, typing, filing, coordinating resources. Breaking secretarial work down into its component parts, so that different persons do each task, reduces the amplitude of work.

- Rate: the speed with which changes occur. Changes might refer not only to the work activity or tasks (e.g., typing, writing, lecturing, planning), but to the speed with which changes are introduced. Does the changeover from a conventional manual to an electronic filing system occur within a week, a month, or several years? Does a new supervisor reorganize the office space the first day of work, or gradually over the first several months?

- Synchronization: the degree to which cycles and changes are in phase. Major renovations often disrupt work activities because use and nonuse cycles occur simultaneously. Scheduling highway repair at night or on the weekends, to avoid intensifying the congestion that already exists at peak travel hours, would be a means of improving synchronization.

- Regularity: the degree to which the preceding time characteristics themselves remain stable and unchanging. There are slow days and hectic days. Sometimes we are overwhelmed by the amplitude of changes within a day. It is not unusual for a professor to meet with a student for five minutes; consult with a colleague for 20 minutes, during which time the phone rings twice concerning entirely unrelated matters; bang out a memo about an upcoming seminar; glance over notes for a lecture; run to the lecture, stopping to talk briefly with a student; give the lecture. Were this an entirely regular structure of time, most would find it highly stressful. But it is not regular: There are days when we stay home, write, and refuse to answer the telephone.

● Orientation: the degree to which attention is focused on the past, present, or future. The design and furnishings of the setting can contribute to time orientation directly: Antiques direct us backward while computers focus our attention forward. The preceding characteristics also help focus attention to particular time directions. Regularity focuses attention, in terms of work, more to the present than either the past or future. Unstable and changing conditions may focus attention either to the past or future, probably depending to some extent on how the changes are interpreted.

We know something about the effect of the pace of work from studies of assembly-line processes (Blauner, 1964). We know much less about how this wider range of time structures influences behavior in organizations, for persons at different levels in the organizational hierarchy; for different kinds of persons, at different stages in their work career, working on different kinds of tasks. It is possible that alternative and imaginative time structures could compensate for what are otherwise routine and uninvolving work activities. Flextime, for example, in which individuals are allowed to arrive early or come in late and stay late, or work longer days to obtain an extended weekend, involves relatively simple efforts to restructure time. The advantage for the employee is the possibility of more creative time management, which allows structuring of work on an individual, and variable, schedule. Developing an understanding of how new technologies (a form of physical change) can be used to create alternative time strucures for work that support changing employee expectations and work to the mutual advantage of the individual and organization is a major challenge for organizational ecologists.

This might be approached in several different ways. One could systematically compare organizations that seem to be backward with those that are innovative, along selected dimensions of behavior: commitment, motivation, initiative, conflict, cooperation. Time is typically structured in a consistent pattern throughout an entire organization. Lynch (1972) talks about entire regions of patterns, but one could imagine organizations with traditional sections in which change is systematically retarded, while other sections within the same organization would be futuristic. These sections might adopt the latest in electronic communications, alternative work patterns, and authority structures. Membership in each type of section would be voluntary. The point is to be able to assess, even in the most rudimentary ways, what some of the effects of change are before instituting them on a broader basis so that there is some sense of what the consequences and benefits will be, especially the unanticipated and unintended consequences (Bauer, 1966).

Both the processes of physically modifying the environment, and of changing one's physical relationship to the environment, focus attention by altering the physical relationship between the person and the setting. These are social processes. Decisions about the nature and/or use of the physical setting are made by individuals and groups to accomplish particular ends. What these ends are, and what role we expect the environment to play for us, is shaped by a plethora of personal characteristics and circumstances, including the kinds of activities and role responsibilities our jobs demand. The characteristics of the environment that these personal circumstances may direct one's attention to are, in turn, subject to interpretation by others with whom the individul interacts at work, at home, through the media, and in trade associations (see Figure 2.3). Personal characteristics, and the social context within which we work, offer us the third and fourth ways of creating the environment.

Personal Characteristics

The potential list of personal circumstances is enormous. Depending on how these are defined, they range from demographic characteristics, such as race, sex, income, and age, to abilities, such as manual dexterity, human-relations skills, problem-solving ability, amount of information, basic intelligence, life style and taste, health and physical condition, and previous work experience. These kinds of personal characteristics are discussed in some detail in Chapter 3, as they influence how we create and use our physical surroundings. Two acquired personal characteristics related to organizational status are worth mentioning briefly here because they play an

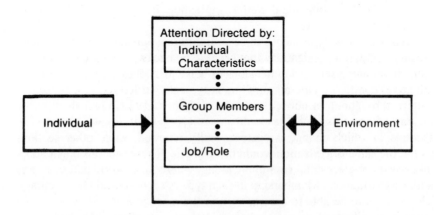

FIGURE 2.3 Factors Influencing Individual Environmental Assessment

important emotion-laden role in how individuals assess the adequacy of their physical surroundings, but are generally not included in lists of personal characteristics. These personal circumstances concern job-related accomplishments, and time and tenure in the organization. They are recognized by all organizations, are an important determinant of environmental form, and are problematic for almost all organizations (see Chapter 7 for more discussion of this issue).

Job-Related Accomplishments

Job-related acomplishments refer to changes in personal status that stem from outstanding achievements or significant personal and career development at work. Such accomplishments include winning a major legal case, attaining a higher educational degree, successfully completing a certified training program, securing a major research grant, publishing in professionally accepted journals, showing consistent ability to solve problems, and the willingness to accept responsibility and provide leadership. Outstanding quantity or quality of output, and other marks of endurance, such as fewest accidents, least days missed, or most years employed, can also be considered signs of achievement.

People who experience such accomplishments expect, and are typically rewarded through, promotions accompanied by changes in job title and salary level. They are also often accorded more freedom of movement, and larger and/or better-quality furniture, equipment, and space. By changing expectations regarding the level of appropriate environmental support, job-related accomplishments direct attention to the nature and quality of the physical setting, which may have been overlooked, or more likely, simply accepted in the past. For upwardly mobile workers, the current physical setting is satisfactory as long as it is seen as a temporary way station rather than as a permanent outpost. The problem for management is how to reflect job-related accomplishments in visible environmental supports, in ways that are not arbitrary and do not undermine activity functions.

Time and Tenure

Unlike job-related accomplishments, which refer to activities that set one apart from fellow workers, time or tenure changes refer simply to the passage of time. The accomplishment here is in remaining a loyal, hard-working organizational member for much longer than is true of the average employee. The person who has worked for 15, 20 or 25 years is likely to view the entire setting quite differently than the less experienced employee. In some cases, old-timers will expect special dispensation for their long service. In other cases, long-time employees will have adapted to a lower set of expectations. As a consequence, they may be more accepting of the environmental setting than those just arriving on the scene, who may have higher aspirations fed by greater familiarity with other work settings they have briefly worked in or been exposed to as part of job interviews, school field trips, or through television and in newspapers and magazines.

Old-timers' concerns, in fact, may not be so much a case of what they can get, but of what they will not give up. Space was less expensive 20 years ago than it is today, and office size reflected this. People starting to work 15 years ago accepted working at a desk in an open area, with the expectation that over time they would move to a more private office. Asking these people, 15 years later, to set aside their long-held expectations and move into open-office plans with modular landscape design often creates tremendous resentment. Thus, amount of time in the setting per se will direct people's attention to particular characteristics of the physical environment. In a study of Kodak's facilities, Riland and Falk (1971) found that employees with five years' service or less had more favorable views about moving to an open landscape-design office than did those who had been there longer. These kinds of individual differences need to be understood and taken into account as a means of determining what the environment is, or more precisely, what it means, for different individuals.

How employees interpret, and whether they accept, any of the formal organizational devices for directing attention to selected aspects of the total situation depends, as noted earlier, on the social context within which they create their environment. People learn through their interaction with others, both within and outside the setting, which kinds of decisions to consider appropriate and legitimate, and which to reject. The physical environment of the organization is attended to and acquires meaning, as do other organizational decisions and actions, within specific social contexts and over time.

The Social Context

Salancik and Pfeffer (1978) argue that conventional approaches to understanding peoples' attitudes at work fail to take into account the social context in which work occurs. The same point can be made concerning individuals' assessment of and satisfaction with their physical surroundings. Their basic premise is that individuals are adaptive organisms who shape their attitudes, behavior, and beliefs to conform to their social behavior and situation. Like Weick (1969), they argue that rationality is a postdecision process in which individuals try to make sense out of what it is they have done; that is, they look for factors in the setting that provide socially acceptable justifications for their behavior. An important source of information is available in the person's immediate social environment: other people one observes and interacts with in the setting. These others provide cues, in the form of their own behavior and in conversations, which individuals use to construct and interpret events in the setting. They also provide information on appropriate attitudes and behavior.

Salancik and Pfeffer (1978, pp. 226–27) argue that the information made available by the group constrains and directs attention to, and makes salient, selected aspects of the situation. By doing so, it defines which kinds of justifications for behavior, including response to and use of the physical environment, are socially acceptable, and which are not.

The concept that our attitudes and behavior are influenced by others in the situation, as they teach us, through example and direct instruction, how to be civilized, how to behave appropriately by learning and following implicit and explicit norms and values as they have evolved within a specific micro-culture, is hardly a novel idea in social psychology. It is an important idea, however, because it conflicts with a trait orientation in which individuals' behavior is viewed as guided by strong, internal, and enduring states that are relatively immune to changes in external circumstances. Its significance for understanding how physical settings are created in organizations resides in its directing our attention to factors that lie outside both the individual and the physical elements themselves.

For any individual, the enacted physical environment is both social product and process perceived in particular ways. We respond not only to physical elements, like the color, size, and arrangement of the office, on the basis of ur own personal experience and circumstances, job requirements, and role responsibilities, but respond as these are, in turn, subjected to influence processes initiated by our friends, family, and colleagues. Others in the social setting attempt to instruct us on which of those aspects we may have attended to on our own or we should in fact continue to pay attention to, and in what ways. Much effort is made to isolate these processes from a study of environmental effects. We should instead be striving to incorporate them into the study of organizational ecology.

There is additional sense in which the social context influences our behavior, in relation to the physical setting. If we accept that behavior is influenced by information provided by others, the physical setting is the most immediate and visible sign of the social process and of communication in any setting. As a form of nonverbal communication (Becker, 1977), it often says what we choose not to put in words. The presence of separate lounges for different status groups communicates instantaneously an organization's regard for status distinctions, and the expectation that people at different levels in the organizational hierarchy will not socialize together. A company cafeteria says, "We expect you to eat here," just as a professional library communicates expectations about keeping up with the literature. These kinds of environmental messages (Becker, 1977) do not operate in isolation from other social processes, but neither is the reverse true. Both the physical setting and the social context are part of the same social processes. They both constitute an informational environment that is created by individuals and then, in turn, influences their behavior by directing attention in selected ways. In addition, the physical environment may communicate expectations by physically eliminating or inhibiting certain behaviors by making their performance extremely difficult; it is tough to play baseball or do a square dance in a corridor.

The physical settings of organizations are created through a combination of the processes described above. Some of these processes are deliberate. The decision to move from bullpen to open-office landscape, for example, typically involves persons formally responsible for making decisions about environmental form and use: facility planners, plant managers, architects, human-factors specialists. These same processes also occur informally, as individuals rearrange their file cabinets, move their desks, create storage space on top of storage cabinets, and conduct meetings in cramped offices or corridors rather than in designated conference rooms.

Thus, changing the way we experience the environment by altering the way in which we structure such things as time and movement patterns, or the physical elements themselves, is a process of organizing that occurs continuously in all organizations. It is engaged in by all participants, whether or not they are accorded formal recognition and responsibility for such administrative decisions.

The process of designing the physical setting can be formally assigned to particular organizational members or to outside consultants (e.g., design professionals, organizational-development experts), but the process through which the environment is created or made sense of is individually controlled, although it develops within a particular social context and is greatly influenced by it (Salancik and Pfeffer, 1978). The environment can be designed by one group or individual for another, but it cannot be created, mandated, by one person for another. What can be designed are potential environments: environments that contain a number of possibilities. Whether these possibilities are realized, whether the potential environment becomes the user's effective environment, the environment of focused attention, is outside the realm of formal organizational control. The organization expends enormous resources, however, in trying to influence the direction of attention through conventional approaches like incentive systems and training and publicity programs. It can also direct attention, as I have tried to show, through the ways in which it structures and manages time and space. The role, and effect of, such attention-focusing mechanisms, including physical design, are often misunderstood, however, because of a failure to distinguish between intention and attention.

THE EXPERIENCED ENVIRONMENT AND
ENVIRONMENTAL DETERMINISM

I argued earlier that the Hawthorne researchers misinterpreted the data on the effect of the environment on behavior because their working assumption was that the physical environment directly affects behavior, the way winds propel a sailboat. Another way to view environment-behavior relationships is in terms of attention processes. From this perspective, one reason the environment may not appear to influence behavior stems from linking intent to measures of effect. What needs to be linked are processes of attention.

To understand what affect the environment has on behavior, one needs to identify those aspects of the total situation the users attend to, as distinct from those aspects the initial designers intended they notice. The environment appears to have no effect when selected intentions are not attended to and acted on. An environment not having the intended effect should not be confused with its having no effect (see Figure 2.4).

To complicate matters further, those who make formal decisions about the nature and/or use and management of the physical setting may do so for different purposes, and with varying understanding of the implications of the decisions. Three approaches to environmental decision making can be identified.

Naive Environmental Determinism

Some decisions are based on the belief that intention is synonymous with effect. Decisions to locate disparate community-service groups in a multiservice center, to coordinate and integrate services so the whole individual or family is served, illustrate this approach. The notion is that a

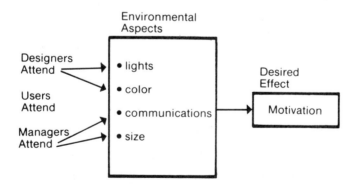

FIGURE 2.4 Attention Processes and Environmental Effects

physical setting which encloses different services within close spatial proximity will, by itself, magically break down rivalries, competition, and jealousy between different service agencies so that the individuals being served have easy access to a complete range of services. This case of naive environmental determinism is typically characterized by attention to the gross aspects of the physical setting (e.g., there is a single building with different services located within it), and by inattention to subtle aspects of the physical setting (e.g., nature and location of the reception desk or location of services within the building) that are required to increase the likelihood the overall concept actually works (Gomez, 1979).

Cynical environmental determinism occurs when decisions are made largely for symbolic reasons, with no real expectation that substantive changes in behavior will result. The primary objective is to demonstrate to others that "something is being done," without diverting limited energy and resources from more valued objectives. Such decisions support a "norm of rationality" (Thompson, 1967).

Experimental Environmental Determinism

This is the rarest form of environmental decision making. It is characterized by the fact that those making the decisions do not know what the exact outcome of their decision will be, and do not pretend to. Such an approach to environmental decision making is often done when all other rational decisions have failed, and when the situation is desperate. The change to participatory management at the G.M. Tarrytown plant represents such a situation (Guest, 1979). It is a dangerous position to assume because it undermines the norm of rationality whose bedrock is not only that decisions are made to attain specified goals, but that the paths to the goals can be specified. While such decisions may be viewed, when planned or implemented, as innovative and positive risk taking, they may as easily be viewed as made in desperation or as an indication of loss of control. It depends largely on the unknown outcome. As Weick (1969) argues, the outcome is used to define the intention.

COUNTERPRODUCTIVITY AND ENVIRONMENTAL MEANING

Determining whether one of these approaches is effective or counterproductive is more problematic than it first appears. The terms noted imply that some action or decision works to make attainment of a goal or objective more or less difficult, expensive, or inefficient. An implicit assumption is that there is a single goal, and a means of attaining it. In fact, as Pfeffer (1980) has pointed out, behavior in organizations serves both substantive and symbolic functions. The audience for the substantive action may not be the audience for the symbolic. Behavior that is largely devoid of substance may be extremely effective for a particular audience. This is the case when the audience essentially is looking for reassurance, and is not directly enough involved with the ongoing activities of the organization, in a way that it can closely monitor the substance of the behavior, rather than its form, or symbolic character. The oil companies' advertisements concerning their contribution to improving the quality of the environment are directed primarily to shareholders and the public at large, not to their own employees, who have a different set of concerns.

The difficulty arises when management makes decisions that do not reflect the kinds of information the intended audience desires, or when it fails to distinguish among audiences. In the academic context, administrative statements about affirmative action increasingly are scrutinized by concerned minorities, in terms of number of women and of other minorities hired and promoted, actual salaries, and other substantive indicators of organizational behavior. They are not satisfied with eloquent statements of intent, or references to single individuals, departments, or even colleges. One of the major functions of management from this perspective, is to direct attention to some aspects of decisions, or to some decisions rather than others. Management can be considered to fail when it loses control over the direction of the attention of its various audiences (Pfeffer, 1980). Management's problem is the fact that different immediate needs influence the direction of our attention to the physical setting. These needs change for the same individual over time, as well as differing among individuals, both within and between job classifications. As a consequence, what appears to be the most unambiguous (standardized) environment may be quite unstable and ambiguous for various organizational members. We turn next to a consideration of the role of ambiguity in the development and function of physical settings.

3

INFORMATION TRANSFORMATIONS

The importance of considering ambiguity in the creation of physical settings initially and over time lies in the information-processing principle that information results from the reduction of ambiguity. All information is ambiguous in the sense that it is open to multiple interpretations. Meaning is not inherent in the information. Meaning results from the ways in which individuals selectively process, or attend to, available information. To take any action, we must transform ambiguous information into unambiguous, or less ambiguous, states, even if only temporarily. Until we determine whether the thump in the night is a fallen branch or a leg against the window, we remain immobilized. The first question on hearing such a sound is "What's that?"; and the very urgent purpose is to transform an ambiguous bit of information, the thump, into something less ambiguous. The application of these kinds of transformation processes is mandatory for any kind of effective behavior to occur (Weick, 1969).

The reduction of ambiguity creates stability, which is essential to functioning. It allows action to occur. But equally important are transformations in which stable, unambiguous states are treated as ambiguous and flexible. Stability becomes dysfunctional in the face of changing conditions. New conditions require new responses, and these evolve only when the opportunity exists for existing patterns to be treated as ambiguous, or open to change. Yet treating all information as ambiguous, while maximizing flexibility, minimizes effective action, which requires stability. Thus, neither ambiguous nor unambiguous states, by themselves, support effective organizational or individual functioning. Weick (1969) argues that innovation and effective adaptation to changing conditions result from periodical transformations of either information state, the ambiguous or unambiguous, into its opposite. Our purpose here is to explore the value of applying the concept of information transformation to the study of how physical settings develop and function in organizations.

Weick (1969) does not define "ambiguous" other than as a state of affairs open to multiple interpretations, or embodying multiple possibilities. For our purpose, ambiguous and unambiguous physical settings are ones that those designing, managing, or using them think of as having either a single use or purpose, or ones that are considered to have multiple uses and purposes. A tight fit (unambiguous) setting is thought to constrain all but a few behaviors. In contrast, a loose-fit (ambiguous) setting is thought to encourage an almost infinite range of possible behaviors. Railroad tracks and the behavior of a train constitute a tight fit while the design of a public plaza or park is thought to provide a looser fit. In either case, how the setting is defined is a function of attention processes, rather than being inherent in characteristics of the setting itself, although these many influence attention processes in the ways described in the previous chapter. Thus different individuals may view the same setting differently, and a setting may indeed be transformed from one information state to another through the application of cognitive processes that allow attention to be directed to existing possibilities that have been overlooked.

AMBIGUITY AND THE DESIGN PROCESS

Physical settings are created through a series of attention cycles characterized by such information transformation. At each stage of the design process, different parties transform available information into its opposite state in order to make sense of and act on it. These processes become problematic for an organization when the transformations do not occur at what are considered appropriate places or times, or are stunted in some way.

Stage 1: First Transformation

The process of creating the environment begins with identification of the problem and an environmentally oriented solution, both of which are a function of directing attention to some aspects of the situation rather than others. As the first stage following identification of the problem, current design practice requires some sort of a program, or explicit statement of ends, the design should suport. Programs generally take the form of an explicit statement of objectives, but they may simply be an implicit set of very general guidelines barely held in consciousness. Explicit-appearing programs are, in fact, often laden with the heavy baggage of implicit objectives and values (Silverstein and Jacobson, 1978).

Ideally, to develop a program, the client should assess all the kinds of activities occurring in the organization presently, and the effectiveness of existing environmental-support systems in facilitating these behaviors. The kinds of activities that will or should occur in the future should also be identified, as well as the necessary support systems to facilitate them. Few programs even approximate a description of such relationships in any depth. Not only are such relationships multifaceted and complex, but they are rarely known with any certainty. Information about these relationships is essentially highly ambiguous. As a result, in practice, these complex relationships are pared down to a relatively few simple size and adjacency requirements (Steele, 1973).

The first transformation, then, has occurred. The ambiguous and multifaceted behaviors of organizational members and physical-setting characteristics have been transformed into an unambiguous-appearing program document. The process of simplifying the complex by transforming the ambiguous into unambiguous information fosters a sense of stability that permits the process of creating environments to begin. But as the process continues, new participants successively transform each preceding stage of the process from what appears to that stage's participants as unambiguous into ambiguous information (see Figure 3.1).

Stage 2: Second Transformation

Most architects realize that the situation is much more complex than the typical program suggests. To develop a design whose complexity and level of sophistication more nearly match what the architect assumes to be the complexity of the situation, the unambiguous program is treated as a highly ambiguous set of guidelines. These direct attention to problems the client has attended to, as well as to the implicit environmental solution, but with skepticism. Space requirements specified are treated as only a minor part of the overall design problem, and in some cases even these and the definition of the problem are challenged (Silverstein and Jacobson, 1978). The ambiguous behavior in the organizational setting that was transformed into the unambiguous program has thus been operated on by the architect to create an ambiguous set of design requirements that can be satisfied by many different design solutions.

Stage 3: Third Transformation

To oversimplify the process, at this point, the designer begins to generate alternatives. These are often based on extensive discussions between selected members of the organization and the design team. The purpose is to clarify, for the architect, what the client wanted (and thought was clear), on the one hand, and to clarify, for the client, what the architect views as a clear

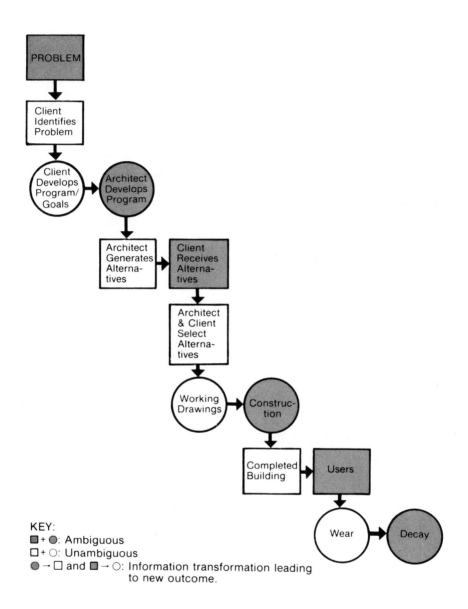

KEY:
■ + ●: Ambiguous
□ + ○: Unambiguous
● → □ and ■ → ○: Information transformation leading
      to new outcome.

FIGURE 3.1 Simplified Model of the Design Process as a Series of Information Transformations

and unambiguous alternative, on the other. These discussions often involve changes in aspects of the program and the design. Finally, an alternative is developed and selected. Those who have been involved in the process see the alternative as clear and unambiguous. They know what their intentions are, and how the physical design is expected to support them. Yet once the design is selected and working drawings authorized, the design once again becomes ambiguous to the next set of participants, the contractors.

Stage 4: Fourth Transformation

Working drawings are intended as a very precise guide for the contractor. But even the supposedly totally unambiguous information package represented by the working drawings is usually considered ambiguous by the contractor. Architects and organizational clients have project managers whose job is to help the contractor interpret the drawings and to reduce the ambiguity always found in them. The transformation of the unambiguous working drawings (ambiguous for the contractor) into the actual building and physical facility completes what is generally understood to be the design process. The building is ready for occupancy. It is presumably totally unambiguous. It exists in brick and mortar. How much more unambiguous could it be? Very much more. All of the information transformations that have occurred in the development of physical settings described thus far are, if occasionally painful, accepted. Upon occupancy, the transformation processes continue, but now with much less attention paid to them, and with a far greater sense that they are inappropriate.

Stage 5: Fifth Transformation

Rarely is the kind of cybernetic planning model described earlier accepted. Consequently, both the architects and the organizational members who hired the architects and have worked with them have a stake in seeing the newly finished building as truly finished, or unambiguous. The many organizational members who had nothing to do with the earlier processes have no such stake. For them, the unambiguous building becomes ambiguous once again. Possibilities that the designers attended to are overlooked, considered unimportant, or counterproductive. Possibilities the designers overlooked are found and attended to. In both cases, the actual users may not create the same environment the designers intended. But at this point, formal and informal pressure is placed on them to react to the building in one way; that is, to attend to selected parts of the whole or, in many cases, to attend to the whole and overlook particular elements or subsystems they may consider dysfunctional.

Upon occupancy, rules are formulated about the use of the environment, some formal, and others in the form of expectations communicated when organizational members violate the unstated definition of appropriate use. The more unambiguous the informational environment, the more rules are applied (Weick, 1969). This occurs because it is assumed that all the potentialities are known and can be operated on. Rules also reinforce existing authority lines that might be threatened by alternative, and unintended, use of existing environmental resources, whether or not these are in some sense more effective. The more ambiguous the informational environment, the fewer the rules that can be applied. If one is unsure about just what or how a facility can be used, it is difficult to develop detailed rules and regulations concerning its use.

The number of formal rules, then, corresponds to the level of ambiguity at which the environment is bureaucratically pegged. Increasing rules and reducing ambiguity can be beneficial: Safety may be insured, chaos and anarchy avoided, and a sense of tradition, identity, and security nurtured. What is problematic is not the existence of rules, but the premise on which they rest. Rules defining the level of acceptable ambiguity of the physical setting are based on the assumption that different individuals can perform at comparable levels in a standardized and unambiguous environment defined for them by others. I have been suggesting, using the concept of attention processes, that such a level of ambiguity cannot be formally enacted, although it can be formally proposed and encouraged. The assumption that a uniform, unambiguous physical setting is both necessary and sufficient to elicit desired behaviors appears to be an even more tenuous one.

We know very little about how people use time, space, and other environmental resources to accomplish their behavior in the organization. Even when genuine attempts are made to provide supportive physical surroundings, as has occurred in educational settings and playground facilities (Spivack, 1974; Cooper, 1974), these efforts often do not have the intended effects. Often attention is directed to different aspects of the total situation than the designers or managers intended to be the case. Of central interest to a study of organizational ecology should be why some of the potential environmental resources become part of an "enacted" or "effective" environment (Weick, 1969; Gans, 1972), while others go unnoticed.

The answer can be found, in part, in the kinds of personal resources, social processes, and administrative constraints that operate within the setting to transform it from an ambiguous, potentially rich setting into an unambiguous, relatively impoverished one, and vice versa. Particular human capabilities, social norms, and administrative processes are required to release the potential of existing environmental resources, and particular environmental resources are required to release existing human potential, and thus maximize organizational effectiveness. Neither human nor environmental potential can be realized in isolation from each other.

THE POTENTIAL ENVIRONMENT

The objective physical-setting resources are those resources that can be measured or counted by direct observation: number of desks, chairs, storage units, rooms; their weight, distance from each other, color, shape, size, and height; the nature of the material and its properties, such as soft or hard, natural or man-made, flexible or rigid. As noted in the preceding discussion, these objective characteristics of the physical setting are both the result of social processes, and subject to future individual and social processes, often at different points in time and by different individuals. The objective qualities of the physical setting are unimportant except as they become the focus of attention. By "focus of attention" I mean that some possibilities, but not others, are acted upon. Attention is best discovered by the actions one takes vis-à-vis the physical setting. These actions may occur outside the individual's awareness, but they are a function of the individual's personal resources as these interact with constraints imposed by others.

The assumption is that available environmental resources may not become part of the enacted environment for two kinds of reasons. The first is the absence of necessary personal resources: intelligence, skills, physical capability. Secondly, available environmental resources may not become effective resources, or part of the enacted environment, because of constraints imposed on organizational members by other setting members (Salancik and Pfeffer, 1978), by community and cultural norms, and by administrative policies that discourage or forbid certain kinds of behavior (including building codes and regulations). These constraints are embedded within the social context.

Personal Resources

Personal resources include the knowledge, physical and intellectual skills, competencies, and abilities the individual possesses. The notion of "partial inclusion" of these (Thompson, 1967) suggests that individuals, like physical settings, have available more potential resources (skills, special abilities) than may actually be elicited (i.e., noticed and used for activities defined as work). The types, level, and distribution of personal resources in the organizational setting will influence how the available or potential environmental resources are used and distributed over time and in space, as well as the different types of resources needed.

This suggests that identical environmental resources, in terms of what can be objectively measured and counted, will have very different implications and impacts depending on who is in the setting. Differences in the nature and types of personal resources organization members bring to the work setting may produce a dysfunctional or an effective work setting even though the potential environmental resources are identical; stairs that are a link for a young person may be a barrier for the older person. The physical setting may also equalize performance by persons with unequal personal resources by acting as a prosthesis or compensatory support system.

The Environmental-Docility Hypothesis

Lawton (Nahemow and Lawton, 1976) has provided a useful way of thinking about the interaction of individual differences and environmental characteristics, within a framework he has called the "environmental-docility hypothesis." Using Murray's notion of "press," or environmental demands, the basic hypothesis is that "the more competent the organism—in terms of health, intelligence, ego strength, social role performance, or cultural evolution—the less will be the proportion of variance in behavior attributable to physical objects or conditions around him.... With high degrees of competence he will, in common parlance, rise above his environment. However, reduction of competence, or deprived status, heightens his behavioral dependence on external conditions" (Nahemow and Lawton, 1976, p. 316).

The emphasis in Lawton's formulation is on the relationship between the characteristics of the individual (level of competence) and the role of the environment as they interact to create or maintain a given level of performance. Three persons with very different visual capacity may be able to read the same book. But the role and importance of the environment will be very different for each. The person with 20–20 vision simply picks up the book and reads it. The person with 20–80 vision needs eyeglasses, which compensate for the visual deficiency, to maintain the same level of performance. And the blind person needs to have the book translated into braille. Competence, in the sense of level of performance, is a function of individual capabilities and of environmental support ($C_p = I_c + E_s$). An extremely resourceful and creative teacher may be able to devise ways of getting the most from available environmental resources, while a less talented teacher with a much richer array of environmental resources may not use them to anywhere near their full potential. The value of a resource-rich environment is that it may allow the less competent, or more inexperienced teacher, to operate at a higher level of competence than would occur in a normal environment.

In work settings, selection procedures are assumed to result in employees at any particular job-classification level having about the same abilities (at least in terms of those considered relevant to their behavior in the organization). This rarely happens in practice. Individuals are different, and administrators and managers see themselves serving a function analogous to that of environmental support: They provide extra supervision or support for a new employee or one whose abilities or motivation is viewed as normally operating at less than some desired level. Yet little attention is paid to how the environment might raise the level of performance in a similar way. Thus, within a given job classification, individual employees are considered to have identical capabilities at the same time that other kinds of management practices, such as supervision, recognize individual differences. The possibility that one individual might need more privacy to accomplish a given level of work than might another individual, because they differ in their capacity to screen out distracting noise, for example, is given virtually no consideration. Yet research on the effect of environmental stressors on performance (Glass and Singer, 1972) suggests that previous experience with noise may affect one's ability to endure it.

In the context of office environments, Sloan (1972) has been involved in several designs in which he has improved productivity by taking into account individual differences in aggressiveness, sociability, and privacy needs, as these have been assessed through various types of observations, surveys, and interviews. Those who need more privacy are located in areas away from major traffic and circulation paths, away from other desks, and may be given more visual privacy by the hanging of banners from the ceiling. Organizing space in these ways is a means of accommodating individual differences within job categories, often without significantly altering the overall space standards. But more importantly, it shows that variable spatial provisions can be made within the same setting if they are made on a basis of function, where equity is defined in terms of individuals obtaining environmental supports that most closely match their own needs, whether or not these are the same as those of the person sitting next to them.

Social and Organizational Constraints

As described in Chapter 2, the same kinds of informal social processes that have been the focus of attention ever since the Hawthorne studies (Roethlisberger and Dickson, 1939) influence the kinds of possibilities one sees in the physical setting, or at least the kinds of possibilities one is likely to act on. Groups of workers develop expectations about what is an appropriate furniture arrangement, office decoration, or use of space and facilities. In a study of college classrooms (Becker et al., 1973), we found that students rearranged chairs, from a circular arrangement back to the typical rigid-row arrangement, even before the teacher arrived at the room.

When organizational members attempt to use their skills, knowledge, and capabilities to create environments more comfortable, efficient, safe, or pleasant, they often find their actions restricted by formal and informal administrative policy. Restrictions are often justified in terms of increased costs or the waste of time the modification would cause, but once again the underlying issue often seems to be control for control's sake. Steele (1973, p. 134) provides a good example:

A middle-level manager decided that his desk had faced the door of his office for too long. It was time for a change, so he turned it around to face a side wall. The next day he found a memo on his desk from the president's assistant saying that it had been found that the most effective way for managers to arrange their offices was with the desk facing the door so others would feel welcome. He was instructed to return his desk to its old position, with the firm implied threat of no longer being considered an effective manager if he did not. He later discovered that there was only one exception to the desk-toward-the-door rule: the president's office.

These kinds of informal norms influence which parts of a facility are used, how, when, and by whom. They define levels of environmental ambiguity and flexibility. Such norms critically influence different individuals' ability to perform at comparable levels, as well as the organization's ability to remain innovative in the face of continually changing conditions. From the standpoint of organizational development, we need to understand the conditions under which the physical setting is viewed administratively as ambiguous or unambiguous because these states, and the ability to move between them, influence individual job performance and satisfaction and, ultimately, organizational stability and flexibility.

STABILITY AND FLEXIBILITY IN THE PHYSICAL SETTING

As already noted, effective organizational functioning requires processes that support stability and flexibility (Weick, 1969). The question is, again, not whether flexibility and stability are desirable or not desirable, but rather, how and where they are achieved in the organization, and with what frequency.

As a tentative proposition, in relation to the physical setting, it seems that the environment is treated as unambiguous in the following cases:

• The environment may be newly created. Right after a renovated or new building is occupied, the official designers' or planners intentions are most salient. They expend great effort focusing all participants' attention on the same selected aspects of the physical setting to which they themselves attended. Those responsible for the design regard diverting attention to other aspects as inappropriate and counterproductive, if not subversive. Searching for alternative ways to use or manage the space is associated with mistakes stemming from bad planning, and reflects negatively on decision makers.

- The environment may be highly visible to nonorganization members (e.g., visitors to a school, customers of a firm). Visual order is associated with effective control and discipline. Visual diversity openly acknowledges the reduction of central control. It is often associated with disorder and ineffectiveness. Therefore, organizations generally wish to present an image of control and consistency, of stability, to visitors. The physical setting is a powerful communication medium that directly influences first impressions. Most administrators and designers want to maintain control over what is communicated.
- We may mistrust occupants, consider them dangerous or threatening, or simply undesirable (e.g., of low status). Many administrators and managers believe that such persons, when faced with an ambiguous environment, one which allows them to project into and onto it their own perceived needs and work or life style, will express behaviors that those in official control of the setting consider disruptive, counterproductive, or subversive. Their enacted environment and that of the planners or managers do not coincide, or at least that is the threat. The absence of centralized control is associated with a tendency toward organizational disorder (Porter et al., 1975). Therefore, administrators' ideas about the setting will prevail in this case.

We treat the environment as ambiguous (that is, we look for new potential in it or consider its total destruction) in the following cases:

- The facility may have existed for a very long time and/or may be obviously decaying or dysfunctional. Derelict and abandoned warehouses, decaying houses, and railroad stations are familiar examples. We begin to think of these as schools, restaurants, and recreation areas. At this point the original intentions of those creating the setting are no longer salient, and the persons who created them are often no longer present to defend and support them. Conditions may have also changed so drastically that many concerned participants view the original intentions as inappropriate. The new ambiguity about what the setting could be frequently generates controversy among competing groups, each of which tries to direct attention to certain aspects of the existing setting as a means of justifying a proposed way of recreating it (including its total destruction). Discussions about historic buildings, such as Radio City Music Hall, illustrate this process very well.
- The environment may be invisible to nonorganizational members (e.g., the factory floor, as opposed to the customer-reception area). In many cases, organizations fail to distinguish between areas that might more legitimately be treated as unambiguous and controlled settings, such as main-entrance lobbies or other public zones visitors and nonorganizational members occasionally enter, and more private work settings that are outside the

public's view. In a study of bank branch offices, for example, we found that the employees' lunchroom was subject to the same level of visual control as the main banking area. This makes little sense except as an attempt to preserve central authority over a low-status group. One of the characteristics of open-office landscaping is that it transforms settings that may have been semiprivate into semipublic ones. Behaviors such as failure to maintain a clean desk may be tolerated when the settings are out of view, but are controlled as they are made more public because they are now viewed in terms of their corporate image, which is less ambiguous and more inflexible than the image appropriate for individual work stations.

- We may trust occupants, consider them desirable, of high status. Bank presidents select their own furniture and arrange their office as they please. Middle-level managers use assigned furniture and their arrangements of it are restricted. The higher the status of the employees, the more the organization trusts them, on the one hand, to share their concerns and values and, on the other hand, the greater the value the organization places on the individual's unique talents and abilities, which it wants to exploit by providing a more ambiguous setting the individual can shape to support his or her own work habits. External control is lessened because internal control is assumed to be high. Higher-status employees are more trusted to share and accept their supervisors' values, and to direct their attention to similar aspects of the total situation, than are persons lower in the organizational hierarchy. The chicken-and-egg problem may pertain: Were employees lower in the hierarchy provided with equally ambiguous work settings in which they had greater freedom to structure their surroundings in ways that matched their individual work style and habits, it is possible that they would have a greater commitment to the organization and a higher level of performance. Studies of worker participation suggest that this, indeed, occurs with some frequency (Katzell et al., 1977; Lawler, 1973; Guest, 1979).

This nonexhaustive list of conditions under which different levels of ambiguity and flexibility in the physical setting obtain suggests that higher-status persons, in nonpublic locations in older buildings are likely to be allowed to treat their work setting as highly ambiguous, open to change, flexible, and unique. A low-status employee in a highly visible public location in a new building should experience administrative pressure to treat his or her work setting as unambiguous, inflexible, unchangeable, and standardized. The front receptionist in the main lobby of the headquarters building provides a familiar image. Persons with intermediate status working in different locations in buildings of a different age and condition should experience levels of ambiguity in their work setting that fall somewhere between these two extremes.

The implications of these different levels of administratively sanctioned ambiguity for organizational behavior rest on the notion that different individuals may require different levels of environmental support to perform at comparable levels (Nahemow and Lawton, 1976). This would suggest that all work settings should be treated as flexible and ambiguous, allowing individuals to create their own proximate environment as they see fit. Yet this may produce an environment in a constant state of change, with little stability and a sense of impermanence. If we acept Weick's thesis that organizations need to attain both stability and flexibility in order to survive, then a totally ambiguous work environment, characterized by constant change in response to individual needs and requirements, should be as organizationally ineffective as a setting characterized by absolute standardization and rigidity. If, moreover, innovation results from the periodic transformation of information into its opposite state (the flexible to the stable; the ambiguous to the unambiguous), as Weick suggests it does, then the relevant questions for organizational ecology center around the appropriate scale at which the physical-setting transformations should occur, and at what intervals.

FLEXIBILITY AND ENVIRONMENTAL SCALE

In terms of the physical setting, stability and flexibility vary with the scale or level of the facility system being considered. These scales or levels include:

- The total system: all facilities, space, equipment, and furnishings that an organization controls, including major circulation and transportation systems (e.g., roads, private buses, fleet cars, or airplanes) that connect various subsystems to each other or to parts of other systems.
- The primary subsystem: in the cases of very large organizations, the primary subsystem may include all of the space, equipment, and furnishings located in one or several buildings that are physically separated by large distances (e.g., branch plants or offices in different cities) or by smaller distances (e.g., a college campus). Thus, in the cases of small organizations, a single building may comprise the total system, while in large organizations, a single building may comprise a primary subsystem. The distinction is important since the degrees of freedom available, or the level of influence experienced on operating practices, are generally quite different. Identifying the total system becomes a critical (Aldrich, 1979) prerequisite for understanding influences processes—that is, factors that affect the form and use of a facility and its physical resources.
- Secondary subsystems: all of the space, equipment, and furnishings located within a floor or wing of a building, or in specially designated areas

like cafeterias, libraries, and conference rooms. Like a nested series of boxes, each of these subsystems forms the total system for those subsystems embedded within it.

- Tertiary subsystems: all of the space, equipment, and furnishings located in offices occupied by individuals and small groups, or in individual work stations.

Each of the systems and subsystems forms its own, and is part of a larger, sociotechnical system. The more inclusive the system scale, the greater the number of people directly involved in operating decisions. These systems are a function both of physical resources and of formal and informal expectations that define appropriate use patterns. Together, they determine the form of a setting. Permanence and stability are more characteristic of some of these systems and subsystems, and the physical resources and informal and formal norms that constitute them, than of others. Figure 3.2 shows one way of thinking about physical-setting scale in relation to the issues of stability and flexibility. For purposes of illustration, the total system is viewed as a single building, and tertiary subsystems are individual offices or work stations.

Figure 3.2 suggests the following: As the level of the physical setting is viewed at larger and larger aggregations (e.g., the entire facility), the amount of physical variety in the environmental form and the frequency of physical change to this form will decrease. The inverse is true as level of environmental scale diminishes. At the level of the personal office, frequency of alterations in its internal arrangement, or the kind and location of its equipment, increases. This relationship is based on both the Principle of Requisite Variety (Ashby, 1956) and Lawton's (Nahemow and Lawton, 1976) environmental-docility hypothesis. Both suggest that there are many differences among individuals, and that these differences should be reflected in the complexity and variation of processes of environmental support applied to them.

Figure 3.2 also shows that the level of ambiguity is inversely related to the level of the physical setting, and that the umber of rules related to how the environment can be created (relational changes and physical changes) is inversely related to the level of ambiguity. The lower the scale of the physical setting, the more ambiguity, and the fewer the rules that should be applied to its use. One further relationship is suggested: The frequency of periodic reversals of environments considered to be ambiguous or unambiguous is related to environmental scale. The facility infrastructure is relatively unambiguous, with the possibilities well defined. Yet at some points this state must be questioned: The facility has to be viewed as open to many more possibilities than have currently been attended to . The problem is this: How often should these information reversals occur? We simply do not have data

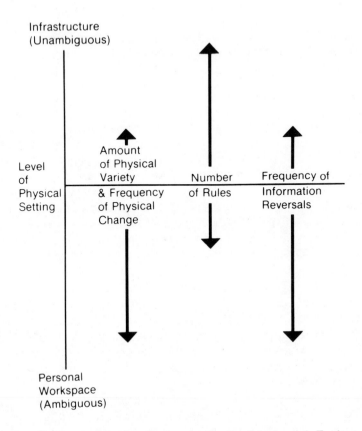

Infrastructure
(Unambiguous)

Level
of
Physical
Setting

Amount
of Physical
Variety
& Frequency
of Physical
Change

Number
of Rules

Frequency of
Information
Reversals

Personal
Workspace
(Ambiguous)

FIGURE 3.2 Physical-Setting Scale, Ambiguity Level, and Environmental Flexibility

on the appropriate rate or frequency of information reversal for any organization, or even on the most rudimentary ways of monitoring the need for reversals before they are long self-evident.

I have been using ambiguity and variety in a more or less interchangeable fashion. This is based on the assumption that ambiguous work settings, when acted upon by individuals, express variety in work style, habits, and preferred environmental supports. I have suggested that greater ambiguity in the physical setting is generally associated with higher organizational status, and I have discussed the role the physical setting may play in compensating for individual deficiencies in the constellations of personal resources. The physical setting may also, under some conditions, compensate for deficiencies in the nature of the work or task activity itself. It is to this role of the physical setting we turn to next.

JOB CHARACTERISTICS
AND ENVIRONMENTAL COMPENSATION

In large organizations, environmental supports are typically standardized for individuals within job categories. The most ambiguity and variety in terms of both physical characteristics of the environment and rules regarding its use are applied to or available for those whose jobs also, on the face of it, contain more variety and challenge; consider executives versus secretaries, for example.

Dull and tedious work is simply dull and tedious. No theory of the environment can overlook the fact that the nature and characteristics of the work itself are most important to the individual (Herzberg, 1966). Yet the nature of work itself cannot be totally isolated from the physical context within which it is carried out.

According to Herzberg, the conditions of work, including characteristics of the physical setting, are extrinsic job factors. He views them as contributing primarily to job dissatisfaction. Improving these characteristics reduces dissatisfaction, but does not necessarily improve job satisfaction, which he views as affected by intrinsic job characteristics, such as job variety or feedback. Satisfaction and dissatisfaction are treated as separate dimensions, rather than as polar opposites of a single dimension. In contrast to Herzberg (1966), the premise, here, is that characteristics of the physical setting may affect both intrinsic and extrinsic job characteristics, and thus job satisfaction. In the former case, they do so by structuring social relations, for example, in ways that facilitate job feedback. In the latter case, they affect the pleasantness and comfort within which work is carried out, for example, by providing preferred lighting and thermal levels. The physical setting also contributes to performance by providing a level of environmental support that matches, or compensates for, variations in individuals' personal skills and abilities. Thus, the physical setting has the potential to affect the individual's sense of competence.

As a direct support system for work activities, the physical setting was identified in a national Harris poll of office workers, in 1977, as a major impediment to efficiency. Major problems found were unsuitable office furniture and inadequate office tools, equipment, and materials. Distractions and the lack of privacy were the most negative attributes of offices because these prevented adequate concentration. These kinds of problems influence one's ability to carry out work effectively, as well as acting as "hygienic" factors (Herzberg, 1966) that influence the total work experience.

Characteristics of the physical setting, then, may compensate for what may be considered intrinsically unrewarding jobs, such as clerical work for example, by providing a level of environmental support that contributes to effective performance, and thus one's sense of competence and self-esteem, as well as to satisfaction with general working conditions. This level of support is likely to be valued for all kinds of jobs. Sundstrom et al. (1980), for example, found that self-ratings of performance and job satisfaction by clerks were inversely related to level of privacy. The argument that employees doing routine work not only do not require, but also do not prefer, levels of environmental support (in this case, privacy) typically provided for those whose work is more challenging was unsupported. Extremic job characteristics may also compensate for intrinsically unrewarding jobs.

There are many clerical and service jobs, for instance, which are considered intrinsically unrewarding and are typically poorly paid, and yet which benefit by responsible, bright, motivated people doing them. External conditions, including the characteristics of the physical surroundings within which the work is performed, become an important organizational resource for attracting and maintaining such people. One of the attractions of office decentralization made possible by electronic telecommunications is that it increases the pool of better-educated, more capable, and responsible people that can be tapped. The ability to attract such a workforce is one reason I have learned, many major companies have moved from places like New York City to rural areas in Connecticut (Williams, 1980). The quality of the physical setting (one's home, in the above example) provides justification for accepting and remaining in a job that otherwise would be considered socially unacceptable for these particular individuals. The environment becomes a salient reward that directs attention away from the less satisfying intrinsic characteristics of the job itself. It may also be the case that changes which appear not to affect intrinsic job characteristics do, in fact. Clerical work done at home is likely to be done with greater autonomy than the same kind of work done in a traditional office setting.

The work environment also includes much more than what traditionally is considered the task environment. A secretary's task environment may be the desk at which he or she types, but the work environment may include restrooms, a cafeteria, or sun deck. It is this total environment, including the geographic location, that has the potential to contribute to overall job satisfaction and performance, and to compensate for aspects of the job that may be intrinsically unrewarding. This is aside from the influence the physical setting has on several important job characteristics themselves, such as feedback and autonomy (Szilagyi and Holland, 1980; Oldham and Brass, 1979).

Summary

To summarize this chapter, I have suggested the following:

- The process of creating physical settings is characterized by a series of attention cycles, in which different organizational members transform the information available in the environment into meaning by focusing on some aspects of this information rather than others. These processes can be directed but not controlled administratively.
- Some of these information transformations are considered more appropriate administratively than others, usually depending on whether they are done by formally recognized organizational members with explicit responsibility for such decisions, or by members without such formal recognition.
- Information transformations in which stable, and often standardized, situations are treated as flexible and ambiguous were suggested as necessary to promote comparable levels of performance among persons with different types and levels of personal resources.
- Characteristics of the physical setting, including its geographical location, as well as its micro-environmental features, were suggested as potentially compensating for work which is intrinsically unrewarding.
- The meaning and role of the physical setting may vary as a function of the nature of the work activity itself.
- Periodic transformations of aspects of the physical setting from states considered stable and unchanging to flexible states, and vice versa, were suggested as a means of facilitating innovation and avoiding stagnation because they force redefinition of roles and goals, and allow individuals to create environments that support their potential.

While there has been considerable research into certain aspects of environment-behavior relationships, the intent of my discussion has been to suggest that a substantial, relatively untapped, research agenda exists. I have tried to show, using models of organizing processes (Weick, 1969) and of social-information processing (Salancik and Pfeffer, 1978), that our understanding of how the physical setting contributes to organizational behavior can be improved by conceptualizing it as a social process amenable to similar kinds of analyses appropriate to other aspects of social structure and behavior. We turn next to a consideration of how views of work and of workers have contributed to the form, use, and management of physical settings in organizations.

4

THE SCIENTIFIC-MANAGEMENT LEGACY

Despite the fact that decisions about the nature and use of space and equipment in organizations are political ones (e.g., they concern allocation of scarce resources on the basis of values), the available literature on interior architecture and space planning (Pile, 1968; Duffy et al., 1976) and on office management (Robichaud, 1958) is largely devoid of discussions of power and politics (Lipman et al., 1978). Explicit and detailed consideration is given to matters of efficiency, as noted by Lipman et al. (1978, p. 30):

> Spatial planning is viewed as a direct, a functional means to these [efficiency] ends; it is a "management tool." Considerations other than technical efficiency—including the possible personal desires of office personnel—are held to be subservient.... The distribution and exercise of power—a concept seemingly inseparable from that of management—appear to warrant neither the emphasis nor the analytical attention granted to those [concepts] they [researchers] associate with productivity and profitability.

Issues of power and control receive little attention largely because the uneven distribution of power among employer and employees is generally taken for granted among those studying office planning. A set of contrived social relations is treated as a structural necessity. The purpose of this chapter is to look at the ways in which social conditions, and in particular, certain conceptions of work and the worker, have influenced thinking about appropriate design and technology for the office. The watchword may be efficiency, but the key to understanding much of the nature of office design lies in issues of power and control.

The rise of office landscaping, in which large open bull pens as well as individual offices are replaced by space organized with partitions of varying heights to create different office or work-station sizes and configurations, has been justified, for example on the basis of improved efficiency, particularly in terms of intraoffice communication. Yet not only is there no evidence that suggests that the major inefficiency or unproductiveness of office workers stems from inadequate communications (as opposed to, for example, routinized work or insufficient privacy for adequately concentrating on a task), but evaluations of office-landscape designs have consistently failed to show improvements in productivity, or in effective communications and interaction (see Chapter 6 for a detailed review of this literature).

Brookes and Kaplan (1972), for example, found that while office landscaping increased the aesthetic features of the office and made it more sociable, it was a less utilitarian and efficient place to work in than the conventional offices it replaced. More recently, Clearwater (1980) found that the primary benefit of changing from a conventional office to a landscaped office setting was an improvement in the aesthetic features. This aesthetic improvement included a sense of increased status and professionalism, as well as a simple liking of the fact the office environment looked better. There was not, however, a level of dissatisfaction with the functional aspects of the conventional environment before the change, and there was no reported increase in productivity or in the functional contribution of the office after the change. Perhaps the most interesting aspect of the study was that the basic justification for a landscaped office design, which resides in the improvement in communication processes, was not at all supported. On several different measures of communication processes, including interoffice communication processes, communication with different divisions, the development of friendships, and interaction with supervisors, the landscape office was found less adequate than the conventional office. This study and others which consistently show that a landscaped office design contributes to communication problems, rather than improving communication processes, suggest that a major reason for moving to the new form of office environment is to create the impression of increased efficiency through the adoption of the latest in office design.

The new democracy supposedly characteristic of landscaped office design, reflected in a more open environment that promotes more open communications, has also not generally materialized. Those who had power in conventional offices still have it. The rush to adopt landscaped office design can be explained, in part, because it lowers costs of rearranging the office environment (*Contract*, 1980a) and, in part, by the need to maintain the image of modernity in a highly competitive marketplace. It would not be acceptable, however, if, at the same time, it did not support established views of work and workers.

The physical setting is simultaneously a symbol of efficiency and an instrument of power. Focusing attention on unequal social relations (e.g., power) is culturally suspect. It undermines the facade of efficiency. The physical setting functions nonverbally to promote power relationships we choose to ignore or suppress in our discussions of organizational decisions. It is difficult to grasp the dual role of environment as symbol of efficiency and instrument of power without critically examining in some detail the development of scientific management, and its basic premises about work and workers. Scientific management continues to influence how environments are created in organizations. Its widespread use, in practice if not in name, is likely to diminish, however, as organizations move toward more democratic forms of work organization in an effort to bolster lagging productivity.

SCIENTIFIC MANAGEMENT

Developed by Frederick W. Taylor at the turn of the century, scientific management was an attempt to substitute a set of highly rationalized procedures, appropriate to the rapidly developing mass-production technologies, for the kind of ad-hoc decisions about the design of work made in small craft-oriented shops. To get the most out of expensive machines, it seemed obvious that standardized work procedures and practices needed to be developed. The design of tasks and jobs was central to the notion of scientific management. Taylor (1911, p. 59) argued:

> The work of every workman should be fully planned out by the management at least one day in advance; each man should receive complete written instructions which described in detail the task which he was to accomplish. The instructions specified not only what was to be done but how it was to be done and the exact time allowed for doing it.

For example, instructions specified the exact weight and size of shovels which should be used for handling various kinds of materials, and the exact spacing of rest breaks for maximum workday productivity. All discretionary activity, all worker control over how to do work, was systematically eliminated. Those who succeeded in doing their task right, and within the time limit specified, were to receive additional pay of from 30 percent to 100 percent of their ordinary wages (Taylor, 1911).

Work was broken down into its constituent parts and partitioned among various workers for maximum simplicity and efficiency. To further insure efficiency, special attention was paid not only to what each worker should do, but to exactly how the work should be done.

Under scientific management, the manager assumed the burden of gathering together all of the traditional knowledge which in the past had been possessed by the workmen. This information was then analyzed, and reproduced as rules governing the most efficient organization of work. No task was considered so simple or complex that it could not be studied by management with the purpose of attaining more information about the job than the person performing it had.

Taylor argued that the workman would not develop this information because he had neither the time nor money. Yet the experimental study of work had always existed. The self-use of such methods by the craftsman is part of the very practice of a craft. What was new, as Braverman (1974) has pointed out in a trenchant analysis of scientific management, was the shifting of the study or work from those who performed it to those who managed it. The value for management of control of the study of work was that by separating complex thinking and mundane performance, personnel costs could be reduced. Rather than having a highly trained person do both activities, always being paid at the level the complex thinking demanded, it was much cheaper to pay someone very low rates to do only mundane tasks, and pay a much smaller number of persons a high wage for doing only complex thinking. Scientific management did not invent management's right to control labor, but it moved it to new heights by asserting the "absolute necessity for adequate management of the dictation to the worker of the precise manner in which work is to be performed" (Braverman, 1974, p. 90).

Taylor's techniques were intended to insure what he called a "fair day's work." He defined such work as all the work a worker can do without injury to his health, at a pace that can be sustained throughout a working lifetime. In practice, the level of activity was often extreme, and could be performed by only a few carefully selected persons. He believed that most workers failed to produce a fair day's work because they "soldiered." Essentially, this was the deliberate attempt to work slower than possible and convince the employer that one was going at a good pace. In today's terms, he was referring to the development of informal social norms to restrict productivity. He believed that the only way to counter this tendency was to give total control to management for the process of work, leaving nothing to the worker's discretion. The problem, from a management perspective, was that under craft technology, the craftsperson often knew much more about the process than the manager, and could dictate the work process.

Breaking down work into its most basic components and having any one individual work only on one component created boring and tedious jobs, and disgruntled and hostile employees (Walker and Guest, 1952; Blauner, 1964). Management's response was to select workers for the job who were as perfectly matched to the demands of the job as possible. Workers had to be physically and mentally capable of the work, but a major concern was to insure that employees were not overqualified for the job. As Taylor (1911, p. 59) wrote in a famous passage:

> Now one of the very first requirements for a man who is fit to handle pig iron as a regular occupation is that he more nearly resemble in his mental make-up the ox than any other type. The man who is mentally alert and intelligent

is for this very reason entirely unsuited for what would, for him, be the grinding monotony of work of this character. Therefore the workman who is best suited to handling pig iron is unable to understand the real science of doing this class of work. He is so stupid that the word "percentage" has no meaning for him, and he must consequently be trained by a man more intelligent than himself into the habit of working in accordance with the laws of this science, before he can be successful.

Taylor's example now appears to many as overstated, yet college graduates often find jobs closed to them because they are overqualified. The underlying justification is not that the person cannot do the job. It is that an overqualified person will cause trouble: not take orders cheerfully, nor happily do dull and repetitive tasks; will ask questions and propose alternative ways of organizing work. Overqualified persons may take initiatives that spill over into areas management considers its sole prerogative. For scientific management, this included all discretionary decision making, all control over how work should be performed. The problem, as Braverman (1974, p. 133) notes, is that management has "not yet found a way to produce workers who are at one and the same time degraded in their place in the labor process, and also conscientious and proud of their work."

Although motivation had not been an issue in craft-organized work, the breakdown of work into its constituent parts immediately created motivation problems and resistance to work. Many employees intensely disliked working on routine, simplified jobs. Porter et al. (1975) note that as far back as 1924, studies began to appear that showed that employees on simplified jobs were bored and, in response to their boredom, took unauthorized breaks from their work whenever possible. Thirty-five years later, Worthy (cited in Porter et al. [1975]) found, in a survey of nationwide retail organizations, that employees' morale and productive output were lower in jobs which were highly segmented and simplified. In a 1950s study of 1,000 assembly-line workers, Walker and Guest (1952) found high levels of absenteeism, turnover, and job dissatisfaction among employees with repetitive, machine-paced assembly-line jobs. Porter et al. (1975, p. 278) report findings from an unpublished study indicating that turnover among assembly-line workers was reported by one company to be over 100 percent in a single year. Braverman (1974, p. 32) cites more recent statistics from an article in *Fortune* that showed that absenteeism at General Motors and Ford had reached the point by 1970 where "an average of 5 percent of G.M.'s hourly workers are missing from work without explanation every day.... On some days, notably Fridays and Mondays, the figure goes as high as 10 percent." Tardiness had also increased, along with complaints about quality, arguments with foremen, complaints about discipline, and grievances. He noted further: "The quit rate at Ford last year was 25.2 percent.... Some assembly-line workers are so turned off, managers report with astonishment, that they just walk away in mid-shift and don't often come back to get their pay for the time they have worked." When unemployment increases, these rates decline, reducing the requirement of employee dependency, if not of desperation, underlying this approach. These kinds of statistics suggest that at least part of the power of scientific management is as a symbol of efficiency.

Rather than attributing the decline in motivation and pride in work to the new ways in which work was being organized, the problem was attributed to character flaws in the workers. They were viewed as intrinsically lazy, and needing constant and close supervision. Taylor and his followers knew that work, as they organized it, was unpleasant, but they believed that workers would accept any kind of work practices as long as they received a substantial monetary reward, and as long as appropriate selection procedures could be developed to insure that overqualified people would not be hired.

It is difficult to imagine how anyone but overqualified persons could be hired. We have spent billions of dollars to educate our children to develop their intellectual potential. With the exception of the educable retarded, almost all persons are overqualified for punching a computer keyboard thousands of times each day, or for stringing together set paragraphs in sequences devised by someone else. Schools have failed miserably, if their role is viewed, as it is by some educational critics, as one of lowering children's aspirations and preparing them for jobs that are dull and repetitive, but well-paid.

Ironically, employers faced with the possibility of choosing a poorly educated and low-skilled worker or a better-educated, more skilled worker generally opt for the latter. They do so not for reasons of wanting increased skill or ability. For the emerging class of white-collar manual laborers, doing most jobs does not require even a high school diploma. The requirement of such a certificate is more a certification of responsibility, motivation, and reliability: "Sure, we can find out quickly if a girl can really punch cards. But will she come in every Monday? Will she stay after 5 o'clock when we're pushed for overtime?..." (Braverman, 1974, p. 337) In the absence of available alternatives, the answer is "for awhile."

SCIENTIFIC MANAGEMENT AND HUMAN ENGINEERING

The logical extension of scientific management was the development of human engineering, in which workers themselves are treated as machines. This was done for two reasons: to increase control over the work process and to determine a fair day's work in a quasi-scientific manner. Time and motion studies have served as the primary means for translating the human-as-machine metaphor into a set of operational standards.

Time study involves the measurement of elapsed time for each component operation of a work process. Its prime instrument is the stopwatch. Frank Gilbreth, one of Taylor's prominent followers, refined the time-study concept by developing the notion of motion study: the investigation and classification of the basic motions of the body, regardless of the particular and concrete form of the labor in which these motions are used. In motion and time study, the elementary movements were visualized as the building blocks of every work activity; they were called, in a variant of Gilbreth's name spelled backward, "therbligs." Therblig charts used by industrial engineers, work designers, and office managers give to each motion a name, a symbol, a color code, and a time in ten-thousandths of a minute. Motions are described in machine terms: bending is "trunk movement with hips as hinge" (Braverman, 1974, p. 174).

Many systems of standard data are available; the most popular is methods-time measurement, described by Braverman (1974, p. 175):

> In this system, the time standard used is the TMS, which is defined as one hundred-thousandth of an hour, equal to six ten-thousandths of a minute or thirty-six thousandths of a second. It offers refinements of the therblig to apply to many conditions. Reach, for instance, is tabulated separately for objects in fixed or varying locations, for objects jumbled with others...."

Such information is used to determine the "human factor" in work design. The time taken to perform any activity can be calculated, including "humane" allowances for rest, toilet, and coffee time.

The prime value is that the measures are seen as objective and scientific. The human-relations-oriented Hawthorne studies and the hundreds of others spawned by it have had little impact on the sanctity of such engineering approaches. They have, in fact, spread from industrial to office settings. As a consequence, the blue-collar worker's dissatisfation with the assembly line is mirrored in a white-collar worker's response to increasing compartmentalization of work. According to a Special Task Force on Work in America: "The office today, where work is segmented and authoritarian, is often a factory. For a growing number of jobs, there is little to distinguish them but the color of the worker's collar: computer keypunch operations and typing pools share much in common with the automobile assembly-line" (*Work in America*, 1973). Secretaries, clerks and bureaucrats may have a higher education, but their prestige, status, and pay is lower than for most blue-collar workers. The same report noted that in addition to expressed dissatisfaction with dull and routine clerical positions, other signs of discontent among this group included turnover rates as high as 30 percent annually, and a 46 percent increase in white-collar union membership between 1958 and 1968. A survey conducted by a group of management consultants among a cross section of office employees found that they were producing at only 55 percent of their potential. Among the reasons cited for this was the boredom of repetitive jobs (*Work in America*, 1973, p. 35).

THE MIDDLE-CLASS MYTH

Wearing a white collar is no longer synonymous with being middle class. This was not always the case. One hundred years ago, even the largest firms employed only a handful of clerks, and most of these were semimanagers in terms of the present distribution of functions. At that time, a clerk was assistant manager, retailer, confidant, management trainee, and prospective son-in-law. From 1870 to 1970, the percentage of gainful workers in clerical positions increased from six-tenths of 1 percent to 18 percent, or more than 14 million workers. The nature of clerical work as a total occupation declined in direct propostion to the number of clerical workers employed (Braverman, 1974, pp. 294-295).

Clerical work has been subjected to the same kind of rationalization and atomization that occurred earlier in industry, and is growing at an ever-increasing pace as a result of computer technology. As office work changed from something merely incidental to management into a labor process in its own right, the need to systematize and control it began to be felt. By the 1920s, scientific management was being applied to the office, for the same reasons it had been applied to industry earlier.

As part of the concern with making all office operations as efficient as possible, office layout was subjected to detailed time and motion studies. The intent was to eliminate what management considered wasted motion because the time taken for trips to a water fountain, for example, when totaled among a large workforce, constituted a significant amount of time spent in unproductive labor—that is, not directly working on an assigned task in an apparent manner.

The same attitude can be seen today in most large offices. Placing everything at the worker's fingertips, from storage units to cafeterias, may be appreciated by users when such arrangements support activities they consider important to fulfilling their jobs. Such arrangements can be counterproductive, however. Trips considered wasted motion provide the opportunity for learning what others are doing, exchanging ideas, recharging one's batteries, collecting one's thoughts. The problem, for the user, is that the benefit, to the organization, of "efficient" design is direct, in the form of reduced space standards, shorter lunch periods, time spent on what are considered activities unrelated to productive work. Elaborate employee cafeterias heavily subsidized by corporations, for example, serve a double-edged purpose: they provide cheaper food, and exert pressure on employees to be back at work (or for the cafeterias to be empty) when lunch periods are officially over.

Human engineers have helped management reorganize office work by developing standard data on time and motion in the office, just as occurred for industry. With access to *A Guide to Office Clerical Time Standards: A Compilation of Standard Data Used by Large American Companies* (Braverman, 1974), one can learn that opening and closing a file drawer takes .04 minutes, opening a center drawer takes .026 minutes, getting up from a chair takes .033 minutes.

Using such data, performance standards that clerks are to measure up to can, and are, devised. Performance against these standards is easily built into the equipment or office procedure: e.g., on office machines, devices such as stroke counters and automatic sequential numbering; prenumbered documents, processed in sequence; number of boxes of punch cards finished in a day. What characterizes and unifies all of these measures is not that they accurately indicate all the relevant costs to an organization, but that the data are easy to collect.

SCIENTIFIC MANAGEMENT AND INDUSTRIAL PSYCHOLOGY

Employee hostility, property destruction, absenteesim, and poor-quality work, all in response to highly segmented and repetitive work, have focused attention on issues surrounding the quality of work. But rather than exploring the nature of work itself, the concern has primarily been with the adjustment of the worker to the ongoing production processes as these have been designed by the industrial engineer. More basic reconsideration of work processes generally emerges only when all other routes have utterly failed, and the whole enterprise is in danger of collapsing (Guest, 1979).

In response to the persistent failure of selection procedures to produce persons who enthusiastically and responsibly perform routine and repetitive tasks, organizations turned to human-relations experts. Braverman (1974) derisively refers to these experts as the "maintenance crew for the human machinery." Their job, as he sees it, is to address the problems of management: dissatisfaction expressed in high turnover rates, absenteeism, resistance to the prescribed work pace, indifference, and hostility. Human-relations experts become a symbol of management's concern, which is used to focus attention away from the characteristics of the job itself.

For many engineers and accountants, QWL is largely irrelevant within the bounds of reasonable (arbitrarily defined) work conditions—that is, ones that offer no immediate threat to life or limb. Their concern for the nature of work conditions is simple and easily articulated: do what is necessary to reduce the direct operating costs. Efforts to improve the quality of the work environment, justified on the basis that such changes contribute to important personnel concerns, such as motivation and commitment, are treated skeptically. The problem lies not with the concept, but with how it is applied in practice.

QUALITY OF WORK LIFE
AND THE PHYSICAL SETTING

Decisions to upgrade the visual design of the office environment by providing office landscaping, for example, may have little to do with major issues of concern to employees. Office landscaping may actually worsen work conditions by reducing the amount of space available to employees (Canty, 1977) or by making their idiosyncratic work style more visible and therefore more open to question. Style of work, as much as quantity and quality, becomes an issue.

Engineers and accountants accept without any qualms the importance of the layout and design of the work environment in terms of production flow, materials handling and human-factors design. They are typically skeptical about the value of considering the design of the physical setting in terms of employee needs, preferences, or work style. Changes in the design of the workplace justified as psychological improvements, but in fact having little or no relation to user preferences or requirements, confirm their skeptical attitudes. They discern no changes in behavior or performance (and rarely look for them systematically) and conclude that improvements in the physical setting have little relation to the kinds of changes in employee behaviors they consider meaningful.

The only justified conclusion the engineer can make on assessing the impact of the change in the physical setting is that a specific landscaped office installed using a particular set of decision-making processes, and based on a particular set of criteria, has not had much of an impact on employee behavior. And even this conclusion is suspect since systematic evaluation is rarely done. In the absence of systematic evaluation of design changes, it is impossible to say, with any certainty, what effects they had. But should we expect anyone to work harder in response to design changes that may include smaller offices, carpeted columns, and colored panels they did not select and may detest?

The problem is that a change intended to improve the QWL (and justified in these terms) is taken as synonymous with actually improving it for those who life with it on a daily basis. As noted in an earlier chapter, intention and attention are confused in this regard. The unfortunate consequence is that the potential benefits of careful design of they physical setting, from the user's perspective, are undermined.

Management's expressed concern for improving efficiency and productivity is real, but solutions are sought within existing concepts of control and power, whether or not these actually contribute to these objectives. Attempts to improve the quality of work life, through changes in the physical setting, will continue to bear little relationship to measures of performance as long as no attempt is made to assess not only the intent of changes as they relate to QWL, but the meaning of these changes as they are attended to by the rank and file. This would require some fundamental shifts in concepts of control and effective management, particularly in terms of encouraging and using employees' assessments of their environmental-support requirements; that is, returning to a situation where those who perform the work study and control how it should be done.

Office design that fails to improve the quality of work life for employees, and which, by doing so, may actually decrease organizational effectiveness, will not, however, easily fade away, for two reasons. First, in the absence of systematic evaluation studies, the effects of different ways of organizing and managing space are assessed by personal beliefs. Many managers underestimate the importance of the physical setting's influence on behavior. Second, most office design will be influenced by calculations of immediate and direct cost savings. Such direct costs are easier to measure than costs related to employee dissatisfaction. They also have a long history of being considered the most relevant costs to measure. New developments in office design, such as the landscaped office and the use of modular systems furniture in it, are accepted by organizations not because they improve, as is often claimed, the quality of work life, communication processes, or work efficiency. They are accepted because, in practice, they are often used to reduce the total amount of space per employee. This significantly reduces direct operating expenses. Work efficiency and quality of work life thus provide the symbolic, not substantive, justification for such office design.

CONTROL IN THE WORKPLACE

In addition to reducing the amount of space and equipment per person, which lowers direct operating costs, the goal of design becomes one of removing as many options as possible from the worker so that discretionary activities are difficult or impossible. The premise is that discretionary activity is unproductive. More importantly, it seems to counter a well-established moral order in which employees are viewed as legitimately excluded from decision making for reasons tenuously related to efficiency.

Control is an important part of an organization's and a supervisor's role. The issue is meaningless framed in terms of control versus no control. The issue is how much control given, to whom, for what purposes, and with what consequences. Scientific management maintains that individual differences are irrelevant and should be stamped out through standardized design of jobs, potent and uniform incentive systems, close supervisory practices. The intent of these practices is to insure uniform behavior of all employees in particular positions in the organization. Porter et al. (1975) argue that this philosophy underestimates both the degree to which it is possible to eradicate such individual differences, and the negative organizational consequences of doing so.

If individual differences cannot be stamped out, and attempts to do so are counterproductive, why do they continue? The answer seems to lie in a view of control as a value in its own right, irrespective of its effect on efficiency. The absence of control is equated with an inherent tendency toward disorder and dissolution in the organization. It is also seen as undermining a necessary social order. Yet systematically denying large segments of the workforce meaningful control over how their work is organized, including control of the physical setting in which it occurs, creates a tendency toward disorder, apathy, and alienation (Blauner, 1964; Walker and Guest, 1952; Guest, 1979).

THE PHYSICAL SETTING,
THE PROFESSIONAL, AND THE MANAGER

In most organizations, control, purpose, social integration, and self-involvement are all problematic. Historically, the focus has been on how the organization of work and the physical setting contributes to alienation (or productivity) among factory machine operators and assembly-line workers. Human-factors specialists and operations researchers, in particular, have done an enormous amount of work on how the equipment and office layout can be organized to promote efficiency and productivity (McCormick, 1976), particularly in industrial settings and among lower-echelon office workers: secretaries, clerk-typists, keypunch operators. In contrast, very little work has been done on how the environment affects the people the organization expects to be in control and to make decisions. Outside of a concern for status distinctions as reflected in office design, very little systematic empirical attention has been paid to executive productivity: how office design affects managers, executives, scientists, or lawyers. Different conceptions of both this kind of work, and the persons who do it, have contributed to this neglect, both from a scientific-management perspective and a broader ecological orientation.

Scientific management has not yet made as much of an impact on these groups as it has on lower echelons because of the difficulty in atomizing the activities of a teacher, nurse, or middle-level manager into a completely standardized sequence of routine tasks resulting in essentially identical products. These kinds of organizational members have more in common with what Blauner (1964) calls "craft" industries than with the kind of repetitive and routine detail work associated with typing or keypunching.

Craft industries depend on the special skills, judgment, and experience of journeymen workers as these have been developed over an extensive apprenticeship period. While the need for management control over craftspersons gathered together under one organization has long been recognized, what distinguishes craftspersons from other kinds of workers is that management is not automatically assumed to have the authority to determine the exact processes of work. These are determined by the craftspersons themselves. By this definition, a teacher, nurse, systems analyst, junior executive, and human-factors researcher are craftspersons.

These kinds of professions have an additional feature that distinguishes them from other professions, particularly when located in service operations like schools and hospitals. Less emphasis is given to productivity, at least as measured in standard units, since these are extremely difficult to define. How does one determine whether a nurse or teacher is productive? More emphasis is placed on individual responsibility and initiative, and on internal standards of performance. Partly for this reason, almost no attention has been paid to how office layout and design affects this group of workers and the overall operation of the organization.

The physical setting of work, which receives so much attention by operations researchers and human-factors specialists as it concerns lower echelons of workers, where control and productivity are the issues, is relatively ignored for higher-status professionals. Not only is the physical setting relatively ignored in terms of constraint functions, but its contribution to the kinds of behaviors that are considered of great importance (e.g., communication, development of innovative ideas, coordination and integration of different organizational functions) is overlooked. Because higher-level professionals are assumed to have more control, and because the ability to do the job well is considered to rest upon the kinds of skills and abilities that reside within the individual, the contribution of the physical setting to effective performance or to QWL has not received much attention.

This is beginning to change, for a number of reasons. For one thing systems furniture is becoming a common solution to interior space-planning requirements. It now accounts for something like 50 percent of all new installations (*Contract*, 1980a). Because the furniture involves a system that presumable integrates functions, it by definition requires, for effective installation, a look at the total personnel of a facility, including professional and technical workers as well as lower-level secretaries, clerks, receptionists. For the most part, the kinds of analysis accompanying systems-furniture installations are still rudimentary. While they are concerned with information flow and communication networks, they are less often concerned with informal work patterns and multifaceted needs for privacy and accessibility among persons at all levels in the organization.

The fact that such relationships have escaped scrutiny reflects a greater preoccupation with issues of control than with effectiveness per se. Tinkering with the design and management of executive-support systems is highly suspect because of its possible repercussions for existing power and political relationships. Scientific management stops at the top floor. It does so, ironically, because of its narrow emphasis on efficiency, which presumably is not an appropriate concern for highly paid executives.

The intense interest, today, among top management in Japanese management styles, in which there is a greater recognition of the interdependency between managers and rank-and-file employees, is likely to help focus attention on overall organizational effectiveness. This will include concern for the way in which mangers relate to each other, as well as to those working for them. The ways in which the physical relationships of organizational members affect communication patterns, including the opportunity for interaction and the exchange of ideas central to mutual understanding and integrated work efforts, should receive more attention than they did under a scientific management approach to the organization of work, in which relatively little attention is paid to social relations among persons.

THE LEGACY: ENVIRONMENT AS A CONSTRAINT

Scientific management's legacy for environmental design and facility planning has been to focus attention almost exclusively on the constraint functions of the environment, stemming from a pessimistic and negative view of workers, and the meaning of work for them. Workers are viewed as lacking intrinsic motivation. They are viewed as motivated more by money than by the nature of the work itself or how it is organized. The problem with this view is that it is largely a self-fulfilling prophecy. Much of the work available as organized under scientific-management principles is routine and unrewarding. Few people enjoy this work. In the absence of other alternatives, most will do what they must to get by, and nothing more. The fundamental problem is with the organization of the work, not with the average worker. Scientific management's belief that individuals possess stable characteristics and traits that can be identified and used in ways that create an effective match between these characteristics and those of the job they are hired to do draws attention not to the nature of the work and workplace, but to selection processes. If one believes the selection processes are effective, poor performance is most likely to be attributed to characteristics of the worker. The next step is to create environments whose basic function is to constrain what management considers inappropriate behavior, and which provide minimal support for what human-factor studies have found people require to complete a job. These requirements are typically based on models of human physical, biological, and cognitive capacities and limitations. Most of these models of human behavior ignore the social context of work and individual needs for control and recognition. Work is organized, and support systems provided, on the basis of how management wishes people were, rather than evolving from a genuine understanding of who they are within ongoing social contexts. There is a failure to distinguish between what people can do, in terms of their physical and mental capabilities, and what they will do.

In most organizations, from elementary schools to insurance companies, management exhorts its people to engage in what it considers desirable behavior, whether it is quietly doing math problems, processing accident claims, or digging a trench. Yet rather than creating social and environmental supports that might encourage desired behaviors, much effort goes into the development of rules, procedures, and environmental supports that emphasize punishment of transgressions. We ask students, or employees, to concentrate on their work, place them in settings with minimal acoustical or visual privacy, and then punish them if they fail to concentrate or try to avoid the setting.

Rather than designing support systems that encourage people to behave in desired ways because they also support individual work styles and preferences, scientific management has emphasized designing support systems that attempt to restrain people from engaging in behaviors we know they prefer. Our approach to children's behavior illustrates the difference in strategies very well. Faced with two children fighting over the same toy, most adults try to persuade one of the children to let the other child have the toy awhile. If this strategy fails, as it often does, a common response is to punish one of the children for continuing to fight over the toy. An alternative strategy is to provide one of the children with another toy or activity.

The environment, in the second case, is used to encourage alternative user-preferred behaviors rather than as a means of directly preventing an undesirable behavior. The goal is essentially the same: eliminating undesirable behavior; but the approaches differ radically. As I noted in the first chapter, environments rarely eliminate behaviors that those engaging in them consider important. They simply make them more difficult to engage in, or cause them to be relocated, often, as a consequence, generating resentment and hostility.

From an ecological perspective, efficient and effective environmental supports (and control) are those that result in people engaging in desired ways without simultaneously creating a series of unintended negative consequences, for either those persons directly affected by the environmental support, or those indirectly affected as they cope with the behavior or activities (or their elimination) set in motion by the original choice of supports. Environments become a symbol of efficiency and an instrument of power when they ignore the personal and organizational consequences of the negative behavior they attempt to control. Measures of productivity that ignore the wider systemic effect of narrowly defined efficiency designs are similarly symbols of efficiency that direct attention away from comprehensive and systemwide decisions that promote effectiveness over time.

THE LEGACY: PROFESSIONALIZATION

A second major legacy of the scientific-management movement, as it affects how physical settings are created in organizations, stems from the objective of breaking comprehensive and integrated work activities down into the smallest constituent parts. Essentially, the goal is to limit decision-making capabilities to the professional and specially trained expert. Whereas craftsmen studied their own work activities and continually sought ways of improving the kinds of tools and other environmental supports they required, scientific management created separate professions, such as industrial engineering, to conduct these kinds of studies and to recommend what the best supports and working procedures were. The effect was to exclude all of those who were not officially designated experts in some area from participating in any decision making in that area. The reluctance to systematically solicit feedback from employees about the adequacy of their environmental supports reflects this fundamental premise that only those specially trained in the environment should and can make such decisions.

The exorcising of laymen from all decision processes overlooks a fundamental distinction between the ability to identify dysfunction in environmental-support systems, and the ability to generate better solutions for it. Specially trained persons, such as architects or space planners, often can generate solutions that are far better than those by the average layman. But to do this effectively, they must know what the problem is. They generally do not know this and have only the most primitive strategies and tools for finding out. In exorcising the average worker from any decision making, scientific management blurred this distinction and has made the work of the professional more difficult, and in some cases impossible.

Ironically, the strengthening of the role of the professional has succeeded so well that it is beginning to backfire. Because people realize that some sort of recognition as a professional is a prerequisite for some degree of control and autonomy in one's work, workers with any specialized skills are beginning to view themselves as professionals. They want to be treated accordingly: given higher pay, more discretionary decision making, more general autonomy.

PROFESSIONALIZATION AND THE
ROLE OF THE PHYSICAL SETTING

Most professions only approximate the ideal type found in the ministry, law, and medicine, the traditional and original professions. For this reason, Vollmer and Mills (1966) suggest that it is more useful to analyze and describe the characteristics of occupations in terms of the concept of professionalization. They assume that many, if not all, occupations may be placed somewhere on a continuum between the ideal-type profession at one end and completely unorganized occupational categories, or nonprofessions, at the other end. Professionalization can be defined, then, as a process by which an organized occupation, usually, but not always, by virtue of making a claim to special esoteric competence and to a concern for the quality of work and its benefit to society, obtains the exclusive right to perform a particular kind of work, control training for and access to it, and control the right of determining and evaluating the way the work is performed (Vollmer and Mills, 1966). Professions (generally defined as including individuals engaged in similar types of behaviors and who belong to formally organized trade associations or professional societies) have evolved for essentially political and economic reasons: to create a set of normative expectations, supported whenever possible by training programs and legal processes, such as certification or a union contract, that insure that only selected individuals are permitted to engage in designated activities. The control of critical information and skills, and the restrictions on the number of persons with these resources, insure high demand and commensurate remuneration. Professional and trade associations work very hard to create a set of conditions where nonprofessionals cannot engage in the professional activity even if they are capable of doing so. Unlicensed medical practice is a criminal offense. Union contracts forbidding plumbers to hammer nails have become caricatures of this hardening of professional boundaries among the crafts.

One outcome of the professions' attempt to create a limited population of qualified persons to engage in particular activities is that they have directed attention to the capabilities, skills, and experience of their members. They attempt to manage and control these through their educational and certification programs. These personal resources are considered scarce, and dependent for their development on special experiences and educational opportunities. For this reason, doctors, lawyers, teachers, and nurses generally focus on personal qualities of professional members—their training, experience, intelligence, special sensitivity—and on suitable recompense for what they consider the discharge of very special duties. With the exception of design professions, whose focus of concern is the built environment, most professions and trade union associations tend to ignore or play down the physical setting's contribution to effective performance, except in circumstances where the environmental conditions are so extreme that they blatantly undermine successful and safe completion of activities (Trist and Bamforth, 1951).

To focus on characteristics of the setting that might be contributing significantly to performance and success in that setting would, from a professional or management perspective, be counterproductive and subversive unless the professional or manager were viewed as responsible for making these decisions. Attributing successful performance to the nature of environmental-support systems when these have been designed by other persons, particularly other professionals, undermines the claim to special personal skills and autonomy central to the definition of "professional." It also undermines the authority of the manager based on the "administrative principle" (Vollmer and Mills, 1966; Freidson, 1973)—in which occupancy in a formal office in an organizational hierarchy, not expertise derived from special educational and training programs, is the basis of authority.

To recognize the importance of environmental supports in a context where one's identity, competence, and self-esteem are closely associated with highly personal skills and knowledge, either based on special training programs or extensive experience, is inherently threatening unless one is responsible for these supports. Otherwise one risks demeaning one's own standing while raising the standing of some other individual or groups. The impression may also be created that personal skills could be replaced by suitably designed machines or that individuals with lesser skills and training could perform as well as professionals in an appropriately designed environment. Simplified legal forms designed to be used by lay persons, and highly sophisticated equipment used to diagnose blood, are resisted by lawyers and medical technicians, respectively, because they appear to undermine their special skills, training, and esoteric knowledge. Such changes threaten their financial security, which is dependent on the scarcity of their particular capabilities.

Efforts to influence directly the nature of environmental supports, therefore, occur in a social and organizational context where two factors undermine the development of effective environmental supports. First, professionalization tends to underplay the importance of broad-based environmental supports (i.e., other than for specialized equipment). Second, the administrative principle (Friedson, 1973) legitimizes only efforts of persons holding certain offices, regardless of their training or education, to make decisions about the organization of work, including the form and management of the physical setting. As a consequence, nonmanagement efforts to create effective work environments are typically viewed by management as relatively unimportant (characteristics of the worker and financial incentives being the focal concern), yet infringing on the legitimate sphere of management responsibility. Such efforts are resisted by management primarily for the latter reason, although the resistance is often justified in terms of efficiency: the amount of work time lost, the chaos of getting everyone involved (see Chapters 7 and 8 for a discussion of these issues). Professionals with formal responsibility for organizing space and equipment (e.g., human-factors specialists, industrial engineers) are more likely to resist such efforts on the basis that the layman does not have the requisite skills to effectively participate in such processes.

This situation is unlikely to remain stable, however, because of the accelerating pace of professionalization of all occupations (Freidson, 1973). Government codes and regulations and union contracts have limited the authority of management, but without really influencing the content of work itself: what the job should be, how it should be performed, who should do it. These decisions, under the administrative principle, are reserved for management. Under the occupational or professional principle, they are reserved for those performing the work. Professionalization enlarges the scope of worker control. Management's role shifts to that of providing necessary resources and services for professionals to carry out their work. As one aspect of increased professionalization, workers' expectations about what they need to get their job done, and what is their due, should change.

The movement toward increased professionalization will occur across the board, but may be most accelerated at the base of the workforce pyramid. At this level, office automation may create pressures from clerical workers to be accorded the more professional status of word processor or programmer.

Professionalization of the clerical workforce will focus on only a few of the key characteristics of professionals, and in particular, on the notion of special esoteric knowledge developed through training programs and work experience, and of development of formal and semiformal associations. The ideals of service to the community and a code of ethics will likely be less emphasized than concern for greater autonomy and higher pay. The original work model for word processing, organized in a fashion similar to assembly-line work, does not seem to be working well (Landau, 1980; Stanford University Symposium on Office Automation, 1980). The more successful equipment installations seem to occur in situations where the machine operators have had relatively great freedom to structure the pace of their work themselves, distribute it according to fluctuating workloads and originator requests, schedule breaks when considered necessary, and arrange their office environment to accommodate what they consider effective and comfortable work patterns.

The sense of being a professional among word and data processors has been facilitated, in part, by the strategies organizations have adopted to make this kind of work attractive. Frequently, the creation of a word-processing job carries with it a new job title, an increase in salary, participation in special training programs run by the equipment vendor or the company, selection of the youngest and most able person, and management discussions which describe the new job as being more professional (Gostinian, 1980).

Part of professionalization is also persuading others that only a selected few are competent to perform a given activity. The new computer-base technology makes it possible to establish authority of expertise in a highly visible way because of the physical presence of the equipment and the fact that others, without training or experience, cannot simply sit down and run the machine. This is true of most supervisors and managers as well as those forming an approximate peer group, such as secretaries. In those cases where managers do use the same type (if not the same piece) of electronic equipment as used by those under their supervision, it is more likely to raise the standing of the lower group rather than lowering that of the higher one.

Increased professionalization will result in which workers wanting more to control over how they perform their work. The weakening of the administrative principle, involving a shift in management function to providing the necessary resources for relatively autonomous workers to carry out their jobs, should change who participates, formally, in creating the physical setting of work, and on what basis. One would expect the workers themselves to become more involved, and for management, in its capacity as provider of necessary resources, to develop an authority based on expertise, rather than relying on the current authority of office.

In order to increase awareness, and stimulate a more active and effective understanding, of the role physical settings may play in organizations, professional training will have to be broadened to include, as one aspect of professional identity, the concept that part of one's skills and capabilities is in managing the available environmental resources from a knowledge base, as well as on the basis of one's own personal experience and preferences.

There are several reasons why professionals, who, I said earlier, tend to downplay the role of environmental supports as a factor in their own performance, may become more interested in how the nature and management of their work environment influences their own behavior. First, it is clear that the further along in the continuum of professionalization an occupation has gotten, the more control it already has in determining the nature of the environmental supports. This is very apparent in hospital design, for example, where the medical staff plays a major role in determining the environmental form, and resists effort by others to influence the design. At this point, many of such decisions are based largely on personal preference, including even such critical considerations as lighting in surgical areas (Beck, 1979) or types of suture materials used (Chu, 1980).

Physicians are likely to continue to make such decisions on the basis of their general authority and position for some time, but increasingly they are going to have to contend with other professions and participants, including management, who are likely to try to upgrade and solidify their own role, and enlarge their influence, by looking for a knowledge base on which to develop their own expertise-based authority. This is particularly likely in the case of relatively insecure professions (nursing and social work, for example) that must deal both with stronger professions as well as management.

Since planning, design, and management of physical facilities play an imortant role in structuring both work and social-interaction patterns, and represent a form of control per se, such professions should be particularly interested in developing an expertise-based authority, in relation to the design and planning of the physical facilities, to express, in visible and symbolic ways, their right to control their own work processes. Since most facilities are shared by different, and competing, groups, the process of design remains a negotiated one. The major difference among groups is in the kind of underpinning one uses to further one's own position.

As Crookston (1975) has argued, this does not mean that every professional should be equally skilled at environmental management. Not all teachers are equally good with small groups of students, or in guiding field experience, or counseling students, nor are all organizational-development specialists equally proficient in both diagnosing problems and developing solutions. Professionals engage in a wide range of behaviors some of the time, and are at least aware that these kinds of skills are valuable in certain situations and should be accessible. The same is true of environmental-space management. The university teacher may be far more specialized in research than in space management. He or she should be sufficiently aware, however, of the role the physical surroundings play in his or her successfully engaging in their research, to either manage these resources themselves (in the case of a laboratory or classroom, for example) or feel knowledgeable enough to call on some other university employee for solving problems with space management that are outside their competence and responsibility.

Since for most professionals, the form of the environment will be of minor interest other than at its most proximate points to their own activities, the role of management is to make available, on request, specially trained persons with an expertise-based authority who provide a service to help in the planning, design, and management of environmental resources at a level or complexity that exceeds the competency and/or interest of the individual. This is already beginning to happen in some large corporations, such as at Kodak Park, in Rochester, New York, where individual operating departments contract and pay for administrative services that include space planning and design.

Within this ecosystem-planning framework, there is an overlap among professional and management responsibilities in settings. The broadening of professional roles and weakening of management's boundaries (although strengthening their expertise-based authority) will be resisted, largely on the basis of its creating inefficiency; although closer to the heart of the matter is the threat to what Freidson (1973, p. 30) has called the "imperialistic" nature of professions and management—namely, the tendency to claim more for professional (or management) knowledge and skill, and a broader jurisdiction, than can in fact be justified by demonstrable effectiveness. This "imperialism" stems partly from a rather narrow self-interest, and is partly a natural outcome of deep commitment to the value of the work, developed by a person who has committed much of his or her adult life to it. It becomes the organization's responsibility, in its role of managing resources, to coordinate and adjudicate, but not control, these conflicting interests. In many cases, what may be most helpful is simply explicating and acknowledging what is already occurring. In addition, organizations need to reexamine some of the asumptions underlying their current approach to planning, designing, and managing environmental-support systems, and how these relate to productivity and organizational effectiveness.

5

RETHINKING PRODUCTIVITY

A major concern of all business enterprises and increasingly of service and educational institutions centers around issues of productivity, efficiency, and effectiveness. Scientific management's contribution to this concern, in relation to the physical setting, was its search for cost savings that could be realized by scientific design of equipment, office layout, and operating procedures. Whole occupations sprang up to service this organizational concern: human-factors specialists, operations researchers, production engineers. The role of the environment within the framework of these occupation groups is twofold: to control or eliminate behaviors considered undesirable by management, usually meaning wasted motion and time; and to develop an understanding of human capabilities, in areas such as information processing and manual dexterity, that can form a rational basis for the design of equipment and operating procedures that will reduce costs.

Yet organizational costs are influenced, particularly over extended periods of time, by providing workers with job characteristics they value—autonomy, meaningful work, timely and constructive feedback about performance, and variety (Hackman and Lawler, 1971; Lawler, 1973)—as well as by such factors as pay, organizational size, and employees' personal characteristics. As a whole, the research evidence suggests that for the worker, the basic issues center around social processes such as recognition, achievement, and autonomy, as well as pay. The question, here, is twofold: how does the physical setting, and the way it is created, contribute to measures of effectiveness; and how is productivity defined and measured, and how does this direct attention to selected aspects of the total organizational system?

SYSTEM GERRYMANDERING

The focus on productivity and cost/benefit analysis is central to any organization. I do not argue with it as a general goal. The way in which it is typically operationalized, or actually measured, seems less defensible, however. Cost/benefit analysis is typically applied to highly visible and easily measured components of a total system. The issue is one of system boundaries. In a manner not unlike political gerrymandering, in which the local political boss fights to have political-district boundaries created that encompass mostly supporters (assuring election victory), many cost/benefit analyses focus on only selected aspects of the total system and, in particular, on those aspects that are most obviously and directly affected by a given change in the organization of work. To assess the overall impact of such changes on an organization, indirect costs must also be calculated throughout as much of the entire system as is possible.

Systems analysts conceptualize change in a part of any system as affecting other parts in the system. A system is dynamic, even in equilibrium. Removing environmental-support systems, such as benches in a park, within this framework, may not eliminate a specific behavior, such as sitting and talking. It may simply transfer the behavior to another location, or create a new seating-support system; planters, for instance, become benches. This in turn may result in the demise of the flowers, the cost of their replacement, the removal of the flower box, building of new flower boxes. A change in any part of the system thus reverberates throughout the system.

Lawler (1973, p. 122) cites a study by Babchuck and Goode (1951) that illustrates negative and dysfunctional aspects of a part of a system considered in isolation. In an attempt to increase sales volume, a department store introduced a pay plan where employees were paid on the basis of sales volume. Total sales initially increased, but in the long run, the program was dysfunctional and counterproductive for the organization as a whole. Employees engaged in "sales grabbing" and "tieing up the trade" and neglected unrewarded and unmeasured functions like stock work and arranging merchandise for displays.

Measures of efficiency based on technological capabilities of new equipment or office systems must also take into account the fact that technological capabilities are not synonymous with human effort or motivation (Cooper and Foster, 1971). Technology is a function of the social context in which it is placed, managed, and used. It is a social product, not an engineering one. In a classic study of technology assessment, Sharp (1952) beautifully illustrates this distinction. He found that missionaries who introduced steel axes into a stone-ax culture to increase efficiency did so;

more work could be accomplished in the same amount of time. But productivity, in the sense of overall output, did not rise. The extra time the steel axes made available was devoted to increased sleep, not to higher output.

A more recent illustration, in a formal organization, of the gap between technological or engineering potential and organizational effectiveness is provided by management's experience with a sophisticated, computer-aided nurse-dispatching system installed in a nearby general hospital. The system cost $160,000, and it must be staffed by two full-time persons, for an annual personnel cost of $60,000. The system is comprised of a number of wall-mounted units in patient rooms and in corridors that are electronically linked to a central computer. Nurses are required to push the nearest button on the wall whenever they enter a room or pass a wall unit. In this way, the nurses' locations are known at all times. When a patient pushes his or her call button, the location of the patient making the call and of every nurse is indicated on a visual display in the central processing room. The central operator must then only call the nurse the display indicates is closest to the patient needing help. The assumption is that a nurse's travel time will be reduced and patients will more quickly receive assistance. Unfortunately, the nurses despise the system, and refuse to punch the buttons. They do not like having a nonnurse operator telling them what to do, and they resent very precise records being kept about their response times. Despite several long training sessions after the system had been installed, the person responsible for managing the system considers it a failure. He is not, however, willing to remove the system, because that would communicate, to the staff, management's lack of resolve. So the expensive failure will continue as a nonworking solution.

The failure to measure these kinds of unintended and unexpected second-order consequences creates a distorted picture of the effects of change in an organization. Jobs designed according to the principles of scientific management, for example, typically do not produce the results claimed by the advocates of the approach. Employees simply do not behave as they are supposed to, and thus the expected economic savings never materialize. Lawler (1973, p. 150) cites some of the costs of organizing work according to scientific-management principles. These include higher turnover on routine jobs—in some cases, in excess of 100 percent per year on assembly-line jobs. Turnover creates the need for job training, and the expense of recruitment, selection, payroll work, accounting, having inexperienced workers on the job, and supervision. Lawler notes recent research indicating that it costs organizations at least five times an employee's monthly salary to replace him. This means it costs at least $2,000 to replace even a lower-level employee and much more to replace higher-level employees.

In addition, high levels of absenteeism on standardized, specialized, and simplified jobs are expensive because workers are likely to use all their paid sick leave and vacation time, and a large "float" of extra workers must be maintained to fill in for absentees. This means that the organiztion gets fewer hours of work per employee, per dollar spent. Even the cheap labor that breaking complex jobs down into simple, standardized sequences is supposed to produce is rarely obtained. The work is so dissatisfying that companies have to pay high wages to get workers even to accept assembly-line jobs. Finally, dissatisfaction typically is reflected in poor-quality work. Lawler (1973, p. 151) notes that the traditional answer to this problem has been to hire more quality-control inspectors and to use more sophisticated control procedures. While these methods may result in some improvement, they are very expensive. By the time the controls are installed, many of the cost savings resulting from the assembly-line approach are lost.

The impact of unsatisfactory work conditions will remain submerged as long as the majority of potential effects, many of which are subtle, are ignored and only those reflecting very gross dissatisfaction—quitting, sabotage, theft—are attended to. A genuine concern for work effectiveness requires the use of multiple criteria. It would actively seek to measure gross and subtle effects: quitting rates and absenteeism as well as frequency and nature of interaction among team members and between supervisor and employee; employee willingness to take the initiative and accept responsibility; cooperation; time spent complaining. Just as merchants have come to accept employee theft as a standard business cost (which they pass on to the consumer) (Becker, 1977), it seems likely that many organizations develop norms of acceptable, or at least predictable, quantity and quality of work and worker behavior that are at the same level as, or a lower level than, would occur if the norms of acceptable behavior were based on how workers actually perceived their jobs and carried them out. Studies in the automobile industry, for instance, have documented the fact that workers are easily as ingenious as operations researchers in developing standards of acceptable work. In fact, one could plausibly argue that the operations researcher simply codify the standards that the workers have created.

Whyte (1955, pp. 15-16) provides what has become a classic quote from a worker about the workers' attitude toward the measurement system and their manipulation of it:

> You got to outwit the son-of-a-bitch! You got to use your noodle while you're working, and think your work out ahead as you go along! You got to add in movements you know you ain't going to make when you're running the job! Remember, if you don't screw them, they're going to screw you! ... Every movement counts! ...
> When the time-study man came around, I set the speed at 180. I knew damn well he would ask me to push it up, so I started low enough. He finally pushed me up to 445, and I ran the job later at 610. If I'd started out at 445,

they'd have timed it at 610. Then I got him on the reaming, too. I ran the reamer for him at 130 speed and .025 feed. He asked me if I couldn't run the reamer any faster than that, and I told him I had to run the reamer slow to keep the hole size. I showed him two pieces with oversize holes that the day man ran. I picked them out for the occasion! But later on I ran the reamer at 610 speed and .018 feed, same as the drill. So I didn't have to change gears....

What is astounding, of course, is the enormous amoung of goodwill and creative energy the organization squanders, at great cost to itself, when work is organized in such a fashion. Its persistence, in the face of so much evidence that it is counterproductive in terms of overall organizational costs, seems explainable more as a central component of a belief system about management control than as a strategy for increasing organization effectiveness, on which basis it is formally justified.

In a few cases the direct cost savings of mechanization, in automobile assembly, for example, may be of such an enormous magnitude that they may mask and even offset the costs of deliberate sabotage of the line and high costs of absenteeism and turnover (Cooper and Foster, 1971); although the data, cited above, by Lawler (1973, p. 150) suggest these savings may be more myth than fact. In any case, the application of the same factory model to the office setting is unlikely to result in productivity gains of the same magnitude except in some very limited areas of office work, such as typing and filing, which represent only about 25 percent of the secretary's time (Tyler, 1980).

Productivity in other office functions is much more difficult to calculate, and whatever gains are made here occur in the context of a total workforce likely to be increasingly hostile to the organization of work not perceived as challenging and rewarding. For these reasons, and because the first cost of facilities and equipment reflects only about 6-8 percent of the total cost of an organization over a 30-year period (about 92 percent of the costs are personnel related) (*Contract*, 1980a), more attention needs to be paid to the way the physical setting, including its equipment and the manner in which it is managed, supports the kind of work conditions and activity patterns workers consider rewarding.

SOFT- AND HARD-DATA MEASURES

The difficulty convincing management to broaden its measures of efficiency and effectiveness to include more indirect, people-oriented costs is well illustrated by the controversy over clean-air standards. Industrial firms and developers can cite the easily documented costs of personnel and equipment required to protect the air, water, and land. Environmentalists have been hampered by a lack of scientific data and the absence of techniques for translating certain antipollution benefits into dollar terms. Douglas Costle, an administrator at EPA, described the situation in the following way: "The upshot is that, while our critics consistently appear to be no-nonsense fellows with their feet on the ground, environmental regulators come across as a bunch of bureaucratic flower-children intent on recreating the Garden of Eden" (*San Francisco Chronicle*, May 7, 1979, p. 10).

The attempt to develop "culturally powerful" measures of benefits (Becker, 1978), usually but not always related to money, is something students of organizational ecology will have to develop to gain credence in the organizational world. As Figure 5.1 suggests, the objective should be some sort of balance between productivity levels and total organizational costs, including those related to work quality, absenteeism and turnover rates, and retraining programs. The issue is not only what outcomes to measure, but how different outcomes relate to each other.

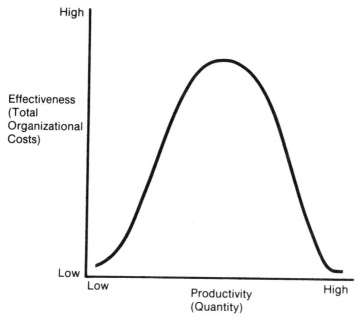

FIGURE 5.1 Relationship between Organizational Effectiveness (Total Costs) and Productivity (Quantity)

SATISFACTION, PRODUCTIVITY, AND EFFECTIVENESS

There is substantial evidence (Brookes and Kaplan, 1972; Oldham and Brass, 1979; Szilagyi and Holland, 1980) that charateristics of the physical setting produce dissatisfaction in office workers. For the most part, however, such evidence has made little impact on how organizations create their physical surroundings. The nature and management of physical settings are seen as tangential to more important resources the organization can manipulate, including such aspects of work as pay scales, job design, and supervision patterns. Such evidence also has had to compete with the typical management attitude that satisfaction with one's workspace is a luxury that cannot be accommodated except in the upper echelons of management. The working assumption is that the added expense of creating more satisfactory working environments cannot be justified because they bear little or no relation to productivity. Thus, measures of worker satisfation with their physical surroundings, and the creation of settings using such measures as an important criterion, are rarely seen as supporting the organization's self-interest.

The bulk of the research evidence does indicate only a weak positive relationship between job satisfaction and job performance (Lawler, 1973), when job performance is defined in terms of quantity of output of the individual worker. Lawler and Porter (1967) argue that job performance, measured in this way, produces satisfaction, and does so because of the intrinsic rewards (e.g., sense of competence, growth) and extrinsic ones (e.g., pay, promotion) one attains by performing well, as these are related to one's expectations of what rewards one deserves.

From an ecological point of view, the question is whether, and how, the nature and use of the physical setting contributes to performance, narrowly conceived as related only to the performance of specific work tasks, as well as how it influences other behaviors the organization values. There is substantial evidence linking job satisfaction with absenteeism and turnover (Lawler, 1973). To the extent that environmental satisfaction is an important facet of job satisfaction, as workers' concern with their working conditions suggests it is, there is reason to assume that the nature of the physical setting can act to reduce some of the costs of absenteeism and turnover already noted. For example, a recent study of German factory workers (Bergermaier, Sundstrom, and Berg, 1980) assessed the relative contribution of environmental and biographical factors to the intention to leave a job. The authors found that environmental factors, including noise, crowding, and air pollution, by themselves, accounted for 9 percent of the variation in the intention to leave, and added significant predictability even after taking into account job satisfaction. Biographical factors, such as age, tenure in the job, and marital status, and environmental factors contributed to job satisfaction, which, in turn, contributed to the intention to leave the job.

The physical setting's importance lies in the kinds of work and social behaviors it facilitates. Whyte (1948), for example, has shown that being a member of a closely knit social group seems to motivate people to go to work regularly. The friendships and social interaction of the group, rather than the work itself, provide the incentive for job attendance. Dividing a large room into small rooms, with six people in each, encourages group development in a way that undivided space will not. Arranging work space to facilitate face-to-face communication provides the opportunity for friendship formation that other arrangements may discourage or prevent.

In several studies of small-group ecology, Sommer (1961, 1965, 1967) has shown how seat location influences participation rates, and how different seat arrangements are associated with cooperative, competitive, or coacting behaviors. Other studies (Sommer, 1961; Hearn, 1957; Howells and Becker, 1962) have shown the effect of office layout on friendship formation. And recent studies, described in detail in Chapter 6, have shown how office layout influences autonomy, performance feedback, and communication. Clearwater (1980), for example, using self-reported measures of productivity, found that environmental satisfaction, environmental functional quality, and ability to concentrate, among other factors, correlated significantly with self-reported measures of productivity. Since the mean self-reported level of productivity was 81 percent for all employees, these data need to be treated with caution. They do suggest, however, at the very least, that employees may use characteristics of the physical environment as a basis for justifying given levels of performance.

This relatively small, but accumulating body of research evidence suggests the kind of relationship, between performance, organizational effectiveness, and the physical setting, shown in Figure 5.2. Overall organizational effectiveness takes into account both direct performance measures as well as other organizational costs, such as those of absenteeism and turnover. Figure 5.2 suggests that the physical setting plays an important role in behaviors that contribute both to performance and job satisfaction. It does so by facilitating social and communication patterns such as feedback and autonomy, that are important job characteristics, and by facilitating directly the performance of work tasks. The location and nature of storage systems, for example, influence the accessibility of information and tools that directly contribute to the rapid and effective performance of work. Reduction of noise and the provision of privacy facilitate concentration and reduce work interruptions. These environmental-support-system characteristics thus affect both intrinsic and extrinsic aspects of the job (Herzberg, 1966). They play an important role in organizational effectiveness.

Obviously, the physical setting is not the only factor that contributes to autonomy, effective-performance feedback, or cohesive social groups. The point of Figure 5.2 is that the physical setting's contribution to such programs and behaviors has been consistently overlooked. Figure 5.2 provides a conceptual model that links environmental preference and job satisfaction with behaviors valued by both individual employees and the organization.

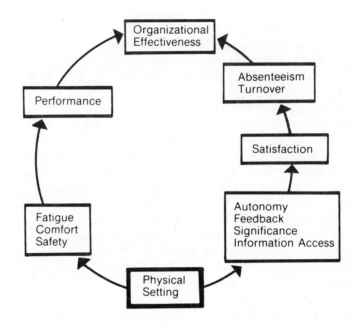

FIGURE 5.2 Model of Physical Setting's Contribution to Behaviors both the Individual and Organization Value

Within this model, the environment becomes a tangible, visible, and under-utilized resource the organization can use in ways the support its own interest by tapping that of its employees.

Failure to identify a wide range of effectiveness measures has contributed to the benign neglect of the role of physical settings in organizations. New measures can be found, and systematic assessments carried out. A more fundamental problem is demonstrating conclusively the effect of any changes, including change involving the physical environment and its use, on a complex system. Limitations in pinpointing causal relations have been underlined for the study of environmental effects, but the issues underlie evaluation of any organizational change.

PINPOINTING CAUSAL RELATIONS

In any complex systems where a cause becomes an effect that, in turn, becomes a cause in a long chain of interdependent actions and reactions, it is extremely difficult, if not impossible, to conclusively prove that a particular change effort of any kind had a specific effect due to that change, and no other. For the most part, we make changes based on the belief that they will have some effect. Rarely do we try to evaluate or isolate the precise costs and benefits of those changes. Even when studies are done, it is, at best, not obvious where exactly one should look for effects or how to measure them. Working models help, but in the social sciences these are usually more heuristic than predictive.

It is extremely difficult to demonstrate cause-effect relations, not only because variables are intertwined, but also because we are generally unwilling to do precisely controlled experiments in field situations. Who is willing to try to install an informal and highly interactive sytstem of supervision in an environment where the only means of communication is by telephone, or by a long corridor between supervisor and staff? Making feedback on tasks performed more specific may also change the nature of interaction between supervisor and staff, the duration of the contact, and perhaps even the location for the meeting. Quality of work goes up. Why? No one can be absolutely sure. But we believe it went up because (we focus on the fact that) feedback was more specific.

Organizations pay thousands of dollars to develop logos. Can they prove the logo brought in more customers? They have not only a new logo, but new advertising slogans, repainted equipment and facilities, and saturation advertising. Assuming someone tries to pinpoint the change to a logo, how can one attribute the effects found to it alone? One cannot. The same is true of millions of dollars spent on landmark buildings like the TransAmerica building in San Francisco. People know it's the TransAmerica building, but as a result, do they buy more insurance from them?

In any complex setting, single variables do not cause single effects. Observable behaviors are multiply determined. As Porter et al. (1975, p. 222) argue, the designation of particular variables as causal and other variables as dependent is partially arbitrary. This is because the design of organizations involves an extremely complex interplay of variables, each of which can function as both a cause and a result of another variable. In other words, the variables in the design of organizations do form a system, but it is a system that does not permit the isolation of unequivocal cause-effect relationships. To use an example from educational settings, while seating arrangements may influence modes and levels of student participation, student behavior may influence the types of arrangements teachers permit. Porter et al. (1975, p. 223) argue it is possible to designate the most likely or most predominant causal chains of factors involved in organization design and, at the same time, recognize that each variable or factor can have a reciprocal effect on the others.

For these reasons, it is very difficult to prove, for example, that a firm's productivity was raised solely by the introduction and use of a new office-furniture system or word-processing equipment. With the new equipment, are supervisory patterns the same? Is scheduling identical? Is the employee allowed greater mobility and autonomy? Is it the supervisor's expectations or the new equipment that stimulated a change in the behavior, or was it the special training program the vendor made available to the employee that the employee interpreted as a sign of upward mobility and organizational concern? While attributing effects to characteristics of the physical setting is often criticized on the basis that other social and psychological factors are more important, we might just as well ask whether it is not the physical setting or its use that caused the observed outcome (when an effect is attributed to a new program or to management training that is accompanied by changes in the sociotechnical system). It is virtually impossible to isolate all the variables, even if we knew which ones to isolate.

PREDICTING OUTCOMES

The question, then, is whether it is possible to identify configurations of environmental and personal resources that support relatively stable outcomes. Assuming one starts with a goal of maximizing a particular outcome, in other words, is it possible to predict a configuration of variables that will result in a significant likelihood that a desired outcome will be achieved?

The nature of the outcomes selected will determine their generality across different situations and groups of participants. As Roger Barker (1968) has demonstrated, certain types of behaviors are nearly invariant within similar settings, despite very different participants over time. It may be easier to predict satisfaction, role behavior, verbal participation, and involvement than test scores, writing skill, or self-esteem. Similar outcomes may also be obtained by different combinations of factors operating together. Excellent reading scores might be produced by an outstanding teacher despite negligible support from the parents at home; or, conversely, a high level of commitment and involvement by parents may offset or compensate for a poor teacher in the school environment.

There is the additional problem that identical objective characteristics of the setting may have very different effects, depending on how they are interpreted by participants in the setting. Reality is socially constructed: What exists is what I think exists. To accurately predict outcomes, we need to understand not only what the factors are, but what their meaining is and how they are interpreted. The same constellation of factors may have very different meaning, and thus effects, depending on the history of the situation and the individuals in it. In a physical-planning context, Donald Appleyard has described the case where neighborhood residents rejected what designers and planners considered to be genuinely positive improvements for their neighborhoods, because they interpreted the changes as undermining their social and economic position in the neighborhood. Unfortunately, most of our predictions of effects are based on relatively objective characteristics of programs and facilities, and not on the meaning attributed to them by their users. This is one reason predictions often fail: We assume intent is synonymous with meaning.

The first order of business, then, is to identify all those variables that may influence behavior in a setting, including influences and factors operating outside the setting in other parts of the school, office, or hospital, in the community, in the home, the state, or nation—without trying to specify how all of these individual factors are related to each other in a causal model. Since the possible permutations based on the large number of variables we have identified so far result in a staggering number of configurations that might result in similar outcomes, I am not convinced that it is possible to identify general causal relationships, especially in a static sense.

It would be more useful to alert participants in the setting (e.g., teachers and students, staff, supervisors), as well as experts who might work with them, to the possible impact of a wide range of social, economic, administrative, cultural, and physical factors operating in their setting; and then, for any particular setting, to begin looking at how these factors operate. Given all the factors potentially active in any situation, one also needs to characterize the factors in terms of their resistance to change. If one accepts the compensatory nature of the variables involved (i.e., different combinations will produce the same results), and the implication this has for emphasizing or strenthening some factors as others change (assuming one values the same outcome), then it becomes imperative to understand which factors are likely to be flexible. Some factors will remain as constraints or demands on the system, thus reducing to a more manageable number the number of factors one can actually begin to consider manipulating in an effort to attain any given outcome.

The framework proposed involves essentially more of a management than a planning perspective. The former implies a dynamic equilibrium maintained by continuous monitoring and feedback over time, with modifications in the system taking place relatively frequently. Dynamic equilibrium is maintained by compensating for a change in one factor (e.g., the loss of an outstanding math teacher) by strengthening another factor (e.g., increasing students' access to highly motivated college-student tutors or outstanding educational facilities, such as museums located outside the formal school setting).

The planning model, in contrast, is more static. It implies not only identification of the factors involved in any system, but a fairly precise understanding of the causal relationships among them. It implies that once a program or facility is planned, relatively little change will occur in it except at major intervals (often initiated by a clear dysfunction of the system for a long period prior to the change effort).

How does all this relate to the manager, or the school or hospital administrator's desire for predictability of outcomes? In this way: I am suggesting that research can identify relevant variables to consider in assessing behavior in any situation, but that research is much less successful, at this point in time and perhaps always, in describing the exact linkages among all variables (because these change and have similar effects in different combinations) in the form of general predictive models. Predictability is further limited by the absence of detailed ecological descriptions (i.e., ones encompassing a broad range of social, psychological, political, economic, and environmental characteristics of the setting) of the conditions under which different studies occur. Ecological research must develop ways of describing the setting accurately along many dimensions in order to make relatively valid comparisons across settings (Stokols and Shumaker, 1980).

Theoretically, over time and with research conducted with attention to ecological description of study conditions, consistent patterns or configurations of environmental and personal resources tied to particular but limited outcome measures could be identified. These more general predictions form the basis for initial planning of programs and facilities to achieve intended outcomes. These planning efforts should be conducted with the clear understanding that each situation will have unique properties in addition to the properties it holds in common with similar settings. In order to maximize a specific outcome in a particular setting, a relatively continuous site-specific econogical analysis should be undertaken. Its purpose would be to identify the role of different factors and to look for factors, not emphasized in a general predictive model, that may play a compensating role in the specific situation. This approach, then, is not a search for general ecological principles that can be applied in an invariant way to any setting, but rather, a quest for bounded predictability. It is a mode of research consistent with the cybernetics model of planning presented earlier.

BOUNDED PREDICTABILITY

Given an understanding of the factors operating within a single context bounded in space and time, such as an office, classroom, or perhaps a school, our chances of predicting outcomes are reasonably good. This kind of bounded predictability is possible because most of the variables operating in the situation can be known, particularly over time as continuous mini-inquiries are carried out that serve to clarify the relationships among the different variables.

Miniinquiries, rather than being viewed as only the most preliminary step to the development of full-blown experimental studies that will eventually lead to precisely developed working models, are the foundation for a continually evolving ecological theory rooted in specific time/space contexts. While general ecological principles primarily emphasizing which factors may play a role in a setting can be developed, specific predictions are made not for all classrooms, or schools, but for a single classroom, or school.

A two-tiered predictability emerges. The first is based on the assumption that over time, patterns of some outcomes may become discernible in relation to relatively basic configurations of environmental, personal, economic, and political factors. In the planning of new facilities or programs, these kinds of data are used to guide the program's initial development. To maximize outcomes for a particular setting, a more refined, continual ecological analysis must be performed, with the goal of achieving a kind of bounded predictability—that is, a reasonable prediction of what will happen in a specified context. Practitioners could be trained to do these types of ongoing mini-inquiries and should be involved with them regardless of who has primary responsibility for them.

Bounded predictability is characterized, then, by continuous interventions sustained by an experimental attitude. Decisions are made with the best available information. To attain desired outcomes, programs and facilities have to be as varied as the users and settings they serve. The more continual the predictions of outcomes made in the settings, the more likely the predictions will be accurate.

A PROCESS APPROACH TO EFFECTIVENESS

The concept of bounded predictability brings into sharper focus the essential ambiguity inherent in the concept of effectiveness. The approach suggested here is similar to what Steers (1976) has called a process approach to effectiveness. Rather than specifying criteria for effectiveness, the objective is to understand what conditions are most conducive to it. A critical component of that understanding is that effectiveness measures or criteria are likely to be different for different organizations (a university and a manufacturing firm, for example), and even for the same organization at different points in time. Steers notes that effectiveness in a growth economy, capital investment, for example, may need to be changed in a recession to capital liquidity. In the fact of a declining college-age population, effectiveness in colleges and universities begins to be defined more in terms of outside funding levels and number of students attracted than in terms of scholarly papers or quality of students. It is not that one set of criteria is completely replaced by another. Rather, it is that the balance among various criteria shifts.

Effectiveness criteria also vary as a function of the time perspective employed. In the short run, productivity defined in terms of strict output measures may make sense, but in the long run, the absenteeism and turnover stimulated by the changes required to obtain high productivity in the short run may impose a significant cost on the organization. The objective is clearly to get a balance, based on a number of fluctuating conditions, among the criteria employed. The problem, of course, is that multiple measures may conflict, especially if they operate in different time perspectives.

Compounding the problem is the fact that the organization deliberately hires persons with professionally centered orientations for assessing effectiveness: economists, operations researchers, human-relations experts. These have been trained to look at the world through a particularly tinted set of glasses. They serve a valuable purpose for precisely this reason. Yet the organization needs to keep each of these orientations in a wider and more integrated systems perspective. Someone has to balance the role each of the orientations should play at different points in time. It is a monumental, but indispensable, task. It requires continuous monitoring of the organization's operating activities and aspects of the organizational environment (political, economic, technological, social), to identify trends which provide a rationale for shifting emphases, for focusing attention on different selected aspects of the total situation, and for having some documented information about just what the organization is doing, not what it thinks it is doing or wishes it were doing. Given this perspective, the value of the physical setting to the organization does not rise or fall solely on the issue of productivity. It does reside in its contribution to a wider, and often shifting, set of organizational behaviors related to overall effectiveness. We turn next to some empirical evidence supporting these kinds of contributions.

6

BEHAVIOR IN
ITS PHYSICAL CONTEXT

Tension between industrial designers and production engineers often finds its source in designs that are considered unusual. The designer labors to create a beautiful object. Sinuous shape, smart color combination, and ingenious mechanical devices are integrated. The drawings are stunning; the model is intricate. The designer's unique talent, special insight, sensitivity, and creativity are apparent. Only one problem exists: The cost and difficulty of designing the machinery for production made necessary by the sinuous shape are astronomical. Moreover, the material specified by the designer cracks under the stress of shaping the exaggerated form, slowing production and raising costs. The design may be unusual, but neglects to sufficiently take into account the materials and processes required to make the concept— which may be very good—work as it is routinely operationalized in the everyday world of the factory.

Organizational-behavior concepts that describe and analyze behavior in a physical vacuum, as though behavior occurs in an undifferentiated field of univalued space, share the same difficulty with the beautiful design. For imaginative concepts and new technologies to be effective, appropriate social-support systems must be developed. Organizational-behavior theorists not only accept the limiting nature of social conditions, but consider them their major research focus. This chapter examines some of the empirical evidence supporting the necessity of taking into consideration the physical context within which social processes are necessarily created and played out.

Every characteristic, goal, program, or activity of an organization and its individual members has a physical-setting component to it. We behave in small or large, cold or sunny, sterile or comfortable rooms; we use different pieces of equipment, at different distances from our coworkers, with varying degrees of visual access to the outside and to other parts of the organization;

we have different opportunities for controlling social interaction, and varying levels of mobility and visibility. We determine some of these relationships and characteristics ourselves. Some are controlled by others. These decision processes with environmental ramifications are as much a part of the environment as the more objective physical elements and relationships that result from them. Together they constitute the sociotechnical system (Cooper and Foster 1971) within which behavior in organizations occurs. It consists not only of the technology, equipment and machines, and office layout, but also the rules and norms which govern how individuals relate to the technology and to each other.

Attempts to understand and investigate organizational concepts, like authority structure, outside the specific physical and technological context in which they are enacted assume that the environment will support virtually any type of social structure or set of relationships equally well. If we turn things upside down, and reverse the usual assumptions of causality, it makes just as much sense to assume that social structures are designed to support particular kinds of physical-setting arrangements. It often seems to be the case that decisions are made not to change the social structure, because of the trouble it would cause for the walls and chairs in the physical setting, or at least for those people like janitors and other personnel responsible for maintaining the structure (Sommer 1969, 1974).

EXPECTATIONS AND RESOURCES

Organizations have certain expectations about employee behavior that are communicated to members. They also have resources available whose purpose is both to communicate the expectations and to increase the likelihood that the organization member will meet them. Similarly organization members bring to the organization certain expectations and resources. Individuals, like the organization, employ their own resources to increase the probability that the organization will fulfill their expectations. The ideal situation occurs when the individual's and organization's expectations and resources mesh in such a way that the organization gets from individuals particular behaviors that it considers necessary or appropriate, and individuals get from the organization what they consider necessary, desirable, or appropriate. The individual and organization work to fulfill each other's expectations by exchanging resources.

Using this model, Porter et al. (1975) propose that organizations and individuals value each other's contribution and seek to maintain relations to the extent that individuals, on the one hand, feel that their needs and goals are met and organizations, on the other hand, are satisfied with individual members' behavior. For our purposes, the main interest is in whether conventional ways of thinking about how expectations are communicated, what resources are employed, and how, are adequate.

Communicating Expectations

An expectation is a notion or an image of appropriate behavior one individual or group holds regarding some other individual or group. Organizations communicate expectations, or what they consider desirable and appropriate behavior, to individuals constantly. We are expected to be prompt, to appear regularly, to do what we are asked to do. Individuals in turn expect the organiztion to pay them, to provide necessary tools (including libraries, laboratories), and to give them materials and/or information necessary to perform the tasks they have agreed to do. Expectations are communicated formally and informally. Organizations use various formal mechanisms to insure compliance with their demands. These include selection systems to exclude those who cannot meet expectations; socialization and training procedures, to teach organization members the organizational expectations, and tell them how to fulfill them; evaluation and reward systems, which provide explicit contingencies linking behavior and rewards; measurement and control systems, which monitor the degree to which the objectives of the organization are being met, and provide the means for remedial action; supervisory practices, which can be designed to help the individual effectively meet organizational expectations. The organization uses these mechanisms to maximize the likelihood individuals will experience a set of expectations or demands relevant to their own personal behavior (Porter et al., 1975).

Porter et al. (1975) do not mention the mechanisms, formal or informal, through which organizational members communicate their expectations, perhaps because they are considered so obvious: quitting, complaining to a supervisor or union representative, refusing to work at an assigned pace or task, missing work, doing poor-quality work. Most of these are informal processes. Once hired, organizational members have few formal mechanisms for communicating their expectations. Unions and grievance procedures are the only two formal mechanisms that have received much attention.

The difficulty in focusing on formal mechanisms, whether used by the organization or individual, is that some of the most potent and pervasive organizational demands on members can be very subtly or implicitly communicated to them. Porter et al. (1975) give one illustration of implicitly communicated expectations: an assembly-line worker who confronts a very fast-paced line and decides that he is expected to produce large quantities of work, but that he need not try to do especially high-quality work. Not much further attention is given to implicit and unintended communication. Despite awareness of these kinds of communication possibilities, rarely is the role of the environment as a communication medium systematically explored as a facet of organizational behavior. This is as true for the resources the organization provides as it is for the expectations communicated.

RESOURCES

A resource can be anything which an "organization member potentially can find useful" (Porter et al. 1975). Salary levels are considered the organization's prime resource, and the prime incentive for the individual. Money is a necessary, but insufficient condition for attracting and keeping high-quality employees. The belief that money can compensate for the most tedious, overcontrolled, and persistently unsatisfying work is a vestige of the scientific-management legacy that lingers today. The quality and nature of equipment, furnishings, wall and floor surfaces, lighting, and other enviromental elements are typically ignored in terms of how they influence motivation, structure interpersonal relationships, or communicate expectations and attitudes. It is not that such environmental elements are not manipulated for programmatic purposes. It is that the manipulations are often arbitrary and capricious and, therefore, ineffective (or only randomly effective).

The possibility that both the development and access to these kinds of physical-setting resources might be more consciously taken into consideration in attempts to, for example, improve morale and raise employee-motivation levels, is not pursued in the organizational-behavior literature. Despite the very clear understanding organizational theorists have about the importance of the study of informal organizational processes, the potential of the physical setting for structuring these informal processes (e.g., making some kinds of social interaction easier or more difficult, or communicating attitudes and values through characteristics of the physical environment users imbue with meaning) is overlooked.

NONVERBAL COMMUNICATION

Communication occurs through multiple channels. We often pay more attention to what is implicit, or unsaid, than to the more formal mechanisms. We assume that the informal is less deliberate (more unplanned) and therefore often a more accurate indicator of true feelings (Weitz 1974; Goffman 1961).

Investigators of nonverbal behavior, for example, have shown that paraverbal behavior (the rate, amplitude, pitch of language) is a more accurate indicator of real feeling than is the meaning of the words themselves

(Davitz and Davitz, 1974; Milmoe et al., 1974). Bateson's famous (1956) "double-bind" theory of schizophrenia is based on the conflicting messages a child receives from a parent: the verbally—"Oh, darling, I love you so much; come here and let me give you a hug," followed by the behaviorally—rigid arms to keep the child at arm's length. Goffman (1961), in his study of Shetland Islanders, noted how much more faith natives had in nonverbal than verbal behavior, and described how they went to great lengths to manage this nonverbal behavior.

Others have written about the role of the physical setting in various types of institutions characterized by suspicion and/or hostility among different participants in the setting. Although the specific settings are often not offices, the kinds of relationships described occur in all organizations. I described some of these in an earlier book, *Housing Messages* (1977, p. 3):

> Consciously and unconsciously we interpret our physical environment in a variety of ways. We try to understand the motivations and intentions of those who designed it, the ways in which it affects our behavior and influences our emotional reactions, and what its symbolic meaning is within a particular context.... [Many different kinds of institutions] managed by one group for the "good" of another can be characterized by the generally paternalistic and negative images they convey to their inhabitants and the occupants' feelings of being neglected, ignored, and treated impersonally. In the context of a therapeutic environment for autistic children, Bruno Bettelheim has written of the importance of what he calls "silent messages," which convey through the minute details of the physical environment the staff's concern for the patients' well-being. He makes a point, often overlooked by designers and administrators concerned with the overall design or form of a building, that an institutions' intentions are conveyed by the smallest details of the staff's behavior and the physical environment.

The physical setting is a communication medium through which all participants in an organization send and receive messages. A large proportion of these are unintended, but their effects are no less real.

As I also wrote in *Housing Messages* (1977, p. 2):

> The kinds of conflicts E.T. Hall has described as a consequence of misinterpretation of nonverbal attitudes communicated through body position and distance may be occurring around us every day as a function of misinterpretation of nonverbal messages communicated through the physical environment; or, ironically, as a result of agreement about what the environmental messages are, but with the social meaning and impact on the groups or individuals associated with the environmental message being very different than it is for groups who may form their identity by not being associated with the same physical cue.

To illustrate the latter point, in a business school at a major university, ther are five different lounges in the building, each with a closed door and a different sign on it: "faculty lounge," "staff lounge," "Ph.D lounge," "MBA lounge," and "undergraduate lounge." No doubt everyone is absolutely certain about the message the different lounges convey. The meaning for an M.A. and a Ph.D candidate is likely to vary tremendously, however. Access also varies. The lounges form a Guttman-type scale: If you can enter the lounge at the top of the hierarchy (faculty), you presumably can enter all those lounges below it. If you are at the bottom of the hierarchy, you can only pass by the doors to lounges for persons higher in the hierarchy. The distribution of spatial resources, determined by rules, creates an almost rigid set of expectations, that no one will enter into another's territory. According to one faculty member, faculty feel as uncomfortable talking with students in the undergraduate lounge as undergraduates feel in the faculty lounge.

The interesting point, of course, is that the organization (business school) makes no attempt to understand what the implications of this kind of resource allocation are for the organization's functioning. Perhaps it is highly motivating for undergraduates. More likely, feelings of alienation and indifference occur among groups, while individual groups' sense of cohesion may be strengthened by their segregation. The possibility that the restriction and discouragement of informal group interaction such spatial arrangements support might result, for example, in undergraduates or master's students becoming less involved in their academic program, less interested in faculty research, and less committed to the school in general remains unknown. Yet at the same time the impacts of such a spatial arrangement are ignored, concern is expressed about faculty morale, and student enthusiasm and initiative. The organization has communicated a set of expectations, through the allocation of its spatial resources, that supports behaviors the organization presumably considers inappropriate and undesirable.

Ruesch and Kees (1964) have called the attempt to influence others, through the intentional and nonintentional display of material things, "object language." They note that in a democracy, where all individuals are presumably equal, objects have the useful function of announcing an inequality that, taste and conformity dictate, cannot be expressed in words. All organization members can, and do, communicate their expectations through the ways in which they use (or fail to use, or misuse) the physical resources the organization makes available.

Places of work generally not only reflect their functional purpose, but are differentiated according to underlying values and expectations. Hospitals must not only meet certain sanitation criteria, or allow certain kinds of activities to occur comfortably and safely. They must also appear to be clean and sanitary. The image of the hospital and of healing can be as important a healing element as the level of skill and knowledge actually available. In a study of the impact of a small-scale renovation of a nursing unit in a general hospital on staff, patients', and visitors' attitudes and behavior (Becker et al., 1978), we found that aspects of the physical setting, including color, lighting, and graphics, increased feelings that the hospital was progressive and modern. The change was based on an image of what is progressive, not on information about the type of facilities and equipment available or the training level of staff (none of which had changed). The hospital effectively manipulated its environmental resources to fulfill the expectations those who used the facility brought to it.

While designers and administrators are usually aware at some level of this function of the environment, they rarely systematically explore how the organization's resources can be most effectively deployed. The problem, in the above example, is not only to communicate modernity. It is to do this without simultaneously communicating the sterility and impersonality associated with modern institutional environments. The environment does this in partnership with staff, but we know very little about how such chains of effects involving the environment and behavior operate.

There is little doubt that patients, for example, consider the behavior of nursing staff to be the primary factor affecting their feeling about the hospital. Aspects of the physical setting may create certain staff expectations and attitudes, however, that, in turn, either support or undermine what patients consider supportive nursing-staff behavior. We found in the same study that after the renovation, significantly more persons thought the hospital was less impersonal and bureaucratic. While the changes were not statistically significant, we also found that more people felt the hospital administration cared about the people who used and worked in the hospital. After the renovation, significantly more respondents also felt that friendly and cooperative relations existed among doctors, nurses, and administrators. These effects were found in a renovation that cost less than $3,000 and used existing hospital personnel to implement the changes.

One explanation for why organizations overlook the potential of physical-setting resources to satisfy expectations of organizational members is that the physical setting is construed unidimensionally, if considered at all. A multidimensional conception of the environment, like Gibson's (1950), makes more sense. Gibson (1950) has proposed that the environment embodies a hierarchy of levels of meaning. These range from concrete meanings (e.g., the ground itself) to activity-oriented meaning (e.g., the ground as something to be walked upon) to symbolic meaning (e.g., the ground as homeland). Even activity-oriented meaning is problematic in organizations. The potential some organization members see, in aspects of the physical setting, for particular activities may not be seen by other members. While the concrete and use meanings of objects and environments are shared by a wide variety of people, the higher levels of meaning are more personal and less predictable.

Effective communication requires understanding how those who will respond to it are likely to interpret the environmental cues. For example, in a recent visit to a large manufacturing plant, I was shown various attempts to introduce color into a bleak environment through the use of supergraphics. The result was disastrous. A multicolored, green and orange stripe greatly offended many of the Irish employees. They attended to the symbolic meaning of the colors within the context of their own political allegiances. Motivation and satisfaction reportedly decreased, and the organization is worse off than it was before.

The answer is not to leave the environment bleak simply because "you can't please everyone." It is to develop and use procedures that increase the likelihood that environmental changes made will support users' expectations and values. Some of these procedures are discussed in Chapter 8. The point here is one made earlier: The failure to take into consideration how different individuals or groups attend to the environment increases the probability that environmental resources will be allocated in ways that undermine organizations' goals.

One way of avoiding the vague implications of a concept like image, and of dealing more directly with expectations, is to follow the example provided by Rapoport (1971). He suggests starting with simple molecular concepts, such as activities and functions. Any activity can be divided into four components: the activity proper; a specific way of doing it; additional, adjacent, or associated activities that become part of an activity system; and symbolic aspects of the activity. Applying this kind of analysis to the activity of information transfer in an office, for example, we find that the activity is one of moving information from one individual to another. The specific way may involve telephoning; typing and sending a letter; typing into a computer a message that will appear on others' monitors when they call for the information; or walking, flying, or riding a bike to, or, in some other way, physically moving oneself to the other person or persons and delivering the message in person. Special kinds of equipment are needed for each specific way of performing the activity. Associated activities may include socializing, exchanging information, playing a game on the computer, or getting fresh air and exercise. Using the symbolic meaning of information transfer may be a way of asserting independence and job autonomy, or demonstrating technical competence, social identity, or status.

To effectively organize physical-setting resources, each of these aspects of even the simplest activity need to be examined. Using this framework clarifies, for example, why the introduction of new equipment or technology into organizations, or an apparently minor change in office arrangement, generates resistance. The assumption that people resist anything new is too simplistic. More likely, the change has altered some of the associated activities or the symbolic meaning which is a valued part of a routine activity

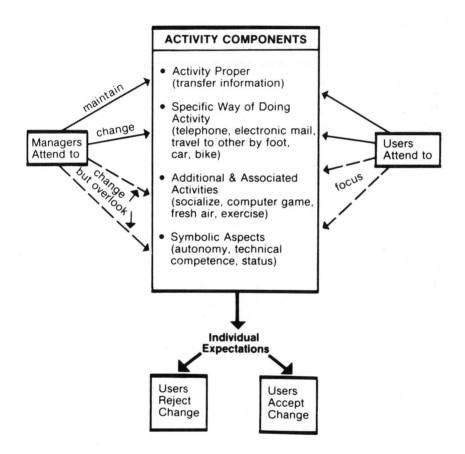

FIGURE 6.1 A Multidimensional Framework for Relating Individual Expectations and Activities to Environmental-Change Efforts

(see Figure 6.1). Information-processing equipment, for example, often allows some of the differences in individual capacity and interest among staff, within a job category, to emerge. Indeed, some of the staff are faster and more adept at learning how to use the new equipment in innovative ways. Those workers who are not so adept become concerned because the new equipment creates opportunities for performance differences that jeopardize their own promotion possibilities. The equipment alters well-established social relationships and hierarchies, and it may develop a new symbolic meaning that alters the standing of different office workers. Administrators must come to grips with these kinds of effects if they are to effectively use their resources to communicate their own, and fulfill their workers', expectations.

If we move from a general discussion of expectations and resources to one focusing on specific kinds of behaviors that organizations expect individuals to display, and look at how the total resources of the organization can be effectively deployed, it becomes clear that many organizations fail to use their available resources in a way that would increase the probability of eliciting desired behaviors.

COMMUNICATION/INTERACTION: OFFICE-DESIGN EVALUATIONS

All organizations want committed members. They want them to like working in and for the organization. They want them to be motivated and willing to contribute all of their personal resources (skills, knowledge, abilities, insights) that the organization considers relevant to fulfilling organizational goals. Most organizations attempt to achieve this end by employing the formal mechanisms described earlier, and by informally giving performance feedback and encouragement to workers. All of these processes are important and contribute to the attaining of expected behaviors. They are necessary, but not sufficient. In some cases, they may be undermined by characteristics of the physical setting that implicitly comunicate or support undesired behaviors.

For example, in one of the most recent and best studies of open-office design, Oldham and Brass (1979) found that a move from a conventional office to an office without interior walls or partitions resulted in significant decreases in employee satisfaction and internal motivation. Their study is particularly useful because it analyzed the ways in which the office design influenced important job characteristics, which, in turn, influenced satisfaction and internal motivation. It demonstrates very well the ways in which the physical setting of the organization can dramatically influence important organizational behaviors.

Data were collected from 81 employees three times: once before the change to the new facility and twice after the facility change. The study tested two different approaches to physical-setting influences: what Oldham and Brass called the social-relations and the sociotechnical approach.

The social-relations approach, according to them, argues that the absence of interior walls and barriers in open-plan offices facilitates the development of social relationships among employees, which in turn, positively influence employee motivation and satisfaction. The basis for this argument lies in the data on small-group ecology (Sommer, 1965, 1967, 1969), which show that the nature of furniture arrangements influences the level of interaction and friendship formation.

The relationship between interaction and task performance is less direct. Oldham and Brass (1979) cite studies by Berkowitz (1956) and by Chapman and Campbell (1957) that found a significant positive relationship between aircrew members' attitudes toward one another and two measures of their combat effectiveness. Chapman and Campbell (1957) found that an individual's desirability as a teammate correlated significantly with the success of the team of which he was a member. The chain of events from a social-relations perspective, then, leads from office environment to interaction level to attraction/liking to performance. The direct first-order consequence of the physical setting is interaction level. The second- and third-order consequences are attraction and performance. Moreover, not only in interaction, in general, supposed to increase from an open-plan environment, but the absence of walls is expected to enhance the performance feedback employees receive from their colleagues, and to encourage persons to communicate about, and to resolve any, interpersonal conflicts that might arise in the organization.

In contrast to the social-relations approach, Oldham and Brass (1979) suggest that the sociotechnical approach argues that boundaries can transform a work area into a private, defensible space in which an individual experiences a greater sense of privacy than if no boundaries exist. Such a private area provides opportunities for personal conversations and the sharing of information, as well as facilitating employees' identification with their task and the equipment and technology available to complete the task.

Several negative implications of open offices, regarding job characteristics and employees' response, follow from this approach. A move from a conventional to an open-plan office should result in a decline in autonomy because the absence of private offices and interior walls increases the likelihood that supervisors and coworkers will interfere with, or infringe upon, an employees' discretion and freedom to work. Supervisor and coworker feedback are expected to decrease in a move from a conventional to an open office because of the elimination of private space desirable for evaluative feedback. It is also expected that there are fewer friendship opportunities because the development of close, personal friendships is dependent upon sharing thoughts, feelings, and values of coworkers. The private space that might facilitate such discussion is less available in open offices.

The findings, as briefly noted above, did not support the social-relations approach. Supervisor feedback and friendship opportunities declined, as did task sigificance and concentration. These direct, first-order effects, in turn, resulted in a decrease in employee satisfaction and internal motivation. An unexpected finding was that employees described their jobs as having less significance after the move to the open office. According to Oldham and Brass (1979, p. 282): "Apparently, when employees were able to observe the entire work process, they could more clearly evaluate the actual impact of their work on others. In this instance, their observations evidently indicated that their work had less impact than they had perceived before the move."

Several other evaluations of open-office design (Hundert and Greenfield 1969; Brookes and Kaplan 1972; Boyce 1974; Dean 1977; Clearwater 1980) have also failed to support the claims of increased efficiency and improved communication made by landscape-design advocates.

For example, Brookes and Kaplan (1972) found in a before-and-after evaluation of 120 employees, who had moved from a mixture of conventional offices to a landscaped design, that perceptions of functional efficiency measured with a semantic-scaling instrument decreased after the move. Perceived increases in noise level, loss of privacy, and visual distractions were the basis of dissatisfaction and of the reduction in perceived efficiency.

These findings support those of Hundert and Greenfield (1969), who conducted an extensive empirical study comparing landscaped and conventional offices. They tested several of the effects landscape design was intended to improve; namely, comfort and attractiveness of the environment, flow of information, morale and personal relationships, awareness of organizational functioning. While more information flowed in the sense of duration, privacy was lost and distractions and interruptions were perceived as having increased. The physical setting of the office made a difference. It simply did not support the expectation of office-landscape advocates.

The failure of an office-landscape design to facilitate communication and interaction both within departments and between departments has also been demonstrated in another recent office-evaluation study (Clearwater, 1980). In an analysis of the effects of a move from a conventional to a landscaped office, after a three-month period, Clearwater found that communication and interaction had not only not improved from a level found in the conventional office, but in fact had significantly worsened. Self-report measures of productivity also did not improve over time. The new landscape-design office was viewed by its employees as being less democratic, and people felt more insecure, unsettled, alienated, passive, and vulnerable. There were no significant differences on these variables among different job categories, which included clerical workers, technical workers, and supervisory professional staff. With respect to differences among job categories, an interesting finding was that supervisory personnel reported the lowest perceived environmental encouragement for personal contact. Every one of a half-dozen evaluative communication items was rated significantly worse in the landscaped than in the conventional offices. All groups were greatly disturbed, distracted, and dissatisfied with the lack of auditory control in the landscaped office. Supervisory and technical workers were the most dissatisfied. The problem was greatest when conversations needed to be kept confidential.

In general, Clearwater (1980) concluded that the move from a conventional to a landscaped office did not support the intentions underlying the move: to improve flexibility, information flow, communication; and eliminate internal barriers which would otherwise hamper a dynamic organizational environment. The actual effects, as noted above, were to make communication and interaction more, not less, difficult. Even with respect to flexibility, Clearwater found that for the individual worker, flexibility did not increase. It could increase for management over time as it altered the space in response to changes in work patterns or technology, but the individual workers experienced no more flexibility or freedom to manipulate their surroundings, to meet their own needs, than they had in conventional offices.

Similarly, Dean (1977) found in a less rigorous evaluation of the American Institute of Architects (AIA) open-office design for its headquarters, four years after it had been installed, that while almost everyone had something positive to say about the open plan, two-thirds of those answering the questionnaire (a total sample of 62 persons from a population of 67) said they preferred working in a conventional, closed-office plan. More professional than clerical employees voiced a preference for closed spaces. Some of the comments of employees are worth repeating here.

An administrator noted (Dean, 1977, p. 34):

I don't know if the arrangement makes communications within the department better. I do know that there are constant interruptions, that everything you say is overheard, which means you can't talk to an employee about poor performance unless you parade him or her into a conference room, and then everybody can see what's happening. For some reason, nobody exercises common rules of courtesy here; the arrangement has brought out different— and worse—patterns of behavior than I've been accustomed to, even when working in a totally open space.

Another employee suggests that courtesy is what saves the situation (Dean, 1977, p. 34):

Only the courtesy and general amiability of the staff members prevent this from being an absolute snake pit. Seated at a desk in a cubicle, one is visually isolated but continually assaulted by distracting noise—exactly the reverse of my preferred work style.

In a study by Boyce (1974), of a British office in which employees' reactions were assessed in a conventional office design and then one year after they had moved to a new open-office design, lack of privacy was also a major complaint. All employees found communication with immediate supervisors to be very easy in the open-office design, but this had been equally easy in the more conventional office from which they had moved.

The increased social density that accompanies open-office designs may, under some conditions, have beneficial effects for both the organization and its employees. Szilagyi and Holland (1980) found, in a study of job characteristics, role stress, work satisfaction, and functional interaction in relation to changes in social density, that professional workers reported less role stress and job autonomy, and more job feedback, friendship opportunities, and work satisfaction. Functional distance, or the number of other persons easily accessible physically to a person, was altered by moving from an older building, in which the professional staff had individual offices that were rectangular in design, with solid doors, small windows, movable furniture, low sound transmission, and a high degree of isolation between work areas, into a modern building; the offices in the latter were described by the authors (1980, p. 29) as

> organized to create a series of small work areas (i.e., three to five offices) with openings leading to the next work area. Individual offices (which were approximately the same size as the old offices) were enclosed on three sides by floor-to-ceiling partitions with the fourth side having a glass front; no doors were on any offices. In addition, custom work units (desk and storage) were in each office and conversational privacy was retained.

It is useful to keep in mind, in interpreting their results, that the increase in social density was moderate and it was not accompanied by an increase in spatial density; that is, office size remained about the same and offices were still private (one-person occupancy). Given these conditions, and that the employees studied were professionals, the findings still suggest the positive effect the organization of space can have on valued behaviors. Increases in the number of colleagues one regularly asks for information, and who ask for information in return, and the reported sense that the changed environmental conditions facilitated work effectiveness by reducing disruption and increasing a sense of order and support, are kinds of behaviors and attitudes that organizations strive to develop in professional employees.

As the authors note, in considering some of these positive effects, particularly in relation to other studies of open offices, which have consistently shown more negative consequences, not only the nature of the physical change, but also the nature of the work performed, must be considered. The professionals in this sample required a high degree of interaction and information flow to perform their work. Any arrangement that assisted this communication function would facilitate work processes and would be viewed in a positive manner by these professionals. Secondly, approximately one-half of the groups finding a social-density decrease were in a new business-development unit. They experienced a change not only in social density, but in new working relationships and new departmental boundaries. These factors, in conjunction with increased distance from others with whom they needed to work, may well have contributed significantly to the reported increase in role stress and to lower work satisfaction.

Problems with the research design, as well as the particular kinds of conditions already mentioned, suggest that these data need to be treated with caution. Their value is that they direct attention to the kinds of effects the organization of space in offices can have on behavior, and underscore the need for further research in this area to ferret out the effects of different types of arrangement as a function of the nature of work involved. The Szilagyi and Holland (1980) study also underscores the point that many of the complaints about office landscaping are not necessarily inherent in the design concept per se (e.g., office landscaping does not require smaller offices).

Given the salience of privacy for employees, and the difficulty open-office designs have had in providing adequate levels of it, it is surprising that there have been few empirical studies of privacy per se in offices. One exception is a study by Justa and Golan (1977). They looked at privacy as a concept whose meaning and behavioral forms vary as a function of changing sociophysical situations. Their study is particularly useful for organizational ecology because it looked at the relationships among the desire for privacy, actions taken to insure privacy, including physical, social, and policy supports, and norms of a particular situation. They defined privacy in multiple ways, and explored the role the physical setting plays in providing adequate supports for different kinds of privacy (e.g., communication privacy versus task privacy, or the opportunity to work without interruptions). They looked at situations in which an individual was either alone or with others, and at the degree of physical closure of the space characterizing the interaction.

They found middle-management executives spent their days in situations that differed in physical design as well as in social structure. Managers met on a daily basis with fellow employees and dealt with unanticipated meetings and emergency reports, spent time working alone on problem-solving and report-writing tasks, and attended to personnel matters, such as salary reviews, hiring, and interviewing. The kind of social- and physical-support systems appropriate to carrying out these different office functions varied with the particular function, as did the definition of privacy itself. For example, privacy ranged from "being able to work without distractions" to "controlling access to information" and "controlling access to space" and "being alone." The underlying characteristic of privacy was the ability to control or regulate inputs and outputs (Altman, 1975). As responsibilities and demands varied over the course of the day, desire for privacy and actions taken to insure privacy also varied.

Physical supports, in themselves, could not provide adequate privacy. Secretaries, for example, served important gatekeeping functions. This was especially true in terms of actions taken to insure privacy, which occurred significantly more often when participants were with others than when they were alone. In these cases, in addition to going into an enclosed office and closing the door (which did not occur when participants were in their offices alone), secretaries were instructed to screen visitors and phone calls.

From an open-office design perspective, the most interesting finding was that the most privacy (complete lack of intrusion) permitted by the office norms was in interaction with others. Even when alone and in an enclosed office, participants communicated, through their secretary and by leaving their door open, that they were accessible. This was part of the normative social structure. Being alone and enclosed and inaccessible was considered inappropriate. Also part of the normative structure was the fact that when participants were with others in public spaces, the nature of social interaction was casual and informal. Thus, the kind of interaction differed significantly as a function of its spatial location, or privacy.

Justa and Golan (1977) conclude that the "ability to regulate interaction and the experience of privacy, given a situation in which there is a desire for some form of privacy, is a function of what is required, what is available and what is acceptable." What privacy a manager could attain, in terms of available physical supports in the form of an enclosed office, may not be obtained because of norms supporting accessibility, except when one is already in interaction with others. Managers must balance their personal-task requirements (working alone without interruptions, for example) with office social norms that exert pressure to be accessible to others at all times. The difficulty with office landscaping is not that interaction or communication in a generic sense is not increased, but that physical supports are not available to provide privacy for specific and varying kinds of interactions that individuals feel require full enclosure. The presence of appropriate social systems, such as secretaries whose function is to screen inputs, cannot be effective by themselves. Neither can physical-support systems, in the form of enclosed offices, by themselves insure appropriate forms of privacy. The social- and physical-support systems are interdependent.

These empirical data undermine the claims of open-office-design advocates that this type of plan increases efficiency by restructuring communications in more productive ways. The increasing use of open-office designs in the face of evidence that overwhelmingly documents the failure of open-plan designs to increase efficiency by improving communications processes (it seems to worsen rather than improve them in terms of meaningful interaction, such as occurs in performance feedback) suggests that criteria other then work efficiency are, in fact, being used in decisions about office planning. As I noted in an earlier chapter, these criteria appear to be direct costs of space per person, which can be reduced by squeezing more people into a given area, regardless of the impact on communication or work processes. As Brookes and Kaplan (1972) point out, there is very little empirical evidence to support manufacturers' claims of increased productivity and of improved staff morale and lower absenteeism. Decreases in renovation time and space requirements appear more justifiable, but these data are not examined in the context of their implications for work efficiency, which may, in fact, negate a significant portion of the direct cost savings realized.

SMALL-GROUP ECOLOGY: PARTICIPATION

Organization members spend inordinate amounts of time in meetings. Decisions of all kinds are made in these meetings: approving or rejecting capital-budget requests, hiring and firing employees and providing performance feedback, determining implementation plans, arguing the merits of one product over another. All these meetings share a common characteristic: Individuals interact with each other as they share information, opinions, and insights. Because meetings often bring together individuals or groups with competing interests, such gatherings often are characterized by tension and anxiety. Organizations seem to assume that where these meetings occur, what the nature of the furniture arrangement within them is, and where individual participants are located, are nonproblematic. Rigid rules generally prevail: The president sits at the head of the table, with his associates on one side; and the higher the associate's position, the closer to the president. Groups with conflicting interests take opposite sides of a rectangular table.

Organizations need to consider these ecological characteristics of meetings as problematical. They affect the nature of interaction and participation patterns, and these patterns, in turn, affect social-influence processes that affect the nature of decisions made. As Spaulding (1978) notes, the positive role of meetings in organizations is typically overlooked or played down in general. Meetings are widely viewed as a drain on energy and a waste of productive time. They often are. But this is a little like eating burnt toast and deciding you do not like bread. Meetings, as typically conducted, provide participants little opportunity to participate. They are designed to facilitate one-way communication, not the exchange of ideas. Even more overlooked is their potential for facilitating the development of social bonds that are important to a sense of group cohesiveness and the trust required to share ideas.

Clearly, not all meetings should stimulate a free exchange of ideas. Spaulding's point is that there are whole classes of meetings where social interaction should be a purpose of the meeting. This is particularly so in matrix-form organizations where teams of people are continually reconstituted to tackle new problems. An important characteristic of these groups is that they are composed of relative strangers. To build a committed, motivated project team from a group of people who do not know each other very well takes some time and a sense of comfort among, if not a liking for, other team members.

Spaulding (1978) argues that the most obvious influence on the development of settings that provide the opportunity for and encourage social contact is the physical arrangement of the meeting rooms. He notes that arrangements that maximize eye contact and minimize distance between persons are optimal ones. For this reason, a squared circle is better than the long conference table, and far superior to the typical lecture arrangement. The importance of the physical arrangement is in its direct contribution not to productivity, but to the kinds of social relationships which underlie team effectiveness and are directly related to productivity.

While very little systematic data are specifically collected in organizations looking at these issues, a great deal of research has been done on nonverbal behavior and interaction in laboratory and school settings. Applying these studies to work settings requires caution. Yet at the very least, these studies underline the need to explore similar processes in work organizations.

In a series of well-known studies, Sommer (1969) was one of the first to systematically and empirically investigate some of the ideas about particular arrangements of people being more suited to certain activities than others. Sommer and his colleagues found, for example, that students' selection of a seat position at a rectangular table was related to the kind of interaction they expected. Corner-to-corner arrangements were overwhelmingly chosen for casual conversation; side-by-side arrangements, for cooperative activity; and face-to-face seating by competing pairs. Students explained that a corner-to-corner arrangement facilitated eye contact and physical proximity, and that the side-by-side arangement made it easier to share things. In another study, students rated diagrams of seating arrangements at a rectangular table. They found that increased distance between seats produced ratings indicating less acquaintance, less friendliness, and lower talkativeness, except where increased eye contact counteracted the effects of increased distance.

Sommer (1969) also found that there are limits to comfortable conversation distance. He placed two sofas in an attractively furnished lounge at prearranged distances from each other. Pairs of subjects were asked to enter the lounge and discuss various impersonal topics. When the couches were placed from one to three feet apart, people sat opposite one another. From three-and-one-half feet and beyond, people sat side by side. Sommer concluded that under the conditions where two people know each other slightly and are discussing an impersonal topic in a large lounge, this would be considered the upper limit for comfortable conversation. Under different conditions, in a larger room, for example, the comfortable distance would change. Differences in noise level, distractions, and even lighting would also affect the distance.

The studies, of how seating position and spatial location influence interaction patterns, that Sommer and his colleagues pursued evolved from a series of studies in which researchers investigating group dynamics in small laboratory groups realized that the interaction patterns they were observing were related to spatial factors (Hare and Bales, 1963); Steinzor, 1950). They began to go back and reanalyze their data to take this new variable into consideration. Steinzor (1950), for example, reanalyzed his data to see whether group members were more likely to interact with people whom they could see. He found that when one person in the group finished speaking, it was the person opposite, rather than someone alongside, who was the next to speak. Others began to look at the relationship between spatial factors, largely seating position, and leadership. Sommer (1961) and Strodbeck and Hook (1961), for example, found that leaders are more likely to select a seat at the head of a table than at any other location, and persons who sit at corners of rectangular tables are likely to contribute the least to discussion. These studies have not received much followup attention. They did stimulate, however, a continuing interest in the spatial factors' influence on frequency of interaction, particularly in school environments.

Several studies have found that participation in the classroom is related to seating position. Sommer (1967a) found greater participation by college students sitting in the front of the room and in the center of each row. Adams (1969) found similar results at the secondary level. He observed and recorded verbal interaction in 32 math and social-studies classes, two classes of each of 16 teachers. Verbal interaction was so concentrated in the center front of the classroom, and in a line directly up the center, that he coined the term "action zone" to refer to this area of the room. Koneya (1976) found that college students judged to be highly verbal consistently chose front-center seats when asked to indicate their preferences on a seating plan. These students, and those judged moderately verbal, exhibited very different response rates depending on actual seat location. Those randomly assigned to the "action zone" participated far more than those assigned to seats outside this area. The participation rates of students characterized as low verbalizers did not vary according to seat.

MOTIVATION/INVOLVEMENT/SUPERVISION

A great deal of research has been done on open-plan schools, some of which is very suggestive for organizations adopting landscaped-design offices in which high levels of interaction among colleagues are expected. Weinstein (1979) provides an excellent review of this research, and in the discussion that follows, I have borrowed freely from it.

In relation to the school environment, Meyer (1971) found that the bulk of the data on teacher attitudes and behavior shows that open-space schools often lead to increased interaction among teachers. When teachers in open space are compared with their counterparts in conventional schools, they have greater feelings of autonomy (Brunetti, 1972; Meyer, 1971), satisfaction (Meyer, 1971), and ambition (Cohen, 1973). Open-space plans have also resulted in teachers placing a higher value on evaluation by their colleagues (Meyer, 1971), and spending less time conducting routine activities (Ellison, Gilbert, and Ratsoy, 1969). Open space generally appears to enhance students' feelings of autonomy (Meyer, 1971), willingness to take risks (Anifant, 1972), and persistence at a task (Reiss and Dydhalo, 1975).

The organizational literature is replete with discussions of motivation, authority, and supervision. Again, the literature on schools suggests that characteristics of the physical setting may contribute in important ways to these behaviors. For example, in a study of day-care centers in Los Angeles, intended to isolate factors predictive of program quality, Prescott, Jones, and Kritchevsky (1967) found that the availability and organization of equipment and materials were among the most effective predictors of the quality of a day-care-center program. The data were qualitative, but suggested that as the quality of the physical space decreased, the amount of teacher restriction and control increased; the teacher's manner was less frequently rated as sensitive and friendly, and the children were less frequently rated as interested and involved; the number of lessons on arbitrary rules of social living increased; and conflict among children rose.

Similar findings were reported by Zifferblatt (1972). She examined the relationship between design and behavior in two third-grade, open-education classrooms in which the teacher's instructional styles, the curricula, and the activities were very similar. In one classroom, students' attention spans were shorter; there was much non-task-oriented movement, and loud conversation. Zifferblatt concluded the behavioral differences were a function of classroom arrangement. In classrooms with more desirable behaviors, the desks were arranged so that only two or three children could work together, and often these desks were placed in less accessible areas of the room, providing a certain degree of privacy. The teacher's desk was also situated in a corner, so that she was unable to direct activities from it and had to move around the room a great deal. Barriers such as bookcases delimited areas for specific activities.

Students' commitment and involvement in classes has also been found to be related to design at the college level. Horowitz and Otto (1973) compared the scholastic achievement of college students in a traditional classroom and in a specially designed "alternative learning facility" that contained a great deal of color, movable wall panels, a complex lighting system, and flexible, comfortable seats. Grades were not affected, but the reported anecdotal information was striking. Attendance in the experimental room was better, despite the fact that the section was held at a less convenient time; students participated more during class; more students from the experimental room paid office visits to the instructor; and there was more informality and group cohesion.

Several studies have looked at performance, with equivocal results. It may be that performance measures used do not tap aspects of learning that occurred, or that they overlook the importance of the process of learning; for example, how one learns material or is introduced to a subject may influence the individual level of initiative in further explorations of the subject.

Schwebel and Cherlin (1972) observed the behavior of students from kindergarten to fifth grade in two middle-class elementary schools. They found that in two of three observation periods, students who had been assigned seats in the front rows were more attentive and engaged in more on-task behavior than students in other rows. When students were reassigned seats on a random basis, those students who had been moved forward showed the greatest mean increase in the amount of time they engaged in work and the greatest mean decrease in time spent in inactivity and unassigned activity. They also found teachers' ratings of student attentiveness and likability changed. Students who moved forward received more favorable ratings than they had before, whereas the opposite was true for students who moved backward.

THE ENVIRONMENT AND EVALUATIVE INTERPERSONAL JUDGMENTS

Another aspect of organizational performance involves the kinds of evaluative interpersonal judgments made by all employees about each other. It is a particularly acute issue for managers and supervisors, whose job requires them to rate performance, recommend promotions and salary adjustments, and provide guidance and positive and negative feedback.

These kinds of decisions directly influence job satisfaction and play an important role in decisions to hire and retain employees, on the one hand, and in employees' decisions to remain in the organization, on the other. There has been relatively little work directly focused on the effects of environmental factors on evaluative interpersonal judgments, but what there is suggests the need for additional work in this area.

The classic studies in this area were done more than 25 years ago by Maslow and Mintz (1956) and by Mintz (1956). In a laboratory setting, they experimentally investigated the effects of a "beautiful," an "average," and an "ugly" room on perceiving "energy" and "well-being" in faces. This is quite different from the human-factors tradition that measures the effect of environmental characteristics, such as color, noise, or vibration, on vigilance, learning, memory, and motor-performance tasks.

They (Maslow and Mintz, 1956, p. 248) described the three different rooms as follows:

> The beautiful room impressed people as "attractive," "pretty," "comfortable", "pleasant." It was 11' × 14' × 10' and had two large windows, beige-colored walls, and indirect overhead light, and furnishings to give the impression of an attractive, comfortable study. Furnishings included a soft armchair, a mahogany desk and chair combination, two straight-backed chairs, a small table, a wooden bookcase, a large Navajo rug, drapes for the windows, paintings on the wall, and some sculpture and art objects on the desk and table. These were all chosen to harmonize as pleasantly as possible with the beige walls. The "ugly" room (UR) evoked comments of "horrible," "disgusting," "ugly," "repulsive." It was 7' × 12' × 10' and had two half-windows, battleship-gray walls, an overhead bulb with a dirty, torn, ill-fitting lampshade, and "furnishings" to give the impression of a janitor's storeroom in disheveled condition. There were two straight-backed chairs, a small table, tin cans for ashtrays, and dirty, torn window shades. Near the bare walls on three sides were such things as pails, brooms, mops, cardboard boxes, dirty-looking trash cans, a bed-spring and uncovered mattress, and assorted refuse. The room was neither swept nor dusted and the ashtrays were not emptied. The "average" room (AR) was a professor's office 15' × 17' × 10', with three windows, battleship-gray walls, and an indirect overhead light. Furnishings included two mahogany desk and chair combinations, two straight-backed chairs, a metal bookcase, window shades, a metal filing cabinet, and a cot with a pleasant looking green bedspread. It gave the appearance of a clean, neat, "worked-in" office in no way outstanding enough to elicit any comments.

Subjects in the experiment were asked to rate ten negative-print photographs of men and women, arranged alternately, on the dimensions of energy and well-being. They were told the study was about impressions, and that the use of the negative-print photographs was to minimize hairline and clothing and to emphasize bone structure and shape. Maslow and Mintz found that the average ratings for energy and well-being in the beautiful room were significantly higher than ratings in the ugly and average room. Subjects rated the faces in the ugly room as having little energy and being more "irritable" than "content." The authors noted that their data did not indicate whether these findings were merely short-term effects that would disappear as subjects adapted, or more enduring. To answer this question, Mintz (1956) did a second study.

In the followup study, the two examiners, unaware that they were also subjects for the study, each spent prolonged sessions testing others in a beautiful and in an ugly room. The study was conducted over a three-week period, with two sessions each week lasting either one or two hours. The examiners spent the whole of one session in the same room, and switched rooms for alternate sessions. Each examiner thus spent three sessions in the beautiful room and three sessions in the ugly room. In addition to the same type of ratings used in the first study, observational data, in the form of the time taken to complete the testing, were collected. Since each examiner tested concurrently, and since the test procedure and the time each pair of subjects entered the rooms were identical for both examiners, the number of times an examiner in the ugly room finished before an examiner in the beautiful room did provided a second measure of the effects.

They found that scores on the rating task were significantly higher in the beautiful room for each of the three weeks of prolonged sessions, and the mean difference in scores for the first week was the smallest obtained during the three weeks. The effects did not decrease over time. The testing-time data were even more fascinating. The total combined sum of times taken showed that the examiner in the ugly room finished testing before the examiner in the beautiful room in 27 out of the 32 situations. The effects did not decrease after the first week. Observational notes taken by Mintz indicated that in the ugly room, the examiners had such reactions as monotony, fatigue, head-ache, sleep, discontent, irritability, hostility, and avoidance of the room; while in the beautiful room, they had feelings of comfort, pleasure, enjoy-ment, importance, energy, and a desire to continue their activity.

While these studies leave a number of questions unanswered, including the effects of moving back and forth between two environments to make the contrast between them continually salient, the studies suggest the significant effects environmental conditions can have on highly valued organizational behaviors, including commitment, motivation, cooperation, and inter-personal judgments. More recently, the effects of other kinds of environ-mental conditions, including temperature and density, on evaluative inter-personal judgments have been demonstrated.

In two studies drawing upon the Maslow and Mintz tradition (Griffitt, 1970; Griffitt and Veitch, 1971), ambient temperature was found related to interpersonal attraction. These studies were done within a reinforcement model of affective behavior (Byrne, 1969). Griffitt expanded this framework and proposed that not only is attraction related to the reinforcing properties or qualities of the stimulus object or person, but also that attraction will be a function of the total 'stimulus situation" to which the person making the judgments is exposed. This stimulus situation includes ambient-situational variables, such as temperature, population density, attractiveness of surroundings. Griffitt (1970) notes the conventional wisdom that people are more irritable when "hot and grouchy," as well as the U.S. Riot Commission's findings in 1968 that ghetto riots were related to summer temperatures.

Since interpersonal attraction has also been found related to individuals' degree of attitude similarity-dissimilarity, Griffitt looked at the effects of different ambient temperatures under conditions where individuals were rating the attractiveness of a stranger who, they had learned through inspection of the stranger's responses on a 44-item attitude scale, generally shared their own attitudes, or who differed with them considerably. Half of the subjects rated this stranger in a hot room (90.6 degrees—effective temperature) and the other half in a more comfortable room (67.5 degrees). Within each temperature condition, half the college-student subjects rated their attraction to a stranger they thought shared their attitudes and half to a stranger they thought differed considerably in his attitudes.

Griffitt found that under the condition of high effective temperature, attraction responses were more negative than under the condition of normal effective temperature. There was no significant interaction effect between degree of attitude similarity and temperature. Essentially, this study, and a second, similar one (Griffitt and Veitch, 1971), in which population density was also found related to attraction, support the hypothesis that under conditions of personal discomfort, interpersonal judgments will be more negative than under conditions of greater comfort. These findings strongly suggest the importance to the organization of taking into consideration individuals' response to their physical surroundings. A more recent study of the effect of noise on evaluative interpersonal judgments suggests even more directly the role the physical setting can play in personnel evaluations.

Using the same reinforcement model proposed by Griffitt (1970), Sauser, Arauz, and Chambers (1978) explored, in a simulation study, the relationship between level of office noise and salary recommendations. The theory asserts, again, that a neutral stimulus, a job applicant for example, associated with a reinforcing stimulus, an enjoyable meal perhaps, will be evaluated more positively than the same person associated with a less enjoyable meal. Using college students, Sauser et al. (1978) had ten students play the role of a personnel manager in a corporation which had just hired five new persons and needed to assign them starting salaries.

The student-managers were told, in a simulated memo from the vice-president of accounting, that starting salaries generally ranged from $7,500 to $15,000. They were to select what they considered the appropriate salary based on the resume of each of the five job applicants. The resume included the applicant's name, birth date, marital status, number of dependents, education (including the names of schools and universities), extracurricular activities in college, hobbies, and previous work experience. The five applicants differed widely in their backgrounds.

Half of the students assigned the starting salary after reading in a noisy office for 20 minutes, and half assigned starting salaries after reading in a quiet office for 20 minutes. The noisy office was simulated by playing a tape of the sounds from an office in a large insurance company: typing, the telephone ringing, talking, paper rustling, people walking and moving. The tape was played at the same 70-80 decibel range that it had been recorded at in the actual office. In the quiet room, the tape was not played at all.

The effect of the noisy condition on the recommended salary level was significant. Salaries were consistently higher in the quiet room than in the noisy room. There were no significant effects caused by the differences among applicants, and there were no interaction effects between applicants and conditions; that is, all the applicants were given lower salaries under noisy conditions. The mean difference in recommended salaries was $971. In a followup study eliminating several limitations of the first study, including the simulated setting, the use of college students, use of only two noise levels, the small sample size, and the relatively short adaptation period (20 minutes' reading before making the salary recommendations), essentially the same results were obtained.

The authors point out that the range of interpersonal evaluations that may be affected by such environmental conditions directly affects many organizational activities, including selection and placement of personnel, salary recommendations, performance appraisals, and grievance resolutions. Increasing our understanding of how the organization of space and the control of environmental variables influence these kinds of judgments is clearly of significance to all organizations. We know, from evaluations of office environments discussed earlier in this chapter, that lighting levels and location, privacy, colors, and storage are sources of dissatisfaction in work settings. We need to begin to systematically assess how such sources of personal discomfort and unpleasantness affect evaluative interpersonal judgments.

Since performance is often linked to performance evaluation, we also need to better understand the interaction between the employee's physical location vis-à-vis supervisors and evaluative interpersonal judgments. A study by Rist (1970) in a school setting is suggestive in this regard. He found that a teacher seated inner-city kindergarten children at tables according to subjectively interpreted social criteria. Those who displayed middle-class attitudes and behavior were placed nearest the teacher and received most of her instruction and attention. Children whose physical appearance, language patterns, and family background departed from the teacher's middle-class "ideal student" were assigned to tables further away from her, were characterized as "slow learners," and subsequently received less attention.

These data suggest that attention to the placement of newly hired personnel may contribute to the level of support and assistance they receive, and thus to their rapid and effective integration into the work setting. The point is not that physical distance causes poor performance. It is that the physical setting acts to control certain social processes, which, in turn, more directly influence a specific behavior.

THE ENVIRONMENT AND
INDIVIDUAL DIFFERENCES

Just as job-enrichment or -enlargement programs will not affect all people in the same way (Lawler, 1973), the earlier discussion (see Chapter 3) on environmental supports and individual competencies suggests that the same environmental conditions will be mediated by individual-difference factors. With the exception of human-factors data, we know very little, however, about what these factors are in relation to environmental conditions in work settings. There is some evidence, discussed previously, that employees lower in the organizational hierarchy respond most favorably to open-office designs and those closer to the middle, least favorably (Clearwater, 1980); that age and marital status mediate the effects of environmental stressors like noise and air pollution (Bergermaier et al., 1980); that professional workers may appreciate increased social density (Szilagyi and Holland, 1980); and that clerical workers prefer privacy in their work environments as much as administrators do (Sundstrom et al., 1980). Given the paucity of ecological research in work settings, research in school settings can at least provide some insight into the potential mediating influence of individual differences on environmental impact.

For example, Bell et al. (1974) measured the achievement of two groups of first graders, one entering an open-space school and one a conventional school. Preschool tests had revealed no differences between the two groups on any variable. Achievement tests administered at mid-term and in June showed the students in the conventional school to be significantly ahead of the open-space students on all reading tests. The percentage of students scoring below standardized test norms in reading was at least twice as large in the open-space school as in the traditional school. They concluded that the egocentric, behaviorally immature child had a better chance of success in the traditional class.

In another study examining the relationship between IQ, achievement, and open space, Grapko (1972) examined the standardized achievement-test scores of sixth graders in one conventional and one open-space school. Students in traditional classrooms achieved higher scores on all four subtests. Further analyses of the results by IQ revealed that these differences were due to the differences in the performance of lower-IQ students. While bright students did equally well in open-space and conventional classrooms, lower-IQ students were likely to achieve less if placed in open space. He speculated that lower-IQ students are less able to function well in situations which are distracting, in which student initiative and responsibility are stressed, and where the discovery approach is emphasized. While generalizing from these findings to adult office employees with extreme caution, they do suggest some individual difference dimensions that bear further exploration.

INTERPERSONAL BEHAVIOR AND DENSITY

Although the increasing number of office-landscape installations has focused attention on issues of density, crowding, and privacy, most of the research in this area has occurred in nonoffice settings: housing, schools, hospitals, and psychology laboratories. Some of this evidence is presented below because the process or experience of crowding is presumed to be similar across settings, even if the specific expression of the phenomenon or its consequences differs. The intent is to suggest the importance of crowding as an issue in organizational designs and behavior.

A major issue in assessing the effects of density is the way in which it has been conceptualized (Loo, 1973; Greenberg, 1978). The influence of number of workers on organizational behavior has been addressed in three different ways. Organizational theorists have shown that the size of an organization or its subunits affects attitudes and behavior of workers (Porter and Lawler 1965; Porter and Steers, 1973). For the most part, size, as studied by organizational theorists, has focused on the sheer number of personnel within a unit. For example, an organization with 1,000 employees is seen as larger than an organization of 500 employees, and a work group of ten is larger than a work group of five. The unit of analysis of organization size varies from the subunit to the total organization. Primary work groups, departments, and factories (in multi-factory organizations) are, therefore, considered to be organization subunits (Greenberg, 1978) Typically, researchers correlate unit size with such organizational indices as job satisfaction, turnover, absenteeism, and productivity (Lawler, 1973). In general, there seems to be a stronger correlation between subunit size and these various measures of organizational behavior than between the overall organizational size and the measures. Job satisfaction is found to be lower, and turnover higher, as a function of size. Productivity, in the sense of the greater output of some subunit, has not been conclusively demonstrated to be influenced by size per se. Like some of the data presented earlier on small-group ecology, organizational theorists (Indik, 1965) have shown that increasing organization size decreases the extent of member participation.

These studies of organizational size do not take into account two of the other kinds of variables that environmental psychologists and ecological psychologists have assessed in relationship to size. Ecological psychologists (Barker, 1968) view size in relationship to task; the way in which they do so is discussed later in this chapter. Environmental psychologists have looked at size in a third way. Their focus has been on size in relationship to some unit of area: number of people per room, number of people per building, number of people per neighborhood. They have focused on the way in which architectural variables influence or mediate the effect of the size per se. In doing so, they have devoted considerable attention to the distinction between density, or the number of people per a given unit of area, and crowding, which has become synonymous with the experience of high density. The conceptual distinction between crowding and density arose from the need to explain why certain situations which involved a given number of people were, under some conditions, experienced as crowded ones, and seemed to have negative effects, while other situations with equally high density did not appear to have negative effects.

Several critical factors underlying the experience of crowding have been suggested (Loo, 1973; Sherrod, 1974; Worchel and Teddlie, 1976; Schopler and Stockdale, 1977; and Zlutnick and Altman, 1974). These analyses focus on the critical element of control. Essentially, for density to be experienced as crowding, which is presumed to be a stressful state, one must feel unable to control the amount and type of interaction with others. Interference with goal-directed activities becomes a major criterion for the experience of crowding. The degree to which the activity engaged in is valued, the type and intensity of relationships among the people interacting, the duration for which the interference occurs and its frequency, the reasons why the interference is occurring, and the degree of boundary separation among individuals that is facilitated by architectural charateristics like seating orientation—all these mediate the effects of interference per se.

As Altman (1975) argues, crowding reflects a failure to obtain a balance between the desired level of interaction and the obtained level of interaction. Level of interaction refers to control over access to oneself or a group. Access includes the ability to control the transmission of information about oneself to others, as well as control over the inputs from others (Sundstrom et al. 1980). As such, the absence of the physical presence of others, or of low visibility among workers, may not be sufficient for the experience of privacy since information may still be uncontrolled in the form of sound transmission. This is one reason manufacturers of furniture systems stress their systems provide conversational privacy: being able to hear sounds of talking without the sounds being intelligible.

Construing the absence of control and the interference with one's goal-directed activities as fundamental conditions for the experience of crowding helps explain why density effects are more apparent when the unit of analysis is more fine-grained: number of people per room as opposed to number of people per building or per block. As density is experienced at more proximate points to the goal-directed activity, the likelihood that other people present will actually interfere with the activity increases. It makes sense, then, that the importance of architectural elements would also be greatest at finer-grained scales, where they have a greater likelihood of ameliorating the effects of density by reducing direct interference with an activity.

Loo (1973), for example, has argued that the reason performance has been unaffected by density in some studies, like that by Freedman, Klevansky, and Ehrlich (1971), is that the researchers essentially created a situation in which degree of interference was very low, as a result of architectural barriers that furniture provided and of tasks which did not require subjects to interact with each other. Sundstrom et al. (1980) have shown that architectural elements, such as degree of enclosure, visibility of coworkers and supervisors, and level of acoustic isolation, are significantly correlated with psychological privacy. They also found that contrary to the expectation that job satisfaction for persons with complex jobs would be enhanced by architectural privacy, while job satisfaction for persons with more routine jobs would be reduced (because of the reduction of social interaction that was hypothesized to compensate for the routine work), job satisfaction for clerks as well as for administrators was related to increased levels of architectural privacy.

Sherrod (1974) has shown that crowding, as a social stressor, may not produce task decrements when the stressor is present, but may do so subsequently when the stressor is removed. His findings parallel Glass's and Singer's (1972) demonstration that the effects of noise, particularly uncontrollable noise, were most evident in situations following the removal of the stressor. Sherrod, following Glass and Singer, proposed that perceived control, or its lack, was the critical variable mediating the effects of density. He had subjects perform simple and complex tasks both during and after exposure to high levels of density under differing conditions of perceived control. Performance of simple or complex tasks was unaffected by density or perceived control while one worked in the dense condition. However, on postexperimental tasks, when others were no longer present, performance decrements were observed in subjects who had not been given the perception of control of the stressor in the earlier part of the study. Like Glass's and Singer's study of noise, this study suggests the importance of perceived control as a mediator of stressful environmental conditions, both during the stressor's presence and after the stressor is removed.

A number of laboratory and field studies which have looked at density at points proximate to the individual have found social withdrawal and/or aggression in response to dense situations. For example, as noted earlier, subjects in a dense laboratory situation rated the hypothetical other person less favorably than did those in less crowded conditions (Griffitt and Veitch, 1971). Freedman et al. (1971) found subjects in crowded conditions felt their partners to be less cooperative and acted more competitively themselves in crowded conditions. Stokols et al. (1973) also found that males in a crowded environment felt more competitive and aggressive toward others than did females. Hutt and Vaizey (1966) found that in response to different-sized groups in a free-play situation, autistic children showed almost no aggressive behavior. Normal children's aggression increased in larger-sized groups and they spent less time in social contact as group size increased. This pattern of social withdrawal also appeared in a study by Ittelson, Proshansky, and Rivlin (1970). They found that provision of private rooms in a psychiatric hospital, which enabled patients to control social interaction, resulted in increased social interaction in areas outside the sleeping/bedroom area. Similarly, Baum and Valins (1979) found that inability to control social interaction in a dormitory setting resulted in increased attempts to avoid social interaction and cooperative interpersonal relations.

This social-withdrawal behavior in the presence of crowded situations is supported by several studies of children. Krantz and Risley (1972) found that when kindergartners were crowded around a teacher who was reading a story or conducting a demonstration, they were far less attentive than when they were spread out in a semicircle. Shapiro (1975) found that noninvolved behavior (defined as behavior that was random, deviant, and onlooking) was most frequent in nursery-school classrooms where the space per pupil was less than 30 square feet and least frequent in classrooms that provided between 30 and 50 square feet of floor space per pupil. The relationship was curvilinear. Noninvolvement was also higher in the least-crowded classrooms, those with more than 50 square feet per child. In a short-term experimental study in which groups of six children were observed in both a large and small room, Loo (1972) found that under high-spatial-density conditions, children spent less time in group involvement and more time in solitary play.

The importance of interference as a condition for high density leading to aggression is suggested by a study by Rohe and Patterson (1974). They formed children's play groups in which environmental resources (i.e., number of toys) were varied. Under conditions of high density/low resources, negative social behaviors were quite high. Under conditions of high density/ high resources, antisocial behaviors were considerably lower. The level of available resources defines the likelihood of interference. If two individuals are competing for the same resource, one's attaining it interferes with the other's engaging in the same activity, producing a sense of crowding and increasing the probability of conflict.

ORGANIZATIONAL STRUCTURE: SIZE

In contrast to focusing on size in relation to a given area, or size in relation to a given work group, ecological psychologists have looked at size in relationship to the structure of particular activities. Unlike cases of crowding, where negative social behaviors are mediated by overstimulation, ecological psychologists essentially argue and have demonstrated that negative effects of size in relationship to activity structure are mediated by understimulation. Size in relationship to activity structure is an especially important variable, given the implications this research has for the development of leadership, job satisfaction, and involvement and commitment to an organization.

Wicker (1979) summarizes very well the development and contribution of the ecological psychological approach over the past three decades, and in the discussion that follows, I have borrowed freely from it. Because "setting" is a specialized term in ecological psychology, some of its essential features are briefly described, before a discussion of some of the research findings.

Ecological psychology was originally developed by Roger Barker (1968) as an alternative to a stimulus-response-oriented model of human behavior. His approach was a radical departure from the rigidly controlled laboratory experiment in which subjects came at appointed times and behaved in response to controlled stimuli (the experimenter hoped). Barker's method was very simple (and very tedious). He and his colleagues followed children around during the day as they went about their normal activities. They recorded, in lay language, what the children said and did, what was said and done to them, and where they went. They called this data-collection procedure a specimen record. Their most striking conclusion was that the behaviors of children could be predicted more accurately from knowing the situations the children were in than from knowing individual characteristics of the children. This was a major departure from the belief that individuals have stable personality traits that they carry from situation to situation and that, in each situation, guide their behavior in similar ways. All the children's behavior was not identical. Some children were more active than others, for example. But all the children's behavior fell within a restricted range. Children could have done many more things in the classroom than they did. Their behavior conformed to characteristics of the setting they entered.

This perspective shifts the responsibility for behavior, at least in part, from the individual to the situation. This, in turn, affects how we think about solving social problems. If we assume that some social problem—apathy or indifference in the work situation, for example—is a function of aspects of the setting rather than of a personal characteristic of the individual, solutions suggested are more likely to focus on environmental changes, such as making the work environment more comfortable or supportive of valued behaviors, than on changing the attitudes of the worker through discussion and feedback about performance. In thinking about changing the setting, from an ecological perspective, it is important to understand that the behavior setting is considered more than the physical setting.

Wicker (1979, p. 12) summarizes the essential features of behavior settings in a single sentence: "A behavior setting is a bounded, self-regulated and ordered system composed of replaceable human and nonhuman components that interact in a synchronized fashion to carry out an ordered sequence of events called the setting program." Let us look at each of the feature separately.

A behavior setting exists in space and time. It is not an abstract concept. It is not just a place, but involves a set of interactions within a place. A behavior setting contains two broad classes of components: people (typists, janitors, administrators) and objects (typewriter, furniture, walls), which exist within a physical boundary—the exterior walls of a room or suite of rooms (depending on how the setting scale is defined). Within this boundary, there is an orderly pattern of behavior that follows a program—a prescribed sequence of interactions between people and objects in the setting. The parts of the setting, human and nonhuman, have a synomorphic relationship with each other. Actions and objects fit compatibly together. They are coordinated. Different positions that people have in behavior settings, such as typist and administrator, can be ordered on the basis of influence and responsibility in the setting.

People in the setting are replaceable and interchangeable. Who fills a position is relatively unimportant as long as each essential job is covered. Behavior settings are dependent upon a minimum number of persons to carry out the setting program. To use Barker's original example, it is difficult to carry on a regular baseball game if the number of players falls below seven or eight. With four or five players, new rules are invented and the game changes.

The last feature is probably most central to the discussion that follows: Behavior settings are self-regulating, active systems. They impose their program of activities on the persons and objects within them. Essential persons and materials are drawn into settings, and disruptive components are modified or rejected. The left fielder who refuses to catch balls hit to left field is told to start playing or leave the field. Maintenance mechanisms, often in the form of social pressure from other participants, act on people to guarantee that the essential activities of a setting (its program) are carried out. Knowing the program of a setting thus allows us to make some limited predictions about how people who are in it will behave. People who enter and remain in a setting behave in ways that are compatible with its program. They will not engage in many other behaviors of which they are capable if those behaviors are not compatible with the program.

This extremely brief description of what constitutes a behavior setting indicates that for an ecological psychologist, the emphasis is on the program, or prescribed sequence of interactions between people and their physical surroundings. It also emphasizes that such a program is maintained by self-regulating processes initiated by individuals in the setting who value the progam. The emphasis is not on the physical setting itself. It is assumed to be compatible with the setting's program. This is not always the case, of course, so one of the implications is that a setting may be maintained by regulating either the human or nonhuman components.

The relevance of the ecological perspective for the study of organizations is based on the notion that behavior settings make differential demands on their occupants, depending on the number of persons in the setting. Barker (1968) developed the notion of "manning" to help explain the ways in which behavior settings attempt to counteract threats to their programs. He was particularly interested in undermanning, which exists when the number of people present is insufficient to carry out smoothly the essential program and maintain tasks in the setting. The theory of manning suggests that occupants of undermanned, in contrast to optimally manned, behavior settings are more likely to engage in more frequent, vigorous, and varied actions to support the setting program, to counteract threats to the program, and to correct the inadequate behavior in other settings; and less likely to eliminate or eject from the setting other occupants whose behavior is inadequate. Occupants of undermanned settings are also more likely to serve in responsible positions, engage in actions that are difficult for them but important to the setting, and participate in a wide range of different activities. Finally, psychological differences include the greater likelihood that persons who occupy undermanned behavior settings will see themselves as being more important to and more responsible for the setting, feel more versatile, be less sensitive to and less evaluative of individual differences among people, and see themselves and others more often in terms of the jobs they do, and less often in terms of personality characteristics (Wicker, 1979, pp. 72–73).

Undermanning puts a strain on the occupants because fewer people have to perform the same actions needed to maintain the progam. But this strain, if not too severe, also has benefits: Occupants serve in more responsible positions with activities that are more challenging and more varied. They feel more important to the setting and greater responsibility for it, and are willing to work harder to support it.

These are the kinds of behaviors and attitudes organizations want to instill in their members. The theory of undermanning suggests that such behaviors and attitudes can be influenced by manipulating the number of people in the setting. A great deal of research has been done to demonstrate some of these effects (Williams, 1964; Wicker, 1979; Barker, 1968). The well-known study *Big School, Small School* (Barker and Gump, 1964) provides a good illustrative example.

That study looked at the differences in voluntary extracurricular activities of high school students in a large and a small school. According to undermanning theory, students in the small school should be involved in more settings, in more responsible positions, and derive greater satisfaction from their participation. In fact, this was what the study found. Students from the small schools participated in a wider range of settings than did the average large-school student, and students from the small schools served in over twice as many responsible positions, and in six times as many centrally important positions, as students from the large school.

In another part of this same study, Willems (1964) categorized students as either "marginals" or "regulars." Marginals had lower tested intelligence and grades and their parents had not completed high school. Regulars had at least average intelligence and grades and their parents had finished high school. According to undermanning theory, the marginals in small schools would experience more pressures to participate than those in large schools because the small school needs everyone participating to survive. Thus, lower admission standards are set. Wicker (1979, p. 89) summarized Willems's findings:

> Marginal students in small schools reported nearly five times as many pressures to participate in the listed activities than did marginal students in the large school;...there was little difference between regulars and marginals in the small school,...but a big difference between regulars and marginals in the large school.... In other words, under the conditions that existed in the small schools, people who ordinarily would be viewed as personally inadequate—as potential high school drop outs, in fact—were not merely tolerated but were valued to such an extent that they were actively sought out by others. In the large school, on the other hand, there were few pressures to draw marginal students into extracurricular activities.

Finally, Barker and Gump (1964) also found that students in the small school were much more satisfied than those in the large school. Students in the small school reported more satisfaction related to the development of competence, to being challenged, to engaging in important actions, to being involved in group activities, to being valued, and to gaining moral and cultural values.

These findings obviously cannot be transposed to the work situation without some qualification. People at work expect to be paid more if they do more work, or more challenging work. There are generally many more applicants for jobs than available jobs, so undermanning rarely occurs as a natural process. People who perform marginally are fired, or pressure is exerted on them to change their behavior, and selection procedures try to eliminate those who do not have certain capabilities. Notwithstanding these qualifications (and the many more that might be raised), the theory of undermanning suggests that important kinds of behavioral and psychological effects are influenced by ecological conditions.

Organizational Implications of Ecological Research

Much of the research cited in this chapter can be applied to work settings only with extreme caution. Yet the empirical work, taken as a whole, suggests that a large number of behaviors and attitudes that are of major concern to organizations may be significantly influenced by aspects of the physical setting. Some of these include:

- expectations about how one should work, and with whom one should
- motivation and commitment
- group cohesion
- active participation/involvement
- performance feedback/sharing of ideas
- job autonomy
- task significance
- job satisfaction
- distractions/interruptions
- perceived efficiency
- friendship formation
- cooperation/competition
- conflict
- social withdrawal
- leadership
- task persistence/attention
- interpersonal evaluations/attraction
- time on task
- supervisory patterns/rule making

Using the framework developed in Chapter 1 and elaborated on in Chapter 5, it is clear that many of these environmental effects are more related to overall work effectiveness than to performance measured in simple output terms. The environment contributes to and facilitates ways of working, and ways of relating to others at work, that employees value: opportunities for friendship formation and increased feedback, for example. These kinds of experiences, in turn, contribute to job satisfaction, which, in turn, is related to turnover and absenteeism.

The gaps in the empirical work presented define a vast research agenda. Yet what research is available suggests rather powerfully that aspects of the physical setting do influence behavior in important ways. The potential significance for organizational-development efforts is enormous. The way the physical setting is created in organizations has barely been tapped as a tangible organizational resource. The next two chapters explore some of the ways in which the physical settings of organizations can become resources rather than liabilities.

7

SPACE POLICY AND STANDARDS

Space policy and office standards constitute a device for allocating the amount of space per person, and the number, type, and quality of furnishings and equipment an individual receives on the basis of a set of rules. There is hardly any other area of organizational decision making that can generate such emotional responses to it. At the same time, these responses often seem petty when others engage in them. Stories about guerrilla furniture moving, in which prized furniture surreptitiously moves from one office to another after dark, or instances in which a distraught manager measures a rival's office and complains bitterly because the other person has two more square feet of space, are good for a laugh—until you yourself are asked to move to a smaller office, a less desirable location, or you see someone else get more expensive furniture or a larger office. The kinds of emotion generated by space decisions, and the typical organizational solution for them, are reflected in the following statement (Robichaud, 1958, p. 267) about office standards:

> Plans for the new office arouse the spirit of revolt in people. A manager will watch to see what is planned for his counterpart. While top management may decry the common tendency of an executive or manager to worry more about what he does not have than what he has, the problem can be solved only by establishing defined organizational rankings and then defining by rank the privileges for private office decor. Standards may smack of regimentation, but they solve more problems than they create, because they insure equity of treatment to all personnel and provide a budgetary means of controlling expense. The latter is significant in view of the wide range of cost which may be incurred in furnishing a single private office.

The underlying purpose of all standards is to provide equity: Some way of insuring fair treatment to all individuals. The question is whether office

131

standards, as they currently exist, actually create equity, along what dimensions they do so, based on what information, and for whose benefit. The regimentation of standards serves the purpose of legitimizing inequality across different levels of the organizational hierarchy, as the preceding quote suggests. Most office standards are based on attitudes and work practices current in the 1950s. Concerns for equity have not diminished, but the workforce has changed, particularly in its expectations about the quality of working life. Electronic technology is also rapidly transforming work processes and the office environment. In light of these developments, there is a need to consider how the form and nature of office standards might evolve during the next 20 years.

THE ROLE OF STANDARDS

In thinking about office standards, and the role they play in organizations, it is useful to think about them in the context of the history of standards in general. Who do standards benefit, and what are their origins, their underlying assumptions, characteristics, and purposes? In an entertaining history of standards, Perry (1955) notes that historically they have been a form of government control to protect citizens and merchants, and to facilitate construction and commerce. The need for standards, and even more so the means for enforcing them to protect unwary consumers, are readily apparent from some of the practices Perry reports merchants engaging in over recorded history.

Many of these were given wide publicity in the early part of this century, to the point of becoming the basis for political movements by an Irishman named Patrick Derry, who in 1866 took over the Office of Weights and Measures in New York City. He promptly detailed exhaustively, in his first annual report, just how the public was being cheated by merchants. Perry (1955, p. 20) quoted from it:

> Here was the padlock a poultry dealer slipped into each bird before weighing it. Here was the lump of putty underneath the pan of a scale, the lump of solder beneath the paper covering the pan, the milk container with the false bottom. Here were iron weights, hollowed, shaved, plugged. Here was the scale with the adjustable face, another with a bent pointer, another with a hidden string leading to a foot with a pedal. Here were "quart" berry boxes holding little more than a pint.

These examples of failures to enforce agreed-upon standards of measurement were preceded by a situation in which there was generally little consensus about standard units of measurement themselves. News media constantly refer to the number of barrels of oil used or imported by the United

States, but for a long period, just how much oil was in a barrel was an open question. This was true for all other units of measurement as well. Take a bushel of wheat, for example. In the early 1800s, Connecticut fixed the bushel of wheat at 56 pounds, while her neighbors made it 60. Connecticut's bushel of oats weighed 28 pounds, but New Jersey's was 32, Kentucky's 33 1/2, Missouri's 35, and in Washington Territory, it was 36 (Perry 1955, p. 57).

The underlying premise of standards was and is quite simple: create uniformity or "one standard to be the same for all persons and all purposes, and to continue the same forever" (Perry 1955, p. 65). With a set of uniform standards of measurement, the ability of the government to protect the consumer would be greatly enhanced, since it would be possible to check a given measure against an agreed-upon reference standard, or some legal facsimile of it. Uniform standards would also enhance commerce among different regions and countries. This is not to say that standards were always embraced, either by producers or consumers. In the early part of this century, Perry (1955) reports, many customers vigorously resisted standards based on level measure (rather than heaped) because they felt they were getting more with the heaped measure. The merchants, of course, built containers to compensate for heaping, making them long and narrow rather than short and broad.

The purpose of these measurement standards was largely economic. They can be defined as procedures and criteria whose primary purpose is to protect individuals' and organizations' economic return on their investment. By "economic return on investment," I mean that measurement standards for currency, for weight, length, and volume were intended to insure that when someone agreed to certain payment for certain goods, both parties received that for which they had contracted. Measurement standards are quite distinct from the much later development of habitation standards, which we know largely as building and safety codes.

Habitation standards have, as their primary purpose, not the protection of economic investment, but the protection of the safety, health, and development of individuals against dangerous environmental conditions: fire, disease, crowding, falling objects, cutting edges, noise, flying debris. Tenement laws and housing codes developed around the turn of this century were the first attempts to regulate environmental conditions (Friedman, 1968). Perhaps the most infamous current example of standards regulating environmental conditions are the OSHA regulations, which range from a concern for safety in factories and businesses, to that for flame retardants in children's sleepwear and the slippery nature of manure on farms.

Figure 7.1 shows that office standards fall somewhere in between habitation and measurement standards in terms of their primary intent, as well as in some of their other characteristics. Office standards here refer not

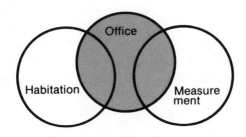

FIGURE 7.1 Types of Standards

to government-sponsored building codes that legislate basic safety in work environments (e.g., fire codes), but rather, to the individual organization's development of standards regulating the amount of space and the quality and type of furnishings and equipment individuals within an organization receive. In most business and manufacturing organizations, precise standards exist which specify how many square feet of space a manager at a particular level will receive, how much storage space, and how much and what type of furnishings. Figure 7.2 shows typical space standards in an engineering department of a major American company. These kinds of standards, and their underlying rationale, serve some of the same purposes as measurement standards (e.g., to protect economic investment). But unlike typical measurement standards, they impinge directly on the kinds of health-related issues habitation standards have typically addressed. Office standards' gray or fuzzy nature stems from this ambiguity.

Figure 7.3 lists some of the similarities and differences among the three types of standards with respect to their fundamental characteristics. The current level of scientific understanding and degree of measurement sophistication distinguish measurement standards from both habitation and office standards. Perry (1955) argues that measurement and standards are the story of science. Standards cannot be developed without appropriate measurement techniques, and these cannot be developed without an adequate understanding of what one is measuring, whether it is electricity, temperature, fire, crowding, or work-related accidents. The hallmark of most of our standard units of measurement is that they are based on relatively basic scientific data. Even standards of weight, which seem so straightforward, required a better understanding of the difference between weight, which is a measure of attraction between two objects, such as an individual and the earth, and mass, which is an inherent quality of some person or thing. Since gravitational attraction diminishes with distance, a person who weighs 200 pounds at sea level would weigh only 199.8 pounds at an altitude of 10,000 feet. A spring scale, which measures the attraction between two objects, will give different

ENVIRONMENTAL SUPPORT

ORGANIZATIONAL POSITION	Square ft.	Partition	Office door	Special Apparatus
Section Manager	350-400	ceiling	Yes	Executive furniture Table & 8 chairs Optional arrange-ment, carpeting
Subsection Manager	144	ceiling or 7'3"	Yes	Executive furniture Name Plate Optional furniture Arrangement
Unit Manager	108	5'6"*	Depends	Name Plate Operation Function
Supervisor, one man cubicle	72-80	5'6"	No	None
Supervisor, two man cubicle	112**	5'6"	No	None
Four man cubicle w/files and tables	169**	5'6"	No	None
Four man cubicle without files and tables	110**	5'6"	No	None
Two man cubicle with files	72**	5'6"	No	None
Two man cubicle without files	60-65**	5'6"	No	None

*Specification includes 24" clear glass on 36" steel, 6" open base.
**Divide by number of persons in cubicle to get sq. ft./person.

FIGURE 7.2 Office-Space Standards for Engineering Division of Major American Company

readings at different altitudes, while a balance scale, which measures mass, will not (Perry, 1955, p. 48).

Thus most of our basic measurement standards have a solid scientific underpinning for the phenomena they measure. This is a major distinction between measurement standards, some of the habitation standards, and almost all of the office standards. Scientists know something about the etiology of disease, about the action of fire under different conditions, and about the effect of different noise levels on hearing impairment over given periods of time. I say "something" because much of the research needed to develop standards for acceptable noise levels, for example, is recent, and many of these standards are controversial precisely because there is a relatively poor understanding of the phenomena and their effects on humans (Nelkin, 1979). Most of such standards attempt, therefore, to regulate only at the extremes of the phenomenon. We regulate the noise level of jet airplanes

STANDARD TYPE

Measurement	Office	Habitation
• good scientific measures	• weak scientific measures	• moderate scientific measures
• externally imposed (Government)	• internally imposed	• externally imposed (Government)
• social control (regulate producers)	• social control (regulate users)	• social control (regulate producers)
• universal	• specific	• culture-specific
• permanent (slow change)	• transitory (rapid change)	• periodic (moderate change)

FIGURE 7.3 Characteristics of Different Types of Standards

only in so far as they fairly obviously damage persons living within certain distances of their landing patterns. We do not attempt to legislate noise at levels that many residents living near airports report as harmful but which scientific evidence has not conclusively demonstrated. A major part of the issue, of course, is what constitutes a fair measure. Should it include only actual hearing impairment, or psychological stress and discomfort?

Habitation standards, as I have broadly defined them, have historically been controversial precisely because these kinds of measurement issues and basic scientific research remain at primitive stages. Yet such standards have been developed, often on the basis of political pressures those experiencing the negative environmental conditions have brought to bear on local, state, and federal government. A public furor is created that leads to the enactment of protective legislation based as much on public conceptions of decency and health as on scientific evidence per se (Nelkin, 1979).

In general, as Figure 7.4 shows, the level of arbitrariness of standards varies as a function of the level of scientific understanding and of measurement sophistication of the phenomenon to which standards are being applied.

Office standards have been shaped largely without the presence of a strong political constituency of users or consumers. Unions have focused their political force almost entirely on conditions of pay and job security, with

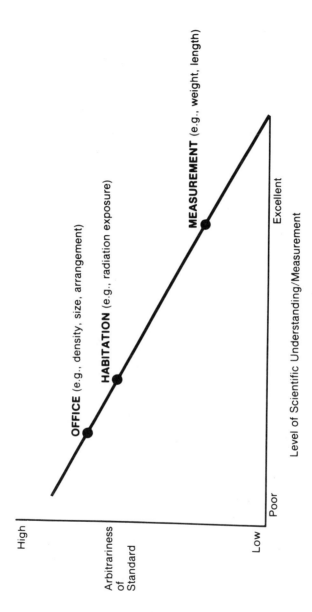

FIGURE 7.4 Arbitrariness of Standards as a Function of Scientific Understanding

137

job conditions largely ignored except under extreme conditions. In the absence of an effective political constituency, office-space standards have largely been developed by corporate managers in conjunction with architects, operations researchers, and human-factors specialists. Their primary purpose has been to reinforce authority lines, to reduce operating expenses by eliminating wasted space and equipment, and to provide a standard that legitimizes unequal allocation of space and equipment across organizational levels while insuring equity within the same level. These functions are of real value in any organization. That is why they emerged originally and have continued to be employed. The question is whether, in serving these functions, standards are inadvertently undermining other organizational objectives, especially those related to employee motivation and job satisfaction.

To be sure, standards for the interior design of offices have changed, but the impetus for it has been a market rather than a scientific or political one. After World War II, the tremendous increase in office work and a shortage of qualified personnel spurred companies to improve working conditions as a means of attracting the kind of people they wanted, and of keeping them (Robichaud, 1958). But the intent of these changes was quite different from that of the institution of office standards, particularly in terms of who benefits from them.

Measurement and habitation standards historically have developed as a social-control mechanism applied to companies and builders in order to protect consumers. Office standards, in contrast, are a form of social control imposed on employees as a means of protecting companies. They do benefit the individual by creating equity within job classifications, but the equity serves mainly to suppress underlying and ongoing discontent (which periodically but regularly shows up, particularly when any office changes are planned) by focusing employees' attention on the fact that "we're all in the same boat." Office standards rarely contribute to satisfaction except at the higher levels of management, where standards directly contribute to satisfaction because they confer status, recognition, and superiority.

Organizations have been free to develop office standards as they saw fit because of the absence of unions and the general assumption, unsupported by scientific evidence, that such standards have little or no effect on human health and welfare. In contrast, decisions about building and equipment design, and operating procedures, have been viewed as affecting human health and well-being. As a result, they have been subjected to government regulations in the form of safety, health, and building codes.

This state of affairs is likely to change, however, for two reasons. First, the scientific community is becoming more aware of and concerned about the relationship between work and mental health, including work's impact on families (Piotrkowski, 1979), and on child and adult development (Kohn and

Schooler, 1973).Second, unions are very interested in organizing white collar and professional workers. For both of these reasons, office standards are likely to be the object of closer scrutiny in the future.

At the same time that office standards, which currently fall somewhere in between measurement and habitation standards, are likely to be pushed closer to habitation standards by union pressures, organizations struggling to cope with skyrocketing equipment and facility costs will be pushing for the development of office standards as measurement standards whose primary purpose is to protect economic investment, as measured by direct operating costs. As available office space becomes scarce, and rents rapidly rise, organizations are unlikely to embrace proposed changes in space planning and management that are currently viewed as unnecessary expenses.

Whether office standards move in one direction or another will depend in part on the outcome of research, now in its infancy, that documents and increase our understanding of the relationship between the nature of office standards oriented toward habitation criteria (e.g., protecting and perhaps fostering health, development, and well-being) and measures of organizational benefit (e.g., productivity, absenteeism, motivation, initiative, attractiveness to preferred employees).

Organizations need to come to grips with the fact that in work settings, space standards have, simultaneously, financial and behavioral implications. Moreover, these two rather separate realms are closely intertwined. The nature and management of the physical setting influence individual satisfaction and well-being, as well as a variety of other behaviors valued by organizations. Organizations that develop space standards on primarily economic criteria risk creating de facto habitation standards that are actually counterproductive economically. Organizations need to begin considering space standards that improve the physical setting in terms of human habitation as an organizational asset rather than as an economic expense.

TRENDS TOWARD IMPROVED OFFICE STANDARDS

Given organizations' concern for containing and reducing operating costs, it is worth noting how the trend toward increased use of open-plan offices and electronic-word and data processing in them, intended as cost-saving programs, will shape and probably improve the physical setting and the nature of office standards for rank-and-file employees. A critical variable appears to be the degree of physical integration, or spatial proximity, of individuals at various levels of the organizational hierarchy.

Figure 7.5 depicts the relationship between work conditions or office standards and physical proximity of individuals at different levels of the

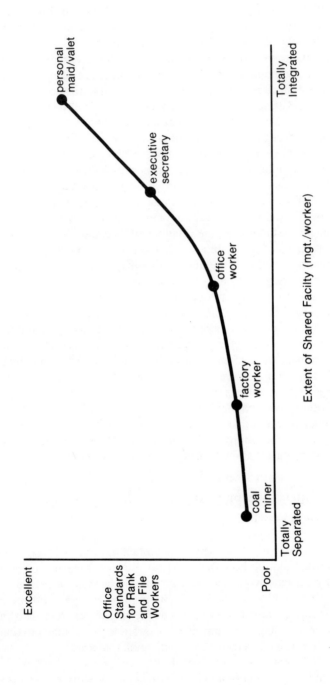

FIGURE 7.5 Relationship between Workers' Office Standards and Physical Proximity of Management and Workers

organizational hierarchy. The basic premise of the curve is that differences among individuals in office standards are maximum in situations where those high in the organizational hierarchy are totally separated physically from those lower in the organizational hierarchy. Under conditions where there is total physical integration of work areas across levels, the discrepancy between office standards or work conditions across groups is minimal. Thus, in the former case, the conditions coal miners work in bear absolutely no relationship to the conditions of work of those who own and manage the mines. At the other extreme, the executive secretary often works in conditions that overlap and essentially mirror those of the boss. At points in between, one sees the factory worker, who often shares the same facility with management (they are in the same building), although they are typically separated by floors, wings. The conditions among levels are quite different, often more so than is true for workers in conventional offices who share the same floor with management. The differences diminish even further in the of workers in landscaped offices because the environmental components, although designed to express subtle differences among levels, are essentially designed within a common framework or design vocabulary. What one sees, to use a statistical analogy, is a regression toward the mean. Extremes at both the low end of work conditions and at the upper end tend to move toward a middle ground. There is differentiation, to be sure, but the variance or range between levels may be less.

This tendency is likely to become even more pronounced with increasing use of electronic equipment by persons at very different organizational levels: the secretary and the boss using the same television-like screen and keyboard at different times, or the executive who uses the identical piece of equipment used by the engineer, accountant, or personnel officer. Much of this equipment is now being integrated into furniture systems (*Contract*, 1980a), so that the most proximate environments of the manager, the secretary, and the individual organizational member begin to merge.

While the manager is likely to get the newest equipment with the most sophisticated options, the equipment that people at different levels in the organization use is indeed essentially identical. Thus, over the long run, although there is economic pressure to reduce the cost of facilities, and this often creates pressure to reduce the overall quality of the environment, the trends in office design and equipment are likely to result in an improved set of working conditions for the rank and file, and by comparison, a slightly poorer set of working conditions for middle-level management. In a sense, the physical setting of work will become more uniform and more standardized, with distinctions among levels more subtle and more symbolic. Concerns about order, control, and variety, particularly among middle-level management, are likely to be acute.

ORDER, DISORDER, AND HUMAN ENERGY

Organizations generally attempt to maximize control through order. The question one needs to ask is, control for what purpose and of what? The answer is usually couched in terms of efficiency, although as I noted in Chapter 4, the underlying objective may actually be support for a moral order, or a sense of how things, and particularly role relationships among individuals, ought to be. If the objective of order is control, and control is defined in terms of effectiveness rather than as a particular structure of interpersonal relationships, then any organization of space that dissipates scarce resources, such as human energy, can be viewed as creating disorder.

Human response to physical facilities is a form of energy consumption. Physical facilities that fail to provide adequate levels of environmental support, for the variety of individuals and activities they serve, burden and financially drain the organization. The definition of "adequate" may include aesthetic as well as functional or task-related considerations. Using Maslow's concept of a hierarchy of needs, ranging from basic needs, such as security and shelter, to higher-order "growth" needs, such as self-actualization, Kaplan (1977) argues that since people are motivated by personal needs to fulfill immediate and long-term goals, an office environment resistant to need fulfillment creates frustration, boredom, and fatigue.

The needs do not disappear simply because they are ignored. People are ingenious in finding ways of satisfying the needs. Creative energy organized to beat the system might otherwise be devoted to the work itself. These higher-order needs for identity and self-esteem, and the results of blocking them, were illustrated in the study by Clearwater (1980) mentioned earlier. Stringent prohibiting of personalized work spaces not only failed, but shift management's and employees' energies from productive to nonproductive uses. Pristine walls became the home for posters, notices, and photographs, despite the energy spent by supervisors to prohibit this type of activity. The principal effect of the tremendous energy mobilized by supervisors to restrict an activity was to generate resentment and anger among a large number of employees.

Typically, organizations view their physical facilities as a liability or expense. And, if not designed and managed effectively, they often are. But by the same token, facilities have the potential to be a programmatic asset. Properly designed and managed physical facilities essentially free or make available human energy that otherwise is dissipated. Individual resistance to unsupportive environments results in a loss of human energy in terms of commitment, satisfaction, motivation, and initiation, since such emotions must compete, for the individual's limited energy supply, with anger, hostility, and apathy. Environments that fail to support human requirements restrain competence and lower performance. Human-energy costs in the form of salaries are the most direct, expensive, pervasive, and fragile of any costs an organization incurs. Organizations need to view office standards in terms of their ability to conserve these energy resources. For office standards to effectively use and conserve available human energy, they need to take into consideration individual differences in work patterns and preferences within job classifications. Variety in environmental supports is required if individuals who differ in their work style or level of competence are expected to perform at comparable levels.

If order is viewed as emerging from diversity, and stability is attained by being able to respond to individual differences in needed and preferred environmental supports, the conception of standards begins to shift. Rather than a set of specifically defined criteria that applies uniformly to all persons within a given organizational category (e.g., level-five people get 35 square feet less than level-seven people), space standards become policy guidelines that detail appropriate performance. The objective becomes one of defining how one wants the environmental supports to perform (Brill, 1974), rather than of specifying in precise terms what the solution is for a general problem.

Performance standards indicate what level of concentration is required, what level of communication privacy, what kind of interaction capability. Different combinations of environmental resources may work very well in meeting these performance standards under different conditions. In an office with a low noise level, higher partitions with greater sound absorbency may be required than in a setting with a higher noise level, which acts as a natural sound barrier. These same settings may differ in the nature of environmental supports required to meet concentration standards for specific activities.

Order, or the effective utilization of available human-energy resources, emerges from variety in environmental supports. Equity, one of the basic purposes of standards, may also be enhanced through variety. Porter and Steers (1973) have demonstrated rather conclusively the relationship between the effects of personal, organizational, and work factors on employee turnover and absenteeism. They interpret the results of the many studies of turnover and absenteeism in terms of met expectations: the degree to which employees feel that their expectations—about pay, promotions, supervision, feedback, coworker interaction—are met. Equity, from the employee's viewpoint, is determined by the level of discrepancy between one's expectations and what one actually experiences (which may or may not be synonymous with equivalency among different workers). In general, Porter and Steers (1973, p. 171) argue that "the decision to participate or withdraw may be looked upon as a process of balancing received or potential rewards with desired expectations." Different individuals will have different expectations, and may seek different rewards: some looking for more money, some for more autonomy, others for better social relations.

The major point, for our purposes, is that equity is not necessarily defined in terms of all employees receiving the same amount of something. It is conceivable, as Lawler (1973) has argued, that the notion of "cafeteria-style" compensation plans which provide employees with a greater selection of rewards toward which to work could be used as a model for the allocation of space and furnishings. Equity becomes defined as the provision of appropriate environmental supports for a given activity and a given level of competence. Competence includes not only skills and knowledge, but physical characteristics, such as strength, endurance, eyesight, and hearing. It also includes personal characteristics, such as need for affiliation and interaction, need for privacy, for expressions of identity.

Different supports for persons at the same level or doing the same job should be perceived as equitable to the extent that individuals feel their own personal needs have been met, or understand and are satisfied with reasons why these needs cannot be met. In either case, the process of space planning would require a much larger level of involvement from the entire workforce than occurs now. As I argue in Chapter 8, such processes are not necessarily inordinately time consuming or expensive, particularly when measured in light of the time spent in ineffective processes and as a proportion of the total building and personnel costs over time.

Principles of Order

Office standards that accomodate individual diversity create elastic environments. These are characterized by their flexibility and resilience. The variety expressed in elastic environments is often resisted in large organizations because it is confused with chaos or anarchy. Chaos is unordered variety. Chaos can be avoided by developing ordering systems that structure the expression of variety and the relationship among separate elements. Ordering systems enable different currents to coalesce and flow into a single stream that has order, or purpose, even while individual components remain identifiable. With respect to the development of space policy and standards, order with variety is attained by integrating the following three functions: the activity, authority and recognition. Each of these functions can serve as ordering systems because they can guide and structure the allocation and management of space and facilities.

Activity Function

As an ordering system, the activity function refers to the ability of environmental supports to comfortably, safely, and effectively facilitate the performance of specific activities or tasks (e.g., a drafting table for the individual developing working drawings, an electronic or manual storage system for retrieving information, a separated area with low sound transmission for conducting performance-evaluation meetings).

Authority Function

As an ordering system, the authority function refers to the ability of environmental supports to reinforce, communicate, and legitimize differences among individuals in their formal responsibility for making decisions and exercising control. These environmental supports may be oriented toward insiders, other persons who routinely interact with particular supervisors or managers, or toward outsiders, persons who infrequently come into contact with them. An employee from a different division or a member of the local community is an outsider, while the members of a single department are insiders. The distinction is valuable because the authority function may be expressed very differently depending on who its primary audience is. Special-quality furnishings, nameplates, office size and location, and degree of spatial enclosure are some of the environmental supports typically used to satisfy this function.

Recognition Function

As an ordering system, the recognition function refers, in part, to the ability of the environmental supports to reward, communicate, and legitimize differences among organizational members on the basis of outstanding achievement, rather than on the basis of authority or supervisory functions (which may or may not be performed outstandingly). This type of personal-recognition function can be called achievement recognition. It refers to such behaviors as producing outstanding quantity or quality of outputs, generating significant increases in sales, developing a patentable idea, or significantly reducing turnover or the number of employee complaints. Pay increases and changes in office size and location are frequently used to reward this function.

Recognition, as an ordering system, must also reinforce and communicate the organization's concern for the individual qua individual, regardless of specific accomplishment or position in the organizational hierarchy. This goes beyond supports that do no more than avoid physical harm. The general ambience of an organization, expressed in the treatment of lighting, color, furnishings, and floor coverings, has symbolic value above and beyond its functional role as an activity support (e.g., number of footcandles needed to perform a recognition task). These other environmental characteristics also communicate status, not only in the sense of specific place in the organizational hierarchy, but in the more fundamental sense of helping employees see how they fit into the larger scheme of things;

that is, do their work surroundings reflect a basic concern for the employee as an individual in society, with needs for identity, for comfort, for stimulation, and even for beauty?

Despite its claims for increased efficiency, landscaped-office design in fact seems to be most successful in satisfying this general or human-recognition function (Brookes and Kaplan, 1972; Clearwater, 1980). This is particularly true for the bulk of the workforce who now have access to environmental qualities, such as carpeting, that were previously restricted to management. For those groups which, in conventional offices, had human-recognition needs satisfied by the speical environmental provisions accompanying their organizational position, the change from the conventional design to the landscaped office does not have a significant effect (Clearwater, 1980). Where organizational position is more ambiguous—for example, in the case of technical workers in an insurance office who fall between clerical workers, on the one hand, and supervisory personnel, on the other—the move from a conventional office to one using landscaped-design principles does not significantly improve their satisfaction. Despite the general upgrading of the environment's appearance, their own position vis-à-vis the other groups remains ambiguous. It is only for the clerical workers, whose human-recognition needs in traditional offices are least likely to have been satisfied, that the change to the office-landscaping system is a significant improvement (Clearwater, 1980).

Each of the above functions, or ordering principles, may, but does not necessarily, overlap with the others. The senior engineer with 20 years' service to the company has recognition needs that differ from those of the newcomer to the firm, and both of these persons differ from the section manager in the degree to which the environmental supports must serve authority functions. All persons have particular activity-function requirements, although these may differ among individuals with identical authority or recognition requirements. Together, these ordering principles determine the spatial form of an organization within any given cost framework. For space policy and standards to be effective—that is, for them to facilitate the creation of an elastic workspace in which the application of human-energy resources results in productive effort rather than in resistance—these different functions, or systems of ordering space in an organization, must be recognized and balanced. They serve as criteria for evaluating the nature of space policy and standards.

Research and planning concerning the role of environmental-support systems in organizations rarely take fully into account the full range of organizational values that forms the social context within which facility-planning and management decisions are made. Current office standards tend to overemphasize authority functions. Behaviorally oriented architectural programmers and space planners, on the other hand, tend to operate on the premise that the physical form of an organization, reflected in space policy and standards, is or should be organized according to a single ordering principle: namely, the activity function. They may document in great detail the dysfunction of environmental supports, in terms of their failure to support specific tasks individuals engage in comfortably, safely, and efficiently, only to have their recommendations ignored in subsequent design and policy decisions, even when such dysfunctions appear to be grossly counter-productive. Both of these approaches recognize that space is organized to reflect status, authority, and activity functions. This is hardly a novel idea. What is novel is the idea that the wrong environmental supports are being used to satisfy these different functions. Most office standards use scarce environmental resources, appropriate for supporting activity functions, to support authority and recognition functions. The most detailed-appearing task analysis, in fact, may primarily support authority functions.

Activity analyses are valued to the extent they at least implicitly support dominant organizational values concerning the nature of work and workers. The human-factors and operations-research-oriented activity analyses have been accepted, while the more recent social-psychological activity analyses conducted by environmental researchers involved in design programming have not, for the following reasons.

First, unlike the more traditional activity analyses performed by operations researchers, environmental researchers with a social-psychological orientation have included recognition, usually implicitly, as the basis for an ordering system in both the questions they ask and the kinds of recommendations they make. There has been a concern on their part to identify aspects of the environment that would contribute to individuals' self-esteem, pride, and self-respect, as well as to their ability to perform tasks effectively. Their activity analyses have accepted individuals' need to control their surroundings in terms of being able to regulate the pace of work, layout of work stations, nature of equipment and furnishings. Secondly, they have also adopted, implicitly, a broader definition of energy expenditure, and have focused not only on what people are physically capable of doing under highly selected conditions of motivation and human capability, but what they are willing to do (Swain, 1973) under the conditions of the workplace and society they actually work and live in. For an operations researcher or time-motion expert, movement that takes the worker away from his or her work station is considered wasted energy and time. It is viewed as a direct cost to the organization because of time lost. Within a broader social-psychological activity analysis, such movement may be viewed as essential for allowing the individual to recoup energy so that time in the work setting is not characterized by energy spent in resistance to the task and the overall work situation. Energy, within this framework, is viewed as a finite resource. Energy depletion can occur from nonproductive as well as productive efforts.

Such an approach to activity analyses is typically dismissed as being softheaded and impractical; that is, designing on the basis of such analyses would cost too much. Yet when organizations argue that they cannot support proposed changes made on the basis of behaviorally based (rather than economically based) activity analyses, they are implicitly evaluating and weighing the costs of satisfying this component of function in relation to the costs of satisfying other components; namely, authority and recognition functions. As presently constituted, these functions are expensive to satisfy. They are bought at the expense of satisfying activity and human-recognition functions for the bulk of any organization's workforce: clerical and non-managerial professional and technical staff.

Elements of the physical-support system, like size of offices or degree of spatial enclosure, which should relate to activity functions, are being used indiscriminately to satisfy authority and recognition functions. The confusion stems, in part, from the fact that those wanting or having systems that support authority and achievement-recognition needs defend them in terms of activity functions: for example, a larger office defended in terms of the need to reinforce lines of authority and communication, or to accommodate a work activity, rather than in terms of the need to have individual achievement and status recognized. All of these needs are legitimate, and all contribute to organizational effectiveness through their impact on job satisfaction.

MULTIPLE-SYMBOL SYSTEMS

There is a need to develop multiple-symbol systems that can support different kinds of ordering systems without exhausting the scarce resources of space and equipment that should be allocated to activity functions across the entire workforce. What is needed is the identification of selected, largely environmental, nonverbal cues that support different levels of individual and professional recognition, management responsibility, and activity requirements. Space policy and standards based largely on authority functions must be able to balance and accommodate programming and design for the three interrelated ordering systems: authority, activity, and recognition.

How might this be done? All actions and objects convey meaning. It is imperative that deliberately designed symbols convey their intended meanings. This is unlikely to occur unless those affected are involved with the development of these symbol systems. Once an initial group has been involved and a symbol system has been devised, the normal social-information processing in which oldtimers interpret for newcomers the meaning of various events in and characteristics of the setting should serve to create a culture which is transmitted from generation to generation.

A multiple-symbol system might not only differentiate among the three basic environmental-support functions, but also be variable within any component of function. For example, it is possible that two different individuals with the same recognition requirements (and rights) might choose to express their position using different, but personally meaningful, indicator cues. Both cues, however, should be within a known framework or population of cues for persons at this organizational level. This population of cues would differ from another population of cues available for persons at different levels in the hierarchy.

Before this takes on the aura of some futuristic society in which rigid social divisions are made public through simple marking devices, let me quickly state that it already is here, formally and informally. Williams (1980) has noted that workers in offices often informally develop communication sysems employing various kinds of environmental artifacts. He has found workers banding together and distinguishing themselves from others by wearing the same plastic pen guard in their shirt pockets or by putting the same calendar on their desk. In many offices, there are strong, widely understood norms regulating who can wear a three-piece suit and who cannot.

Formal cues are commonplace as well. In many institutions, staff members differentiate among themselves by wearing different-style uniforms, hats, and caps, different-colored nametags, or jewelry that indicates outstanding achievement or accomplishment. Shoulder patches and medals on military uniforms illustrate succinctly the desire for recognition of unusual and outstanding achievements, as well as of simple rank. These kinds of apparel/artifact cues occur most often in situations where other kinds of environmental support are unavailable for such distinctions.

Nurses, for instance, do not occupy private offices or even use only a single desk. They move in and around an entire nursing unit. Because they are mobile, their badges of rank must also be mobile. The same is true in the military, at least in battle situations. The increasingly widespread use of electronic equipment inside and outside the formal office environment is beginning to generate similar kinds of mobility. The traditional office is unlikely to be eliminated, but its use by employees is likely to become more variable, more sporadic, and less frequent. Williams (1980) argues that there is already an inverse relationship between office size and office use. The larger the office, the less it is used. Secretaries spend eight hours a day in the office; executives come and go. The additional mobility stimulated by portable electronic minicomputers and remote telecommunications and teleconferencing suggests that badges of rank should become more mobile in the work setting. The use of office size as a badge of recognition, as distinct from supporting legitimate authority or task functions, is a holdover from the days of relatively cheap space and limited mobility.

The development of alternative means of marking distinctions in organizations simply acknowledges current practice. There is nothing novel about the notion of office perks or symbol systems per se. The purpose here, however, is to shift the way environmental characteristics are typically viewed, as serving recognition functions (e.g., flexibility in arrangement of the work station and equipment, degree of spatial enclosure, or choice in equipment and furniture selection) to a view of them as serving activity functions (e.g., facilitating performance by locating storage in a manner that fits an individual style of work). Space standards that allocate certain environmental-support-system characteristics, such as flexibility or degree of enclosure, on the basis of recognition and authority functions, rather than on the basis of activity requirements, are using two of the most expensive organizational assets, physical facilities and employee energy, unproductively.

Given the importance of authority and recognition functions, the role of apparel and other artifact indicators is to create an expanded environmental-support system to serve recognition functions. This is absolutely necessary so that design for activity functions is not viewed as undermining design for authority and recognition. The kind of clarification of the role of support systems I am proposing will generate suspicion and hostility, at least from those higher in the organizational hierarchy. Before a manager or floor supervisor is going to give up 20 square feet of space or see a subordinate working in an office with as much spatial enclosure as in his own, based on activity analysis, the organization is going to have to insure that authority and recognition functions are also supported. To be effective (i.e., accepted) alternative symbol systems will have to be implemented from the top down, and the groups involved will have to participate in determining the nature of them. Zenardelli (cited by Clearwater [1980]), has shown that it is possible, albeit not without some grumbling, to substitute new kinds of status symbols for the old. In a Ford plant in Germany that adopted an office-landscape system, a variety of new status indicators was developed, including the number of plants one had, the size of one's desk, the size of one's individual workspace. Even these alternative status indicators, however, use environmental components that are more logically related to the task function, such as size of desk and individual workspace, rather than developing an entirely new and nonfunctional set of status symbols.

Allocating space and equipment with a clearer distinction among the kinds of functions environmental support is serving should result in a larger segment of the organization working with appropriate and cost-effective activity, authority, and recognition supports. More appropriate supports should increase job satisfaction (Oldham and Brass, 1979; Szilagyi and Holland, 1980) and, ultimately, reduce absenteeism and turnover (Lawler, 1973). In a recent Harris survey (1979), 92 percent of 1,000 office workers surveyed perceived a relationship between their personal satisfaction with their office surroundings and their job performance. Clearwater (1980) also found that workers believed their performance was influenced by the nature of appropriate work supports, in particular the obtaining of sufficient levels of communication and task privacy. Since in many cases, primarily the allocation, rather than the absolute amount, of resources changes, such changes should not increase significantly the costs to the organization. The changes may also be procedural rather than material (increase in mobility or flexibility). In some cases additional environmental support will be required, at some cost to the organization, but this cost should be figured as a percentage of salaries, or personnel costs.

To use an example related to the additional expense incurred by an organization by allowing individuals to take home portable computer terminals, one individual has made the following calculations: Assuming that each programmer earns $3,000 a month, and the cost to the organization of supplying this person with a portable terminal is $100 a month, then a little over a 3 percent increase in productivity on the part of the individual would justify the cost to the organization. Three percent of the individual's time amounts to approximately 14 minutes a day of additional work. Typically, individuals with home terminals work several hours a night. Similarly, providing more spatial enclosures for individuals may cost the organization several hundred dollars as an initial cost. If, as a result, the individual is able to concentrate and work more productively for even a fraction of every day, the cost of the partition is very quickly paid back. As for the argument that less work would be done, the answer is that managers can employ the same criteria they always have. Arguments against such changes in space standards often appear more related to issues of control per se than to effectiveness, productivity, or even initial cost outlays. We turn next to this subject in the context of space policy that favors centralization versus decentralization.

CENTRALIZATION VERSUS DECENTRALIZATION

Issues of control indeed sometimes appear to be more important to organizations than issues of effectiveness or productivity. Organizations, and especially the people with control in them, are generally unwilling to relinquish control. Some of this is for personal reasons relating to the enjoyment of the exercise of power, but much of it is based on the belief that centralized control of some sort is a basic requirement of productivity. Before decentralization of any significant sort can occur, with the attendant increase in variety that is likely to result, changes will have to occur in the definition of control and the conception of what a good manager is.

The processes used for allocating space, equipment, and furnishings can be centralized, and controlled by management. Actual allocation of space, equipment, and furnishings, as well as decisions affecting their use, can be decentralized. The manager's role becomes one of providing support services for localized decision making rather than of making the decisions themselves. The development of such support services, in the form of efficient, effective, and acceptable processes for determining appropriate and acceptable environmental supports for different organizational functions (activity, authority, recognition), within particular cost frameworks, is a time-consuming activity that rarely has received the benefit of sustained creative effort in organizations. Yet support facilities represent millions of dollars of investment in large organizations and their ability to perform designated functions conditions the effective use of additional millions of dollars in the form of personnel costs.

In a decentralized setup, management retains control, but control is now defined in terms of developing and implementing procedures which increase the likelihood that available energy and resources are used to their maximum potential. Control is attained by creating situations where goals are accomplished.

The role of the manager within a decentralized decision-making structure is to develop decision processes and procedures that others in the organization can use, with some training, to accomplish tasks they feel are desirable. The manager creates activities and expectations by the kinds of opportunities he or she builds into these processes. But the actual decisions, and thus the outcomes obtained, may be variable, depending on the kinds of questions those using the process ask, and the conditions they operate within and use as a basis for asking questions and making decisions. The goal shifts from attempting to insure that everyone works at a minimal level of acceptability to attempting to increase the probability that some individuals will work closer to their potential. A well-known organizational theorist estimates that about 40 percent of the workforce engage in jobs that require more skills than driving a car. In other words, 60 percent of workers are using in their work lower skills than they use in driving back and forth to their jobs.

Machines can be assessed in relation to the concept of comparative advantage; that is, the question is not only what someone or something can do, but how good it can do it in relation to someone or something else. Machines are not very good at developing processes others can use to make decisions. This is a capability uniquely held by humans. In a similar way, the question is not whether managers can make decisions about the size, arrangement, and characteristics of space and equipment, but whether they can make such decisions better than those who have to work in the space and with the equipment. A more useful role for management (which in some cases will include union and/or employee representatives) is to develop an appropriate context or framework that facilitates other groups' and individuals' decision making. An important aspect of this framework involves developing procedures for coordinating decisions made at different levels, and in different divisions and departments. The heart of decentralization is a more broadly based distribution of control.

What are some of the organizational benefits of such an approach (assuming that the increase in local control of decisions is a major benefit, in its own right, to employees)? First, the research on worker participation (Katzell, Bienstock, and Faerstein, 1977; Lawler, 1973) generally supports the argument that most employees (not all), given the opportunity to become involved in decisions concerning their work, will become involved and, as a consequence, be more satisfied with their jobs and generally more productive. Both the participation per se, as well as better decisions in some cases, contribute to the positive outcomes. Figure 7.6 suggests an additional way of thinking about the benefits an organization might experience from decentralizing some of its decision making.

Generally, most organizations are organized to maximize acceptable behavior. The nature of this behavior, of course, depends on the particular job, but the point is that it means a range of performance that runs from less-than outstanding to at least marginally better-than unacceptable. It is good enough to get by on. An alternative approach is to slightly decrease the amount of acceptable behavior by increasing both unacceptable and outstanding behavior. Those whose performance is unacceptable can be encouraged to

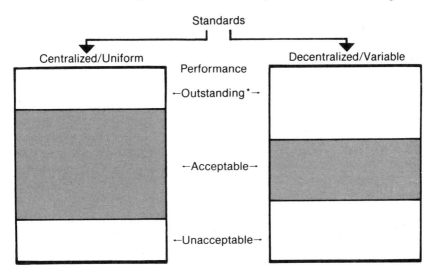

*Definition depends on job. Includes: quality of output/ideas, quantity of output, initiative, cooperation, and enthusiasm.

FIGURE 7.6 Relationship between Performance and Centralized and Decentralized Standards

improve their work, or be fired. The major benefit suggested by this model is the increase in outstanding work that may be stimulated by decentralized procedures that allow individuals to create environmental supports that are congruent with their idiosyncratic work styles and habits, and as such act as a motivator as well as a direct support for task activities.

Other benefits include what, in the housing literature, has been called user personalization: the opportunity for individuals to make decisions about their residential facilities (Becker 1977; Coniglio, 1974). These decisions range from furniture selection and arrangement to selection and application of paints, to the design and construction of storage systems, partitions, and sleeping lofts (Becker et al., 1978).

While it is risky to generalize across settings, some of the findings from the housing literature at least suggest some of the kinds of benefits, in terms of employee motivation and commitment, that might be stimulated by decentralizing some space-planning decisions. Personalization has been found to be related to satisfaction in living in dormitories (Van der Ryn and Silverstein, 1967; Eigenbrod, 1969); to an increase in neighborhood pride and in willingness to maintain and improve private and public spaces (Bush-Brown, 1969); to a decrease in damage in dormitories and improved relations between residents and advisors, and to more group cooperation and identity among residents (Eigenbrod, 1969); and to be a predictor of dropout rates among college freshmen (Altman, 1976: personal communication).

In residential settings, such personalization often occurs at the individual's personal expense and on his or her own time. In organizational settings, it must be viewed as a legitimate component of time at work. The Morse Chain Division of Borg-Warner in Ithaca, New York, for example, encouraged machinists who use heavy equipment on the shop floor to paint their machines, using any number of bright colors, including purples, blues, and oranges selected from a palette of colors made available to them (a centralized framework). They were given time off from their work to paint the equipment themselves.

Being able to paint your own equipment will not compensate for other negative work practices, or for work that is not viewed as having any value in its own right. In situations where tensions among employees and management run high, such a program may even exacerbate the tensions because employees interpret the program as an effort to mollify them and divert them from the real issues. To be effective, the kinds of decisions workers are encouraged to participate in must be viewed by them as important. Decisions about office size, location, and degree of enclosure, and amount and type of storage space, are typically important issues for office workers, not only symbolically, (as an expression of management attitudes) but because they directly influence work patterns. For some people, the opportunity for such personalization may be more important than actually engaging in the activity itself (Becker et al., 1978). Personalization is a form of decentralization which allows individual users to become actively involved with their work setting on a scale where they are likely to be most competent and most ego-involved.

Since organizations are typically concerned about the image their environments create for nonorganizational members, policies with respect to personalization can vary, depending on whether the location is essentially public, or a high-visibility area for visitors and outsiders, or private, and essentially visible only to insiders. In both areas, individuals can be given a choice in their surroundings by providing a coordinated range of elements (e.g., chairs, colors, desks, storage) from which they can select at will, without any individual choice seriously clashing with another. Those working together can also work cooperatively in selecting and organizing their surroundings. Such processes are not without conflict, but they can occur in an orderly and effective manner. (See discussion in Chapter 2, under "visual order," and also Chapter 8.)

SPACE PLANNING AS AN INPUT FUNCTION

Implicit in the foregoing analysis is the assumption that facility planning shifts from a largely reactive to an input function. Instead of decisions made by the finance, marketing, and production units being fed back to facility planning, with instructions to provide appropriate support facilities within a specified time period, facilities and their management should become another block of information which, together with that from marketing, finance, and production, is fed into the decision-making process at its earliest stages as a basis for determining basic policy directions. (See Figure 7.7.)

The approach to facility planning and management that has been developed throughout this book is based on the premise that such a change in organizational structure, involving the upgrading of facility planning into an essentially management function, rather than having it as a maintenance function, is necessary if organizations are to effectively utilize their existing resources, human and material, to their full potential. Facility planning and management, as described here, are intimately involved with concerns that traditionally have been isolated within the departments of personnel, operations research, finance, organizational development, and marketing. For organizations to maximize the resources they can offer to employees, as a means of meeting employees' expectations and securing their commitment to the organization, decisions about space and equipment must be shifted from their back-room status as a building-maintenance function to the front room,

CURRENT: FACILITY PLANNING AND MANAGEMENT REACTIVE FUNCTION

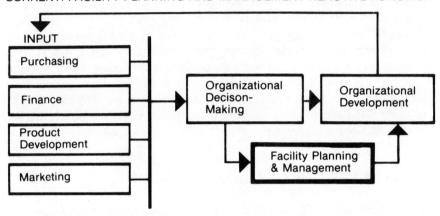

PROPOSED: FACILITY PLANNING AND MANAGEMENT INPUT FUNCTION

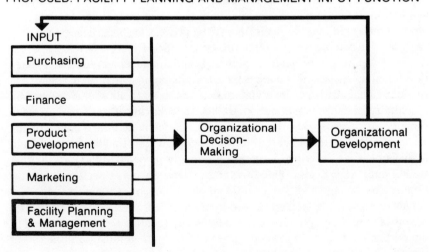

FIGURE 7.7 Facility Planning and Management as Reactive or Input Functions

156

where they can become a critical component of organizational policy. Effective facility planning and management currently fall between the cracks of professional boundaries. Unwarranted assumptions about more comprehensive, social-psychologically oriented facility planning and management processes contribute to this state of affairs. We turn next to these issues.

8

PLANNING ECOSYSTEMS

The previous chapters have pursued the theme that organizations, and those who study them, need to expend more energy understanding the ways in which the physical settings of organizations influence the behaviors of individual members and their relations to each other. The goal of the organizational-ecology practitioner, or what can be called an ecosystem planner (Kaiser, 1975) or a "milieu manager" (Crookston, 1975), is the development of procedures and philosophy that facilitate the coordination of necessary social-, organizational-, and environmental-support systems for the purpose of maximizing the effectiveness, comfort, safety, and dignity with which individuals in organizations carry out their work responsibilities.

We have discussed some of the reasons the study of organizational ecology has been relatively neglected by organizational theorists. These include:

- inadequate conceptions of the environment (Chapter 2);
- inadequate conceptions of the design process (Chapter 3);
- inadequate conceptions of work and workers (Chapter 4);
- inadequate measures of productivity and effectiveness (Chapter 5);
- lack of awareness of, and relatively little empirical data concerning, environment-behavior relationships oriented toward the study of organizations (Chapter 6).

The purpose of these chapters has also been to describe some alternative ways of construing the environment and design process, and to show how these frameworks can be useful in guiding empirical research and facility planning and management practice. I want to turn now to an additional set of factors that has contributed directly to facility planners' and managers' relative neglect of effective ecosystem planning. These are assumptions about what constitutes appropriate and feasible design and planning methods. They include the following beliefs:

- Architects and other environmental experts have the appropriate perspective as well as training and competence to develop appropriate environmental-support systems.
- An ecosystem approach has benefits, but not in relation to the time and expense of implementing appropriate methods.
- There is no organizational payoff in such an approach, and it may even produce worse effects than are obtained with existing approaches.

ASSUMPTIONS UNDERMINING EFFECTIVE ORGANIZATIONAL DEVELOPMENT THROUGH FACILITY PLANNING AND MANAGEMENT

Assumption 1: Mechanisms Exist, in the Form of Activities, Training, and Procedures Used by Environmental Experts, To Provide Services That Support Organizational Effectiveness

Mechanisms may or may not support effectiveness. Results are often randomly effective. What mechanisms exist, for example, to solicit useful information about required physical-support systems? Most organizations have some type of procedure for soliciting employee feedback. These range from once-a-year surveys conducted by the personnel department to completely informal, irregular, and spontaneous discussions between employee and supervisor. If you ask environmental experts in organizations whether they take into account the users of a facility and are concerned about them, the answer, of course, is yes. But that is a little bit like asking hunters whether they believe in conservation. What one needs to know are the specific ways in which concerns with user needs are treated, and how these concerns mesh with other concerns that may have higher priority within the boundaries of professional identity. The following questions are not exhaustive, but answers to them would provide an informed basis for determing whether a particular architectural, space-planning, engineering, or operations-research department of a firm is providing or can provide a specialized kind of service.

How systematically are user-needs data collected? Does the investigator simply talk informally with people as he finds them? Does he or she have a fairly well-defined set of questions that is asked of all respondents? Are the questions asked in the same way, or in ways that are deliberately different in order to take into account the characteristics of different respondents? Are the procedures well-enough defined so that someone else could use them and attain information similar to the first investigator's? How are the questions generated? What are the circumstances in which the questions are asked? Is the language used understandable to the respondents? Is there an attempt to present information separately from interpretations of it?

These kinds of questions are second nature to anyone with social science training. The questions are not arbitrary or academic (e.g., irrelevant or impractical). They are integral to the question of whether information collected is reliable (i.e., whether different people could elicit the same information from the same respondents at different points in time) and valid (i.e., it accurately portrays the conditions as they are observed in action or as respondents perceive them). Procedures that ignore these kinds of issues are likely to perpetuate design and planning decisions based on preconceived notions and untested assumptions. For any client to delegate broad authority for decisions regarding organizational behavior to experts, including many in the design professions, whose training largely if not totally ignores these issues, is absurd. Architects are often faced, for example, with design-linked programmatic decisions outside their professional training and experience. As they themselves argue, they cannot do everything, or in any case, do everything equally well. It is the client's responsibility to hire persons whose training and experience are related to the kinds of decisions that are made, or to develop training programs that help organizational members become more competent environmental decision makers.

Further, how representative are the respondents selected in the data collection? It is not unusual for architects or space planners designing a facility to feel that they are taking into account the users. To support this claim, they may point to repeated discussions with the head nurse, or the floor supervisor, or administrator; with the principal and a group of concerned parents; the head librarian; the director of the chamber of commerce; or the mayor. These kinds of people must be consulted. They are responsible for major decisions concerning the nature and use of the built environment. But they cannot be assumed to speak for everyone in the organization, even those they supervise and presumably know well.

Conflicts of interest define organizations at every level: individual, group, department. To cite only one example, supervisors are assumed to know what those working under them are doing, and what they need to get their jobs done efficiently and effectively. (This is why supervisors are asked for information about their subordinates, rather than asking the subordinates directly.) Even subordinates who are asked for their opinions may be reluctant to identify problems because of the meaning information has in the organization. Expressions of dissatisfaction on the part of line staff are often interpreted by supervisors as evidence of personal deficiency in the persons expressing the dissatisfaction (this is known as blaming the victim). Rarely are characteristics of the situation closely scrutinized.

What incentive is there for a supervisor to report her staff's dissatisfaction to someone else, or to even seek it out, when one runs the risk of finding one's own behavior considered ineffective (e.g., not keeping others productive by channeling their energies away from negative aspects of the work situation)? How many employees are going to express dissatisfaction about their work and its environment unless they are sure they will not be labeled malcontents? Existence of formal mechanisms for reporting "requests for service" is no guarantee, given the meaning of information for organizations, that problems are effectively being identified and resolved. Organizational members quickly learn that it does not pay to make certain kinds of requests or provide particular types of feedback.

Aside from conflicts of interest stemming from the protection of status and position, many supervisors, managers, and executives are simply removed from the realities of the day-to-day life of staff working under them. To have worked as a floor nurse 15 years ago does not necessarily mean one knows the reality of the workplace today. Technology changes rapidly, and certainly people's expectations about what constitutes acceptable working conditions, as well as accepted operating procedures, are different from what they were ten or 15 years ago. Unless one makes a deliberate and intense effort to remain or become familiar with the workplace today, one cannot provide useful information about the situation of those working in it. Most managers, regardless of their profession, have, by professional advancement, removed themselves from the daily grind, or at least have now focused on a different set of problems within the daily routine.

How our role at any moment selectively directs our attention is illustrated by what we attend to as pedestrians and drivers. Most of us are both pedestrians and drivers, but at different times. Our reactions, as pedestrians, to cars that do not stop at crosswalks, that speed, or that make excessive noise are often at variance with our attitudes about these same behaviors we have as drivers. It is not that we do not know what it is to be a pedestrian, but that as soon as we assume the role of driver, the focus of our attention, and of what we consider valuable or appropriate behavior or environmental characteristics, shifts. To understand a given situation, and the people in it, it is necessary to sample people at all levels of the organization, not only those with formal responsibility for decision making. The best advice is this: If you want to know what a postman thinks, ask a postman (not his supervisor, persons on the route). If you want to know what a postman does, watch a postman in action.

Experts' Priorities

Where do the environmental experts' priorities lie? By no means are all architects, accountants, or engineers insensitive to user needs. The question is whether the high priority (based on professional training) the expert holds for the aesthetics of the building, or for its economics, or for its operating efficiency results in decisions detrimental to the satisfaction of an organization's programmatic objectives when tradeoffs between aesthetic, economic, or efficiency criteria and other programmatic requirements (e.g., concern about employee motivation or cooperation) occur.

Many architects, for example, attend to the formal qualities of a building: its shape, cohesion, aesthetic integrity. These factors may take precedence over satisfaction of user requirements when these appear to conflict. Similarly, the operations researcher may attend to efficiency in terms of behavior which is physically possible rather than in terms of behaviors that are probable. This is not necessarily bad.

Architects, operations researchers, and other experts have been trained to be aware of selected issues, and are hired because they have these concerns. Problems occur when one or another of these concerns becomes ascendant to the point where the organization fails to effectively coordinate and balance the various professional perspectives it has brought together. As I noted earlier, boundaries between professions and departments, supported by the belief that one's own particular professional perspective is superior to any other, increase the likelihood that degree of coordination among departments will be low. Unfortunately, most environmental experts are asked to make decisions in isolation from those made by other departments. The surprise should be that the facilities work at all, not that they have various failings.

Communicating Data

How is design and physical-setting information communicated within existing feedback mechanisms? No one would think of asking someone literate only in Chinese to fill out a questionnaire written in English, but in many ways, this is what happens each time organization members are asked to respond, usually in a public situation and with little time to collect their thoughts, to working drawings and other kinds of abstract representations of plans. At the least, one should provide some training in the reading of these plans, prior to trying to elicit feedback about them. Plan implications that go beyond appearances and take into account motivation, social networks, supervision patterns, and communication networks inevitably lead into areas outside the purely architectural realm. The architect, space planner, and plant engineer must be informed about these other realms to be able to make effective organizational decisions. It is the client's responsibility to insure that this information is available to these persons. Why a client would assume the architect or space planner (especially an outside consultant) does or should know a great deal about the operation of an organization, or about its philosophy as it is actually enacted in specific behavioral routines, rules, and regulations, is puzzling.

Assessing the relationship between aspects of a proposed physical design and identified programmatic needs is very difficult. We simply do not know how to do a very good job of it. But we can do a better job than we do now. Architects and facility planners are fully cognizant of the general public's inability to comprehend architectural plans. Yet the plan remains the most common method of communicating with clients. Respondents are often unable to respond at all, or do so with an extremely hazy image of what the implications of the plan are for their own activity—not to mention broader system effects. Architects rarely help the situation by going beyond a description of what exists (e.g., this is a door to the unit, which opens up off the main foyer, and gives a grand view of the entire nursing unit). Much more useful would be a detailed description, using multiple media of presentation (e.g., models, perspective and isometric drawings, tours of partially completed facilities), indicating what kinds of behavior they believe their design will support, and the basis for their beliefs (e.g., personal experience, architectural literature, systematic research).

A design-review session in which detailed behavioral assumptions are made explicit, so that those who will actually use the space can compare them with their own experience and activity patterns, becomes a data-collection instrument in its own right. This kind of assumption mapping provides the opportunity to assess the adequacy of the necessary leap the designer made from available information to decisions on the physical design. It often turns out that architectural decisions the designer felt would support certain behaviors do not. The dynamic relationship among areas and behaviors may not surface until different functional groups review the identical plan, and are helped, by the designer, to look for ways in which the plan will not work for them. This is in marked contrast to the usual process of selling the design concept, often masked as educating the client or user. Architects have a right and responsibility to argue for their best plan, but it should be clear to all participants when one is being persuaded about the plan, and when one is being asked to provide information.

Information users provide may also be very general, and open to multiple interpretations. Therefore, the opportunity to discuss a specific interpretation of a concept, it the form of photographic slides which show different environmental possibilities for defining it (e.g., a cheery and homey look is not achieved by dull yellow and wood-grained formica) provides a yardstick against which different perceptions can be measured. Some sort of such "image negotiation" (Zeisel, 1976), where word images are translated into visual images through discussions of how different environmental possibilities conform to different groups' perceptions, reduces the dismay and disappointment that follow the implementation of agreed-upon word images into physical forms that represent conflicting values.

Assumption 2: Programming and Design Are Discrete Activities

The image of the design process most clients and architects share is one in which programming is a discrete activity occurring prior to design. When this stage of the design process is ended, design presumably begins. This separation of programming from physical design is reflected in large organizations which have entirely different departments for these two activities. My own conception of the design process is different.

In my experience, anyone trained as a designer will begin to design physical alternatives the minute they are introduced to the problem. In an extreme case in my own college, I had called a meeting, involving design faculty and environmental analysts, to simply discuss the process we would use to program and design a renovation for a cafeteria in the building. At least two of the architects immediately started talking about which walls could be (and should be) removed, and where the circulation needed to occur. In part, they did this because they were very familiar with the situation and had been thinking about it for a long time. But in part, their response stemmed from a visual mode of thinking which led them quickly to explore different physical-design ideas. At this stage of the process, their ideas were flexible. They were more or less trying on different alternatives for size. At later stages in the design process, after considerable time and effort has been put into the development of an idea, confidence in the alternative (based on the amount of time working on it and its apparent logic) reduces the designer's flexibility and willingness to continue generating alternatives.

The fact that designers design almost from the minute they are handed a problem has great potential as part of the programming process, for the following reason: Many respondents can more easily articulate what they dislike about a situation than what they like. They can tell you what must be changed, but may have very little idea about how it could be changed. Few people are familiar with the wide range of possible design alternatives. It is necesary to distinguish, however, between asking people about what kinds of activities and experiences they need and want to engage in, and how the present or proposed facilities support or hinder these activities, and asking them to generate solutions for these problems. The architect is hired to provide solutions, or more accurately, to provide the necessary environmental supports for explicitly noted activities the individuals and organization agree are important.

The user's ability to identify dysfunction and desired pattern of behavior, and the architect's early thinking about design, complement each other. Rather than trying to collect information for programming and then giving this information to the architect as a basis for generating design alternatives in a separate stage of design, information should be collected and given to the architect very early in the programming stage. From this information the architect can develop tentative plans. These plans can then be fed back to the respondents as a basis for eliciting their responses to the early and tentative translation of their initial activity requirements into environmental supports. It is often at this stage one can hear the respondent say, "That's not what I meant! If you put that wall over there, I won't be able to supervise these people, and that will be a lot more trouble for me. What I need is privacy for writing, and the opportunity to supervise others easily." The first information collected may have underscored only the privacy needs, not the supervision needs. The tentative physical design thus becomes a data-collection instrument.

Users at all levels are involved in the design process, and this design process is inextricably intertwined with all other organizational processes. With early data, involvement and concern in the organization is likely to increase (assuming the information collected is genuinely intended to influence the design, and not simply to appease the staff). Secondly, the architects are able to elicit much more explicit and specific information prior to their making a more formal commitment to any particular design alternatives. By involving the architect in this process, there is a much greater probability that the architect will be able to effectively utilize the information that has been collected. Its relevance to design is immediate. Third, the likelihood is that this more thorough reiterative design process, involving a broad range of organization members, will result in a better design. Better in terms of user satisfaction, even at points in the future when the initial organization members may have left (Becker et al., 1978). It may also reduce the number of change orders made during the construction process. The cost of elective change orders, in both time and money, is enormous in many projects. If a more systematic process reduced the number of change orders by even as little as 10 percent or 15 percent, the cost savings would be substantial. As far as I know, no study of this kind has been undertaken. It should be. But what should be compared is not the cost of systematic behavioral programming versus the total absence of programming, but rather, whether there is any additional cost for this type of procedure over costs of what would normally be provided by an architectural firm or the client. Behavioral programming of some sort (usually called space planning) already occurs. It simply may be inefficient.

Assumption 3: Systematic Behavioral Programming
Takes Too Much Time and Costs Too Much Money

Organizations often agonize over deciding to spend $20 million or $30 million on a new building or major addition, and then refuse to spend something like 1 percent of the total budget to develop a detailed behavioral program that will guide the allocation of the $20 million in a way that maximizes the likelihood that the organization's programmatic goals will be deliberately and expertly incorporated into the design and construction of the new facility.

Unsystematic behavioral programming done either by the architect's or the client's in-house staff is not cheap. In many cases a project director or principal of a firm will interview top and middle-level management. At $45-55 per hour and up, this is hardly an inexpensive route to follow. On the other hand, using procedures deliberately designed to elicit specific information of relevance to design, and using resources that effectively communicate what one wants people to respond to, would vastly increase the likelihood that the time (and money) spent would produce more reliable and valid information from a wider range of potential users.

For the time it takes to run relatively unplanned and undirected review sessions with uninformed respondents, one could distribute questionnaires to a large part of the organization's population. These can be designed to be easily coded without computer aid (depending on the size of the organization), or if computers are readily available to the organization, for easy computer scoring. Members of the firm can be trained, in a few hours, to code closed-ended questions, and open-ended questions can at least be pursued, if not the content analyzed, in a systematic fashion. Simple questionnaires are available and easily modified for different settings (Sommer, 1972). Any one of these types of instruments will result in much more information, in easily used form, than will almost any undirected and casual attempts to elicit information.

Some firms may feel uncomfortable in or incapable of collecting this type of information themselves. Hiring outside consultants may be beyond the means of small firms (although the cost of the consultant should be computed as a percentage of the total construction costs and operation cost over the life of the building), but it certainly is not unfeasible for firms that engage in large-scale construction on a continuing basis. Such organizations can hire experts whose role is to coordinate efforts to maximize effective use of limited personnel and environmental resources.

Assumption 4: Information Is Wanted

Although I am arguing for the collection of more information, it is not always wanted. Environmental experts, including, but not limited to, architects or space planners, may want to avoid collecting information from a broad spectrum of the organization's members, for several reasons, and with the client's support. Surveys are potentially subversive. They request and legitimize opinions from persons at all levels of the organizational hierarchy. They undermine traditional authority structures because the teachers, the nurse's aides, or the secretaries are asked to provide information and feedback on their own work situation that goes directly to the top without being filtered by supervisors, who may have reason for distorting or ignoring the feedback.

The paying client, usually represented by top executives, board members, and trustees, usually believe strongly in expertise. They do not want others meddling in the work of highly paid consultants or staff members who have been hired precisely because their experience and training provide them with special skills, insights, and expertise. Yet experts are used to provide information only when those with established authority feel they control the nature and use of the information.

Surveys done by independent experts may effectively remove control over the nature and use of information from those with formal authority; conversely, allowing consultants and other experts to control the nature of the information collected as well as its analysis and interpretation may shift power to those without any formal authority. For this reason, information may be resisted unless it can be controlled.

In a study of the use of automated information systems in American local government, for example, Dutton et al. (1978) found that where the information in automated systems can be controlled by, and used to the advantage of, a policymaker, it will generally be used. Where the uses and impacts of the automated information appear to be less controllable, or where the information tends to reduce the discretionary range of the policymaker, it will generally not be used. In this same study, the authors found that automated information's primary use was not in problem solving but in providing evidence and justification for alternatives policymakers had already proposed.

This makes sense within a bureaucratic framework where one of the major resources of those in power is that they control the definition of the problem. Information developed and presented by others may bring to the fore sets of problems, or alternative solutions, that those in power are unwilling to consider. Information, which has broadly been defined as whatever reduces uncertainty, here becomes a force for increasing uncertainty within a political context. It draws attention to various aspects of a situation that decisionmakers or experts may, for a variety of reasons, prefer to ignore. Information is resisted because it may provide convincing evidence that an expert's assumptions, or an executive's, are unwarranted.

Clearly, information is rarely the decisive factor in the policy process

(Dutton et al., 1978). What sometimes appears perplexing, given this fact, is what Dutton et al. refer to as the "policymaker's complaint," or their feeling that appropriate information for decision making usually exists but is not available in a usable form, and that if information in some alternative form were available, decisions would be made more rationally. As I noted above, most decisionmakers favor information only when it is under their control. The "complaint" seems to be rooted in a vision that not only should enough information be available and so compelling as to obviate difficult value choices, but also that it should simultaneously support the values of those controlling the information. If the use of information creates dependence on other experts, the information is unlikely to be sought or used (Dutton et al., 1978). This is a good reason for involving a broad range of organizational members in fact-finding processes.

Assumption 5: Administrators Are Effective Space Managers

For major additions and renovations, organizations assign responsibility for managing the entire process to a single individual or a committee. A hospital construction committee, for instance, may be comprised of the board of directors, and the directors of maintenance, housekeeping, nursing, and hospital administration. This committee is responsible for coordinating and guiding the entire construction project. In other cases, a construction manager may be hired for the duration of the project. In still other cases, an administrator within the organization will be given responsibility for overseeing the planning, design, and construction of the project, in addition to regular duties. Regardless of the specific position or organizational structure created, the function is identical: to represent the organization's interests, and to insure that the architects and contractors work within the budget and meet the programmatic requirements the organization has developed.

Individuals who fill these positions are often unfamiliar with the design process and may fail to fully appreciate (or have full organizational support for) the fact that they are responsible for the design. It is not the architect, who essentially makes recommendations to the organization in the capacity of a consultant. Ideally, the organization's members evaluate the proposed designs, using an explicit set of criteria they have developed and previously communicated to the architects. Separation and isolation from other basic kinds of organizational, personnel, and policy decisionmakers should not, but often do, occur. A number of factors militate against typical kinds of administrative arrangements protecting the organization's interests.

Administrators asked to serve in the role of construction manager may view this role as interesting (for a while) but essentially falling outside the boundaries of their professional responsibility and expertise (and in terms of their training, they are correct). There is also concern about being typed as someone in construction management, because this may restrict job mobility and advancement. For both of these reasons, persons responsible for construction management often do it on a one-time basis. Experience from one job is unlikely to be built into a second, third, or fourth project. This gives rise to persons who are willing to be typed as construction-management specialists.

The linguistic implications of the term "construction management" are worth examining. A construction-management specialist is confined to managing the physical construction of the project. The process through which programmatic objectives are developed, the nature of the programmatic guidelines provided to the architect, and the crucial task of the administration of the unit once it is in operation—in relation to the architectural design—generally fall outside the construction-management specialist's scope of formal responsibility. Yet, decisions are routinely made that directly affect work procedures, staff relations, and maintenance requirements. Rarely are these made with the aid of information about their programmatic effects. The construction-management specialist becomes, without any specific training, a de facto specialist in design, personnel relations, and organizational development.

It is assumed that the personnel department, or the hospital administrator, or individual department heads will attend to matters once the building is finished. As noted earlier, their professional training virtually guarantees that they will not be effective in managing environmental supports. Organizations often make two further tenuous assumptions. One is that somewhere in the programming process, assuming that this was at all formalized, or in the review of the proposed designs at points when they are fairly well developed, the views of a full range of organization members (both by function and organizational position) were incorporated into the program the architects used as a design guide.

The other assumption, related to the design-communication process discussed earlier, is that construction managers or committees are able to effectively read the plans at a level which allows them to understand all the organizational, personnel, and policy issues and, on the basis of these implications, screen the design recommendations the architects make. Unfamiliarity with the method of design presentation and with the full spectrum of problems and activities facing all staff makes this extremely unlikely. The result is that these committees or individuals hand over a great deal of control of the daily operation of their organization to an outside consultant (often the architect) who is likely to be much less familiar with the hospital's operation than the committee itself.

To be fair to the architects, theirs is an untenable position in many ways. If they request more information in order to provide a more effective design, they run the risk of being considered unprofessional and inexperienced (an experienced firm presumably has this detailed programmatic and organizational knowledge). They are put in the position of designing with less information than is necessary, or spending a portion of their architectural fee for behavioral programming.

The responsibility to provide the necessary detailed criteria lies with the organization, the client, not with the architect. Most organizations abdicate their responsibility to see that their goals, programmatic requirements, and organizational strategy are supported by the design alternatives generated at the point of major design work. Organizations relinquish a degree of control in matters of architectural design and environmental-space management control which they would not remotely consider relinquishing in other areas of the organization.

Consultants are hired for many reasons, but rarely is a relatively disinterested consultant given almost unrestricted freedom to determine investment policy or changes in organizational structure. Consultants are asked for advice, but final decisions are made by knowledgeable organizational members. At the very least, consultants are asked their advice and given some freedom to define the problem in areas in which they are recognized experts—that is, where they have considerable academic or technical training and experience. Most exectutives and administrators do not believe architects are experts in organizational behavior, environmental psychology, personnel, or administration. Yet their behavior vis-à-vis facility planning and design suggests that they believe either that the architect will be expert in these areas (perhaps with a little guidance from them) or that other experts can apply their skills with little understanding of how to effectively manage environmental supports.

Assumption 6: Ongoing Space Management Is Less Important than the Basic Design of a Facility

As important as the initial design of the building is the way it is managed, or created, over time. At the time of a major design effort, considerable attention is paid (regardless of its value) to the role of the building, how it will make certain jobs easier, or facilitate organizational objectives. For the most part, once this initial planning and design effort ends, attention shifts away from the building and to other seemingly more manageable human resources. The building seems unchangeable, and since it is newly designed, the assumption is that the building is appropriate. Problems are attributed to the users, who reportedly do not use the building appropriately or resist "innovation" and "progress." The distinct possibility that a very new building is likely to have more problems than an older one, where successive modifications in both the building and its use have created an accommodation or fit between environment and use, is often shunted aside.

The premise of a perfect building exists in the refusal to make immediate modifications to a new environment as unforeseen problems arise, and as the implications of design decisions begin to come into focus. Systematic behavioral programming of major design projects will minimize some of the unforeseen problems, but it will not eliminate them entirely. The perfect building does not exist, even in theory. And if one takes the position that the way in which users create the environment is a positive one and should be encouraged, then by definition, the "perfect" building situation is one in which the opportunity to modify the building occurs. For this kind of process to be effective, some type of ongoing environmental-space management must be built into the overall organizational design and development process.

Assumption 7: Systematic Behavioral Programming Is Not Cost Effective because of Employee Turnover

The major renovation or design of a new building may easily span several years from the time of inception and programming to construction and occupancy. Opponents of systematic behavioral programming argue that staff turnover is so great during this time that it makes no sense to design a facility for people who will soon leave. As soon as someone new comes on board, the old design, tailored to the recently departed employee, will only have to be redone, abandoned, or simply tolerated. This is an argument in support of mediocrity It suggests that since there is staff turnover, and there are individual differences among staff, the best way to cope with this situation is to ignore all individual differences and design for no one in particular. This kind of thinking can be attacked on a number of levels.

Individuals are both similar and different. Because of what is called "partial inclusion" (Thompson, 1967), no individuals bring all their capabilities, interests, motivations, and handicaps into play as an employee. (It is an interesting paradox that many organizations would, in the abstract, argue they want staff to bring more of their capabilities to their jobs, but, in fact, the manifest diversity that becomes visible in such a case is difficult for most organizations to tolerate.) Nurse Smith may be different from Nurse Jones in many respects, but they are probably similar in many others. The ones they are similar in may predominate in their staff role. These similarities derive from common demands of the job, and from similar training and professional development that promote shared role perceptions, expectations, and operating procedures. All nurse's aides, laboratory technicians, or admissions clerks are not entirely different from each other in terms of the environmental supports they require to competently, comfortably, and efficiently carry out their specific responsibilities. Technological innovation and changes in educational and training programs as well as in organizational practices and philosophy may at any time upset the apple cart, but in the design of any facility, there will be aspects of the design that are relatively enduring. Turnover among staff will not markedly affect basic design requirements.

Staff differ, however, in some respects. These differences can be taken into account by construing the environment as one in which different aspects of the physical setting have different degrees or levels of stability and permanence. The less permanent and more flexible components comprise a kit of parts that can be used to construct a broad range of environmental-support systems linked to and integrated with an equally broad range of operating procedures and expectations concerning the use of the available environmental resources.

No facility should be designed for a single person, unless there is only one person using it and that person's activities are unrelated to any other individual's activities and required environmental supports. Organizations are characterized by staff interdependence: large numbers of persons whose activities and required environmental supports are linked. A facility can become dysfunctional upon one occupant's departure only if the entire program guiding operating procedures, work interdependencies, and inter-action expectancies also departs with the staff member. In that case it is unlikely that any environment-support system that was in place would suffice, regardless of how or for whom it was designed. In this case the environment would need to be reassessed to determine appropriate environ-mental supports as a new program developed. This would happen whether or not the previous environmental support had been planned specifically for the departed person, or not. If the existing program is independent of the departing person, then an effectively created environmental-support system would be one which would not fall apart upon the departure of only one of the setting's occupants. It would not fall apart because it was designed to support a number of interdependent activities which are not dependent upon particu-lar individuals for their performance.

Assumption 8: People Always Resist Change

In talking with facility managers, designers, and administrators involved both formally and informally with space allocation and use, a common theme often emerges that has at its center the notion that people will complain about and resist almost any kind of change or innovation, no matter how the planning process is organized. This is generally based on many personal experiences where people have complained about and resisted change efforts. The characteristics of the change processes are generally not considered seriously in making these kinds of assessments, however. Given the autocratic nature of most change efforts, what the personal experiences do suggest very powerfully is that persons who feel they are excluded from decision processes and who experience work patterns or environmental support that objectively worsen their work conditions (e.g., smaller work stations, less privacy and storage), generally resist change efforts.

The problem lies in both the process and the products resulting from it. In situations where workers are included in decision processes, and where environmental changes made support the kinds of work patterns and conditions workers consider necessary for them to effectively conduct their work, change efforts can impressively improve motivation, commitment, and satisfaction (Lawler, 1973).

In a recent study of an office environment, Clearwater (1980) found that in planning a move from a conventional to a landscaped office, 70 percent of the workers were either slightly or not at all satisfied with their participation in the planning process. There was a highly significant correlation between the extent to which employees believed they would like the new office environment and the degree to which they assumed their personal needs had been considered in the design. Participation in the planning process is clearly an important means of individuals communicating their needs so that they might be considered.

The question is one of incentives and threat. What positive incentive does the planning process provide to the employee? Does it support feelings of competence and expertise by drawing on these as a basis for redesign? Does the process provide opportunities to develop a better understanding of the overall operation of the organization? Does it permit the individuals to tap skills and abilities that are relatively dormant in their routine daily activities? Does it permit them to develop skills and abilities that may improve their chances of professional and career advancement? Does it indicate that the organization is aware of its employees and values their contribution? Threat occurs to the extent these kinds of behaviors or experiences are reduced, glossed over, or ignored by the planning process.

Similarly, one can ask, for the product of the planning process, how it recognizes and supports individual differences, job effectiveness, feelings of personal worth within the organizational context. Planning processes that ignore these kinds of issues are, indeed, likely to result in resistance and dissatisfaction. But the problem, once again, lies in the way of organizing the planning process, not in the characteristics or traits of the individuals who experience it.

9

MIXED BLESSINGS:
THE OFFICE AT HOME

Implicitly, the discussion so far has assumed that within the context of a discussion of the role of physical settings in organizations, the physical setting of interest is the office, factory, or some other identifiable and bounded physical facility designed and managed exclusively for the purpose of paid work done by persons hired by and responsible to a specific organization. Telematics, or the merging of telecommunications and computers for the purpose of generating, storing, manipulating, retrieving, and communicating words and data at very high speeds, with essentially no respect for physical distance, has made such an assumption obsolete.

Telematics is linking home and office in ways that are likely to have major implications for the organization's role in planning and managing facilities. Drawing boundaries for organizational control becomes controversial as work begins to extend to the one setting, remote from the traditional office, which is generally regarded as a kind of last bastion of refuge, privacy, and individual control: the home. The purpose of this last chapter is to explore some of the implications of telematics-stimulated work at home.

Piotrkowski (1979) notes that the "home-as-haven" theme is a recurrent one in the literature on work and families. Families have been viewed as an "oasis of replenishment" and as a refuge against the brutality of the industrial world. Some authors (Dubin, 1976) have argued that not only are work and family institutions separate, but that the separation is necessary for the smooth functioning of the social order. Kanter (1977) has argued that in fact, American capitalism was organized in places physically remote from

---

Parts of this chapter were originally written, in modified form, in collaboration with Charles C. McClintock, for a research proposal to investigate the mental-health aspects of doing office work at home.

the home as a means of weakening family loyalties and the threat to work discipline and organizational loyalty they represented. The home became important as a psychological retreat as work became physically and emotionally separated, at least as far as the organization was concerned, from family life.

A number of authors in recent years have begun to explore the relationship between family and work systems (Piotrkowski, 1979; Rapoport and Rapoport, 1971; Machlowitz, 1980). Their goal, in general, has been to explore the ways in which work systems affect families' interaction patterns and emotional life. A working assumption has been that there is a greater connection between work and family systems than many traditional students of either the family, on one hand, or organizations, on the other, have acknowledged. In part, this "myth of separate worlds" has been perpetuated by families themselves, who often fail to connect these settings (Piotrkowski, 1979) to their pattern of family life. The rapid development of telematics, which creates the opportunity, and possibly the pressure, for more work to occur in the home than now does brings these two systems into direct physical contact, and thus raises many fundamental issues about the effects of such technological developments on both the family and work systems.

Like the preceding chapters, this one is intended to identify important issues and ask questions that research may contribute answers to. It differs from most futuristic writing in two respects. First, it employs an explicit, although evolving, conceptual framework that usefully guides one's thinking about likely types of behavioral effects that might be found in both the home and the office. Secondly, it draws on preliminary empirical research directly addressing the social implications of doing office work in the home.

OFFICE OF THE FUTURE

A quick glance at any newsstand within the last year suggested the intense interest the media is focusing on the office of the future and the electronic technology underlying it. The business world is intrigued. It hopes for an almost magical solution to lagging office productivity. Yet the social, economic, and technical aspects of telecommunications technology are just beginning to be explored. Most of the literature on telecommunications' effects on work and social structure is neither systematic nor empirical, and very little of it addresses social-psychological outcomes or implications for mental health (Vail, 1978). Empirical studies of telecommunications and work have focused almost exclusively on communication-modality preferences (Pye and Williams, 1977), on transportation and energy savings due to the substitution of telecommunications networks (Dordick et al., 1978; Tyler, 1977), or on aspects of economic growth in less-developed countries

(Tyler, 1977). The work on productivity is largely based on anecdotal evidence and/or figures supplied by equipment vendors.

The fantastic benefits the new electronic technology will presumably spawn become confused with reality, rather than being treated as the hypothetical scenarios they actually are. A sample of some of the projected benefits underscores the new technologies' widespread appeal. According to one commentator (*New York Times*, October 28, 1979):

> Modern office systems could end the energy crisis overnight. Available information processing technology has made it functionally unnecessary for most white collar workers to do their jobs in a central office environment.

Another management consultant (Vail, 1977, p. 78) on technology in the workplace described what has become a typical scenario involving the family and the home as a workplace:

> Since 1974 (three years ago) Jane Adams has worked for the Afgar Company. During this period she became familiar with the typing and filing routines of the office. But this spring, after she had her first child, she decided she would rather remain at home. Once this might have meant that she would have to give up her job. But not any more!
>
> The company simply arranged to have a remote dictation unit and a computer terminal installed in Jane's home. To avoid tying up her family's phone, Jane's company also had a separate phone line installed.
>
> Today, Jane attends to her household chores, mothers her new daughter, and periodically checks the incoming dictation unit to see if any typing needs to be done. When there is some, she sits at her terminal, transcribes the dictation, and then registers its location in a computer file so that her boss can find it.
>
> Everyone likes the new arrangement. Jane normally works the equivalent of a 40-hour week, but on a very flexible schedule. The arrangement she has with her company is that she will get the work out in a reasonable period of time. Only occasionally does her boss call to tell her something is urgent. Thus, if Jane wants to use a weekday afternoon for shopping, she can do some of her work at night. Or she may prefer to work on Sunday and take Monday off. . . .
>
> Jane no longer has an "office" in the sense of a desk in a room downtown. But neither does her boss. He travels a great deal, so he carries his "office" with him. It fits inside his briefcase and includes: a portable computer terminal that can be hooked up by any telephone to the company's central computer, a microfilm viewer, and a pocket-sized dictation machine that he uses on planes, in cars, and —whenever posssible—alongside hotel swimming pools. A special attachment to this unit stores his dictation and can transmit it on command at high speed by telephone to Jane's recorder.
>
> Jane and her boss still meet face to face occasionally to talk over

problems, and, of course, to attend office parties. Even in this modern age, "electronic parties" are not yet in sight.

Such discussions suggest a potentially explosive change in the relationship of work to family and community life over the next 20 years, but it is a change that is likely to have negative as well as positive consequences. The general image that office automation, including the decentralization phenomenon, will be overwhelmingly beneficial stems, in large part, from the fact that the bulk of the available literature is a form of generic advertising. There will be positive effects, but these need to be assessed in relation to the negative ones. The fundamental question is how to maximize the beneficial aspects of telematics while minimizing the negative ones, as experienced by various individuals and groups affected by the new technologies.

The radical alteration of the organization of work suggested by the above scenarios rests on several technological developments. These include video and audio teleconferencing; computer teleconferencing, which is a print-based communication through keyboard terminals; and the availability of portable minicomputers and related input/output equipment for computer networking and telecopying (Dordick et al., 1978; Johansen et al., 1978). These developments make it technologically possible for an enormous number of clerical, secretarial, and white-collar tasks, which essentially involve information handling and processing, to be performed in remote locations. Estimates of the proportion of persons in the workforce who will occupy clerical, secretarial and white-collar service-sector jobs over the next 20 years range from 60 to 70 percent, with the remainder of the economy consisting of manufacturing and agriculture (Marien, 1978). Thus, shifting the work environment of this large number of persons from office to home could have enormous effects on the structure of work, and the functioning and mental health of individuals, families, and communities.

Treatments of telematics work in the home are unsystematic with regard to causes, consequences, mediating factors, and differential effects according to the status and power of the job in question. It seems reasonable to assume that the age of the worker, the type of work, previous work history, and incentive systems might affect the success of the technical systems as they operate in practice. Even more important may be whether the worker chooses to work at home, as most professionals working with computers now do, or is directed to work at home for purposes that clearly benefit the organization (e.g., lower overhead costs resulting from maintaining less office space). The impact is likely to be quite different for women who view one of the primary benefits of paid employment as the opportunity to leave the house than it is for a woman who, because of child-care responsibilities, could not secure paid employment unless it could be done at home, or for a handicapped person whose physical disabilities make travel to work immensely difficult or impossible.

Discussions typically identify three general categories of individuals who will benefit from telematics work in the home: technicians, such as computer programmers; professional and white-collar persons, such as insurance adjusters and bank officers; and secretaries or clerk-typists who are essentially involved in word and customer-account processing. Since there have been no conceptual analyses, differences among these groups in terms of their work attitudes, power, and needs are generally glossed over. Even less attention is given to interactions in the home as they would interrelate with work activity. In general, there is little systematic analysis of the range of potential effects from telematics work in the home, and scant attention to the potentially undesirable interaction among types of effects—for instance, the cumulative contributions to worker tensions of increased demands from family, as well as the at-least-temporary demands of adjusting to a novel set of work procedures. The following questions, while hardly constituting an exhaustive list, suggest a range of issues that need to be addressed:

- To what extent are the effects of increased crowding and use of the residence mediated by physical- or social-support systems? Can a room be set aside for work without sacrificing other valued activities? What are the costs of modifying the space physically, and what are the implications for other family members?
- Can the design of the residence affect the productivity of the worker and the mental health of family members by increasing or reducing tension through its ability to provide necessary auditory and visual privacy; by helping integrate or separate role responsibilities; by separating incompatible activities?
- What changes in the work role are necessary to accompany telematics work at home? How can characteristics of the work (e.g., networking, lack of visual supervision) be made harmonious with characteristics of home life? How will workers become and remain socialized into the norms of the office and the duties of the work?
- Are increased demands placed on personal and institutional social supports? Do some family members spend more time outside the home, and where do they go? Are friends' houses visited more often, or are friends and relatives invited to visit less often because they contribute to an already increased sense of crowding.
- Do parents make adjustments in their behavior that are undesirable for their children? Are some activities that are valued by children eliminated? Do they occur elsewhere, and what pressure do they put on other facilities or support systems? Does it make a difference what ages the children are, or whether there are children?

These kinds of questions have evolved from and were stimulated by research projects we have done in the Human-Environment Relations Program at Cornell University during the last six years. Several of these studies were concerned with human responses and adaptations to living environments differing in design, management, and location (Becker, 1974; Becker et al., 1978). While these initial studies were not directly concerned with paid work in the home, they remain highly pertinent for the insights they provide into how families function, and the type of environmental-support systems they consider necessary to function adequately.

We found that the design of the setting for living significantly influenced levels of satisfaction and perceived well-being, and altered existing behavioral patterns, particularly in terms of use of different facilities and social interaction. Of particular interest were the following data: The home was consistently described as a type of "refuge," a place to decompress from the stress of work; issues of privacy among family members, as well as among different families, were central to their being able to manage stress and conflict; different family members often had very different conceptions of appropriate design or management of space; and these differences could be a source of frustration, conflict, and tension. For residents of public housing, the above issues were exacerbated by the role of external social-control agents, such as building managers, who established policies that restricted occupants' ability to manipulate their space in ways that they felt could help alleviate tension and dissatisfaction.

These studies have been followed by several small studies in which we have explored the impact of environmental-support systems on family interaction patterns. For example, McLaughlin (1978) investigated the impact of moving from large to small dwelling units on six graduate students' families living in university housing. She focused on role changes in parents and changes in activity patterns among children as forms of adaptation to a new living environment. Time-activity diaries, interviews, and physical-environment inventories were used to collect data. McLaughlin found changes in role relationships, with fathers assuming more parenting responsibilities than they had previously, as well as changes in the nature of the activities, and thus learning opportunities, children engaged in. For example, small spaces reduced the frequency of messy activities and those that require significant amounts of time and/or space to set up. The effort simply became greater than the perceived benefit, at least for the parents.

In another study, Ashworth (1979) explored the kinds of adaptation individuals made in their housing and living patterns in response to the expectations of family members. The focus was on the management of stress and conflict among family members. She found that physical modification of the dwelling unit was an important form of adjustment to changing living patterns and expectations. Rental housing restricted the opportunity for making such adjustments, causing dissatisfaction and limiting the kind of social organization within the family that respondents considered appropriate. These findings are significant for the proposed research because of the large number of urban workers living in rental units whose small size is compounded by rules restricting physical modifications in environmental-support systems which may be necessary to accommodate changes in living and work patterns. Ashworth's finding that particular spatial forms contribute to the mental health of families is supported by recent research on work and family systems.

In her study of working- and lower-middle-class families, Piotrkowski (1979) found that husbands whose jobs were stressful needed "psychological space" to recoup their energies upon returning home. In some cases, children accommodated this need by physically removing themselves from their father. In other cases, the father retreated to a special physical location where the children had learned not to bother him, or the father used outdoor space to maintain distance while still at home. Mothers who worked at home (as homemakers) had little opportunity to physically separate themselves from either their work or their children, and so had a difficult time gaining psychological space and recouping their energy. Depending on the nature of their work and the amount of energy depleted by work (either from physical exertion or mental fatigue stemming from boredom or dangerous work), husbands made themselves more or less "emotionally and interpersonally available." The level of this interpersonal availability was an important determinant of the rest of the family's emotional state and satisfaction. The opportunity to recoup some of this energy and become more interpersonally available may be facilitated by the separation of home and workplace, which provides time to move from the role of worker to that of husband or father (Dubin, 1976). Eric Cooper, one of Piotrkowski's respondents (1979, pp. 90-91), stated succinctly the importance of separating family and work:

> Since I am associated with both worlds—my work world and my home— I separate those two because to me they are two separate things. That's why...when I leave my work at work, I don't want to spend time at home working on work. You know what I mean? I have my home life and I have my work life and I want to keep those two separate because they are two important things. I don't want to mix them up because if something should go wrong at one place, it can have serious effects on the other place because they are so intermixed. I want to keep them separate, so if something goes wrong in one place, I don't have to worry about that in my other place.

Other researchers (Aldous, 1969) have noted the importance for a family of being able to synchronize work and family responsibilities.

While most of the above research is exploratory, it suggests the need for a more extensive and intensive investigation of support systems and role relationships as contextual factors that mediate activity and work patterns, and mental-health effects, of increased use of the home as a work environment. The major gaps in knowledge on support-system and role-relationship effects in the use of the home as a work environment include:

- the need to identify and specify the range of physical- and social-support systems that can mediate the strains and tension that may result from increased crowding in the home;
- the need to assess the relative efficacy of different types of support systems in alleviating interpersonal strains of increased use of the home as a work environment;
- the need to understand how work roles can be structured to accommodate characteristics of telematics work, and the role relationships in the home that are affected by working at home;
- the need to assess whether increased use of the home as a work environment affects mental-health outcomes differently, depending on the type of family structure and/or type of organizational position;
- the need to assess how increased use of the home for office work influences the behavior of coworkers in the traditional work environment.

There is an urgent need to fill these gaps by focusing on effects of support systems and role relationships on activity patterns and mental health in home settings that are used for telematics work, as well as for other kinds of paid work.

The success of work innovations, ranging from flextime to job enrichment, clearly indicates that changes in the routine or the organization of work per se may be greatly appreciated by workers. These can contribute in significant ways to an improved quality of life at home as well as at work. These kinds of changes, in fact, constitute changes in support systems. They have generated in being successful, changes in images of the worker, particularly in terms of responsibility and motivation. They have not, however, significantly changed the organization of work spatially—it still takes place in a formally designated and controlled work site; nor have they directly impinged on a setting outside of this site: the home. As such, the likelihood that these work innovations will fundamentally alter role relationships, as these are played out in either the home or office setting, is relatively slight. In contrast, the introduction of telematics into the home brings two spatially distinct systems into direct contact. Since the advent of the modern organization, each of these traditionally has been operated by different players, with different roles, playing by different rules. Our argument is not that such contact cannot be beneficial, but that for it to be so, changes or adaptations of existing support systems may have to occur.

The gap between a given technology's engineering potential and its organizational impact was made clear in a recent presentation by Porter (1980) in the context of a discussion about the office of the future. Based on extensive experience with telecommunications in an ongoing office setting, he noted that "having an effective electronic-assisted office is not just a matter of buying some hardware and leasing some phone lines. Human and organizational factors must be taken into account, too." He went on to give a list of some of the support programs and design characteristics that were necessary for the hardware to make a positive contribution: support from the top boss; input from the ultimate users of the system, not only in planning stages, but also after the system is on stream; initial and continued employee training; and the opportunity to "play games" on the new system. Fundamental changes in supervisor-employee relations occurred. Top managers were tempted to bypass lower levels of management and communicate directly with the rank and file. The latter, in turn, said things to the top person, through the computer system, that they could not before. Thus role relationships are disturbed, and new support systems in the form of training programs are required. As the computer moves into the home, these kinds of changes become more complex and more intertwined. At this point, our understanding of this phenomenon is woefully inadequate.

One result of not understanding the nature and importance of telematics effects on role-relationship and support systems has been the failure to give serious consideration to the kinds of public and corporate policies that can maximize the benefits of the rapidly developing telecommunications industry for individuals, families, and organizations, while minimizing negative, unanticipated, and unintended consequences. Large-scale housing developments and office projects developed by both the public and private sector are being planned and designed in a knowledge vacuum with respect to employing telecommunications in socially responsible ways.

AN ECOSYSTEM FRAMEWORK

Based on the research program briefly outlined above, we have developed an ecosystem framework (see Figure 9.1) that can usefully guide research to address such issues. The framwork is a simple one, befitting the state of our knowledge. Its basic premise is that there are fundamental and reciprocal relationships between work and mental health (Hunt, Lichtman, and McClintock, 1972; Liebow, 1976). Just as work affects the psychosocial adjustments of individuals, the mental and social conditions that persons bring to their work have important effects on productivity, morale, and general capacity for and effectiveness in work (Neff, 1968). Since work affects the quality of mental health and that, in turn, affects the quality of

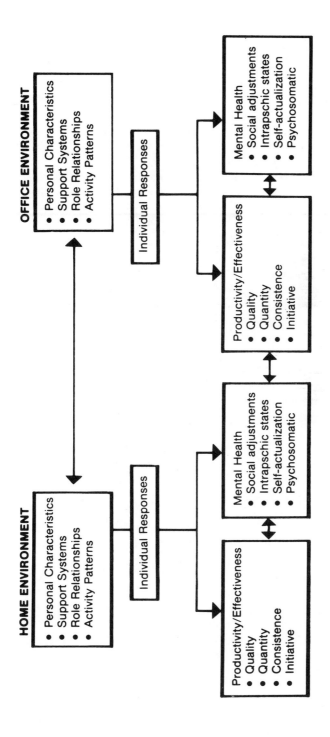

FIGURE 9.1 Ecosystem Framework

183

work, any significant perturbation in either component of the system will have reverberating ramifications.

Our premise is that as work organizations seek solutions to their own economic and energy problems by capitalizing on technological innovations, such as telematics in the home, there will occur a set of second-order, unintended, unanticipated and often undesirable effects (for workers, their families, and their organizations). For example, working at home via computer may reduce personal-transportation costs, but require expensive changes in the size or design of the home to accommodate the new work patterns. It may reduce role conflicts with coworkers in the office, but create role conflicts at home among family members. It may give one greater control over geographic and schedule constraints related to filling a particular job, but impose control by restricting the worker to the home. It may increase physical privacy, but decrease privacy regarding the pace and quality of work if centralized monitoring is in effect.

In trying to assess second-order consequences, it is worthwhile distinguishing between the probability and significance of anticipated consequences (Bauer, 1966). An event may have a very low probability of occurrence, but its costs and/or benefits may be so significant that a thorough understanding of it and contingency planning for it are necessary (e.g., a nuclear-power accident). Also, as is the case with nuclear accidents, the real problem may be second-order effects (e.g., genetic deformation) and not the direct, first-order consequence more easily calculated: number of immediate deaths or serious illnesses.

A key aspect of the framework is that the home and office environments are part of the same ecosystem. As such, changes in one setting will affect the other. Both the mental health of the worker and productivity are determined by an interplay of personal, support-system, role-relationship, and activity-pattern variables in the home and on the job. For example, a change in the physical-support system of the work environment, represented by the introduction of portable computer terminals that move work from the office to the home, would be expected to affect, in the office environment: the need for alterations in the work socialization and other social-support systems in the office; role relationships (e.g., quality and frequency of supervision); the content, duration, and frequency of work activities (e.g., amount of time processing paper). And, in the home environment, such a change would affect the use of residential and neighborhood social supports; role relationships (e.g., quality of interaction between spouses and between parents and children); activity patterns (e.g., amount of time spent interacting with others in the home or engaging in nonwork activities in the home). Of particular importance is that the individual's response to telecommunications-related changes in activity, role-relationship, and support-system patterns within one setting (e.g., the office), which produce higher levels of perceived satisfaction, self-esteem, and sense of competence within that setting, will also influence these variables, perhaps negatively, in the home setting.

The framework also indicates that within each setting, each of the components is influenced by the nature of the other components. For example, one's income (a personal characteristic) constrains the nature of the physical-support system one can afford to purchase. The nature of the physical system, in turn, may influence the type and frequency of face-to-face interaction and activities in which family members engage. Education and social class (other personal characteristics) may also influence the nature and quality of role relationships.

Descriptions of Components of the Model

Support Systems

These systems include social or personal support (networks of friends and relatives), institutional support (public and private agencies), and physical support (e.g., size, arrangement, location, quality of the physical environment, including its furnishings and equipment). These support systems, although different in content, exist in both home and office environments.

Support systems vary in intensity, or frequency of use; in density, or number of persons, settings, or agencies comprising an individual's or a family's set of support systems; in importance, or the degree to which the availability of any particular support system is required for performance of an activity per se, and at a level or in a manner considered by the participant as acceptable; in duration, or the amount of time a support system is used; and in accessibility, or the ease with which a system is used. Accessibility may be restricted by time, financial resources, distance, location (e.g., a short distance but an undesirable location or unpleasant trip quality), knowledge (e.g., appropriate facilities or services may be unused because they are unknown to an individual), and individual or group mores (e.g., "We don't need government help"). Accessibility, defined in this broad manner, is a major influence on the other dimensions on which support systems vary: intensity, density, duration, and importance.

Drawing on the concept of environmental docility developed in Chapter 2, the model suggests that, depending on the individual's intended activities and personal-competence levels relevant to that particular activity, pressures will be exerted on different types of support systems. Or, looked at from the opposite perspective, a given person engaging in a particular activity may require fewer personal competences if particular support systems are accessible. For example, a stockbroker who works at home in a situation where sufficient space is available for an isolated office, and where one's spouse is willing to act as a gatekeeper between the worker and anyone else (including children), will require fewer interpersonal skills and less complex planning and thinking about role boundaries and duties than someone who has neither sufficient space (an environmental-support system) nor an effective social gatekeeper (a personal-support system).

The availability and use of particular support systems (or their absence), in turn, have a series of consequences both for other family members, and for the organization which employs the individual. For family members, a series of support systems that is effective and functional from the perspective of one person (the worker) may be dysfunctional and disruptive for the remainder of the family. The nature of activities children are allowed to engage in, for example, may be restricted to accommodate office work in the home: more quiet, clean, and space-conserving play (e.g., reading) than messy, noisy, and space-consuming play (e.g., learning a musical instrument or setting up a model railroad).

Adaptations on the part of other family members often go unnoticed and are taken for granted. The effects on spouses who decline to accept such roles, or who refuse to allocate space within the home in a work-accommodating manner, immediately sharpen the focus on the nature of such behaviors as deliberate and created adaptations. The recent widely acclaimed movie *Kramer vs. Kramer* vividly portrays the effects on a sky-rocketing career of the removal of personal-support systems that had gone unquestioned.

The effects involve both the difficulty in doing the activities per se, the kind of direct or first-order consequences described earlier in Chapter 2, as well as the emotionally debilitating, second-order indirect effects of coping with the tension and conflict created by trying to manage family and work responsibilities. In many cases both suffer. In the movie, the organization handled Kramer's situation in what is presumed to portray a businesslike manner: the bright, talented, and highly valued art director is fired. Simple enough. The problem is that all of the energy and time that had been invested in helping develop the talent is now lost. An alternative might have been for the organization to help Kramer cope with his situation by providing additional support systems until the crisis was resolved. Organizations typically consider these family problems outside their responsibility or concern, although they are fully cognizant of their negative impact on performance.

Organizations that encourage their employees to work at home, and intrude directly into the home by providing office equipment for home use, will have to face up to the connection between the worlds of work and home in ways they have largely ignored thus far. Ironically, organizations that help may be castigated as much as those that ignore the connection. People may suspect that the help offered will invariably take the form of maximizing the organization's benefit while ignoring or minimizing the benefit for other family members. The thrust of the ecosystem framework is that such an approach cannot work.

Support systems provided to employees by organizations will have to be ones that genuinely enable individuals to accomplish the multiple goals they want to attain. The organization is going to have to become concerned with helping employees balance competing family and work interests, and it will be forced to deal with the whole family to do so effectively. One form this support will take is helping families manage and design their living spaces in a way that contributes to the development of mutually satisfying personal social-support systems, role relationships, activity patterns, and mental-health outcomes. We turn to these next.

Role Relationships

Roles define appropriate, socially legitimized patterns of behavior, and role players are often interdependent. The role of father requires the role of child, as supervisor requires the supervised. As part of interlocking systems, change in one role inevitably creates pressure for change in linked roles. The women's movement in this country, for example, has stimulated as much discussion about men's as women's roles.

The home and work settings are two of the basic settings in our society. It is within these two arenas that most of us engage in our significant role behaviors. Because the roles we play in these settings are so significant, often defining major aspects of our personal identity, pressures to change them are likely to be met with resistance unless they demonstrably improve the sense of satisfaction with these roles.

These family and work roles, however portable and personally con-trolled, have come to be highly place specific. As the earlier quote from Piotrkowski (1979) illustrated, we perform some roles much more often in some locations than others. We often find it difficult to mix roles and locations by becoming the family man at work, for instance, or the boss at home. Such role-place incongruencies often prove uncomfortable for others in the setting, and may be a source of resentment because they invariably put pressure on other persons occupying the setting to also play different roles, at least as members of a supporting cast, that they may find distasteful.

The physical separation of settings has provided a convenient cue for switching roles, and keeping what are often considered conflicting roles at bay. For the most part, the popular discourse on the consequences of telematics use in the home has stressed the opportunity the new technology will create for playing both work and family roles more fully. At least as likely a possibility, however, particularly in situations where only one member of the household is working at home, is the generation of role conflict. At a time when many women, for example, are striving to develop and separate work and family roles, encouragement to do office work at home may constrain and retard the differentiation of these roles. Losing the opportunity that place-specific roles provide for balancing competing and conflicting role expectations may generate conflict, rather then enhancing the performance of multiple roles, as most scenarios suggest will occur.

Doing work remote from the traditional office, and traditional supervisory patterns, may also be a source of organizational conflict. In the office a major basis for organizing work is the degree of interdependence among jobs and tasks. How will this be affected when the medium of interaction becomes electronic? The control of work is based largely on the structuring of discretion in role and interrole behavior (Thompson, 1967). What will happen to managerial and supervisory norms and roles that are based on face-to-face interaction and surveillance? Will conflict and stress increase? How will changes in task assignment be handled? What indicators of effective role performance will develop to replace conformity to the attendance and behavioral norms of the office (McClintock, 1979)? What changes will occur in attitudes toward work and the value of work as the physical and social-psychological partitions between office and home are removed? Changes in work-role relationships, whether intended or anticipated beforehand, are likely to be necessary under conditions of office decentralization. Remote work locations might prompt greater attention to centralized supervision and stricter attention to performance outlines, resulting in less actual or perceived decision-making latitude. Managing work-role and family-role demands might create greater perceived role demands. If office decentralization occurred abruptly, there would be little opportunity to learn new skills, resulting in a reduction in the worker's ability to meet role demands.

Role behaviors may then change as a function of their performance in new settings, for the individual performing them as well as for others also occupying the setting. These new roles, or old roles performed in new settings, may also create pressures for change in the physical setting itself. In the latter case, the pressures may be to recreate the place specificness of role performance in the new setting—to create new physical boundaries, for example, in the house that define what behaviors are acceptable for all those in the setting. Father or mother working in a specially designated place may help define the children's and spouse's appropriate roles, and serve, as did the initial physical separation of home and office, to provide visible and explicit cues for role behavior.

Whether role behaviors change, how, and with what degree of resistance and conflict, will depend on the perceived incentives for change. If performing work roles at home generates sufficient surplus income to purchase leisure-time and/or consumer goods all family members value, the tension created by the new role in the home may be tolerated, if not embraced (McLaughlin, 1980). If the rewards are perceived as benefiting family members unequally, or simply as not being sufficient to compensate for the role changes that do occur, conflict and resistance should prevail. In addition to these external incentives, and influencing both what these incentives are considered to be and their value, are persons who do not directly occupy the setting but who are socially relevant to those who do: parents, colleagues, friends. These significant others help define the situation for participants in conjunction with the individual's personal characteristics and experiences.

Personal Characteristics

Personal characteristics include such defining attributes as age, sex, marital status, stage in life cycle, life style, and income. This potentially enormous set of attributes also includes knowledge, physical and intellectual skills, values, and expectations. Obviously, these are highly interdependent (e.g., values, expectations, education, stage in life cycle). These personal factors influence the nature of support systems and role behaviors considered appropriate, as well as how the available, or potential supports, are used in practice. Identical supports may be considered useless or invaluable or simply irrelevant, depending on what the individual brings to the situation. How these different individual characteristics interact with support systems was discussed in Chapter 3.

One would expect persons who highly value traditional family roles to be more disturbed by the incursion of work roles and activities into the home than persons adopting more contemporary values. To the extent that these value systems conflict, as they often do, the opportunity for working at home may intensify existing tension. Some individuals will also be more capable, because of previous experience, education, and natural tendencies, to handle the increased ambiguity about appropriate role behaviors that work in the home generates. Income defines individual characteristics in terms of the ability to purchase supports in the form of extra space, additional telephone lines, or more storage capacity, which can be used to physically separate activities generated by different and competing roles.

Stage in life cycle, and in particular, the age and number of children present, should also greatly influence the perceived value of the opportunity to work at home. Many of the people currently using telematics equipment in their home are either single, part of a working couple without children, or persons with older children. Most of these persons are professionals highly involved in their own career, ambitious, and in an income bracket that allows them either to purchase support systems (e.g., extra rooms in an apartment or house), which enable separation of work and family activities, or be almost totally work oriented, with an active life involving children being either nonexistent or relatively unimportant.

For the most part, organizations have paid relatively little attention to these personal characteristics, especially as they are distributed throughout a family, because work was assumed to occur in a sphere largely unrelated to the whole family. Formal organizational efforts to place telematics equipment in the home may change the situation dramatically. What it will do to family life, and what implications it has for the formal organization of work, have received little attention since telematics-stimulated home-based work to dae has been on a voluntary and self-selected basis.

As organizations move toward adopting home-based work as an employment policy, and begin to ask current employees to work at home, as well as making it a condition of employment for new employees, individual characteristics, as they mediate the technology, will emerge as an important problem. Questions of work-role socialization become important: Can a first-time employee, either for a particular company, or entering the workforce for the first time, learn the organization's expectations by working at home? Will it take longer? Will special programs be needed? Is there some pattern of home/office work that is desirable for facilitating work-socialization processes for persons at different stages of their work career? Who will determine these patterns, the individual or organization? Will tolerance for ambiguity and the capability of working independently, without self-interrupting, become critical worker attributes? Will the organization need to look at the family situation, or the available environmental supports in the home before hiring a person to work at home, or will these decisions continue to be made on a volunteer basis? These questions only scratch the surface, but they begin to suggest that the consequences and value of the opportunity to work at home will depend on many factors, and a good number of them will only emerge as the phenomenon moves from a largely voluntary self-selection process to a more organizationally controlled one.

Activity Patterns

Activities concretize role performances. Not only what the home-based worker does, but what others sharing the home setting also do, will influence the value of home-based work for different individuals. Activities can be conceptualized in terms of tasks comprising a job (e.g., collecting information, organizing information, analyzing information, writing a report), or in terms of the attributes of the activity itself (e.g., is it noisy or quiet, routine or complex, clean or messy?) and in terms of the contextual attributes, both physical and social, those performing the activity consider necessary (e.g., does it require extensive equipment or space, silence, continuous feedback, others' presence for motivation?) Activities are organized in ways that describe particular patterns through decisions about sequencing, duration, regularity, and frequency. Activities also vary along performance dimensions, including the quantity and quality of the work performed. Telematics work in the home generates new activities, activity patterns, and performance levels. To be valued, these must mesh with the activities and performance levels of other occupants of the home setting.

Coordination of activities becomes a major concern: sharing of resources (e.g., a room or telephone), separating incompatible activities (noisy/quiet), scheduling (reserving a room or telephone for a particular time or day), allocating limited resources (do we buy a storage cabinet, install a second telephone, go on vacation, build an addition?). How these activities are coordinated, and what accommodations are made, and by whom, define major family and work values. As such, they are often emotionally charged decisions and a source of potential conflict. The issue of who makes such decisions, using what processes, and on what basis, becomes problematic.

These issues already exist in the home setting. The introduction of work issues simply adds another layer of complexity and increases the potential for conflict in situations which may already be only precariously balanced. Work in the home may, of course, by generating new activity patterns, also reduce conflict: A mother of young children can remain in the home, doing paid work, without having to send the children for day care; a handicapped person may find working at home reduces tension and anxiety by eliminating fatiguing and uncomfortable journeys to and from work. The question is not one of benefits versus no benefits, but of what benefits for whom, in what time frame. Even more so, the question involves the nature of appropriate supports, in the form of changing environmental-, institutional-, and personal-support systems, as well as definitions of roles and activity patterns, that define conditions that enable interdependent individuals who do not share the same work to balance competing needs, values, and rewards.

The value of defining these conditions lies in the outcomes these conditions generate. These outcomes include both mental-health states (important in their own right), work performance (e.g., quantity and quality of work), and overall organizational effectiveness (e.g., ability to attract desired personnel, maintain cost-effective absenteeism and turnover rates, training costs). Mental-health outcomes are described below since productivity and effectiveness measures have already been discussed in Chapter 5.

Mental-Health Outcomes

There are two distinct yet complementary trends in the conceptualization and measurement of mental health: One focuses on illness indicators, such as psychopathology, stress, and psychosomatic disorder; the other emphasizes conditions of health, such as self-esteem, competence, and autonomy (Hunt, Lichtman, and McClintock, 1972). Within the ecosystem framework, the primary focus is on the latter group of conditions. These are viewed as stemming from the way in which individuals evaluate the adequacy and quality of the other components in the system: physical and social supports, role relationships, and activities, including their performance level.

Individuals must balance their evaluations of these different components against each other, and against the evaluations other members of the household are making of them. High performance levels obtained at the expense of unsatisfactory family relationships, or high performance obtained by one family member at the expense of the performance of another family member, must be weighed against each other in an attempt to determine the overall value of a particular course of action. One's satisfaction with a given course of action, and motivation to continue to engage in it, stem from these evaluations. The ecosystem model expands the work on job satisfaction's relation to such behaviors as absenteeism and turnover, by suggesting that someone may be highly satisfied with a job and yet not perform at an adequate level because of family-generated pressures. Tension and dissatisfaction stem not only from the individual's assessment of the work per se, but also from the employee's assessment of how other elements in the ecosystem are influenced by the performance of the job.

To summarize the ecosystem framework, the emphasis is on the linkages between settings, notably work and home, and, within each setting, on the relationships among key components, particularly support systems, activities, role relationships, and individual characteristics, as these influence mental-health outcomes, work performance, and overall organizational effectiveness. Since all of the elements interact with each other, one conceivably could start with any particular component and look at its impact on others. Or, perhaps more usefully, one could look at the other components in terms of what their characteristics should be, to complement and support the characteristics of the focal component, considered appropriate to retain or strengthen.

Environmental-support systems are particularly important, and a useful focal point, because they are flexible and open to change in ways that role relationships or activity patterns often are not. Equally important, many persons sensitive to social and value concerns of both family and organization may be much less aware of and adept at effective designing, planning, and managing of their environmental systems. Using the ecosystem framework, several of my students have done small pilot studies exploring the issues of office work done at home. The intent was to clarify our understanding of the phenomenon as a preliminary step in moving toward an empirical basis for assessing the home-computer revolution.

PILOT STUDIES

In one study (Reichle, 1980), we focused on characteristics of the home and office settings stockbrokers considered contributing to or detracting from effective job performance. We were interested in whether some behaviors seemed to be office dependent, and resistant to decentralization because of characteristics of the work. Forty-five brief questionnaires were randomly distributed to stockbrokers at Merrill Lynch in New York City and Hartford, Connecticut. An additional 15 brokers were interviewed in the New York City office. Eighty-five percent of the respondents were male, and 75 percent were between 20 and 35 years old. Sixty percent of the brokers had no children living at home; and of those with children, the average number was two. Most of the children were either between the ages of two and five or between the ages of 14 and 20. Sixty-five percent of the brokers had been working at Merrill Lynch less than ten years.

Persons in sales were selected because productivity of sales personnel is something every industry identifies as a key to financial success. This is a highly specialized sales group, but one which was considered especially interesting for an initial foray into the effects of work decentralization since they currently use a substantial amount of electronic equipment in the office setting, and potentially are a highly appropriate group to be decentralized since what they trade in is primarily information that already is handled electronically.

These brokers' work environment already spans the conventional office and residential setting. The average number of hours worked per day at home, by persons under 40 years old, was three; for persons over 40, it was one hour per day. About 50 percent of the time spent at the office (and those under 40 stayed late an average of four days a week at the office, compared to an average of two days a week for those over 40) was spent on the telephone. Their office environment is spacious, clean, and modern and is arranged in an open plan. Information is presented visually in the form of ticker tapes around the periphery of the office, and is accessible to all working in it. Respondents indicated that they were purposely placed in the same room to share the visual information, and to share emotions and knowledge of the market. We will return below to the importance of sharing the emotions of the market.

Reichle (1980, p. 21) found a very general sentiment against working only at home. As one broker said, it would be a "crazy idea and very impractical" to work only from home, because "this type of industry requires moment-by-moment interaction with co-workers for advice and motivation. You try to work [at] home with a two and a four year old.... I have to at times!... It is extremely difficult...."

This quote suggests two very different reasons for work at home being impractical: the distraction of children and the need for relatively constant interaction with coworkers for advice and motivation. The implications of these problems/requirements for the nature of environmental-support systems are quite different, a point we will return to later.

Reichle also found that some differences between brokers were a function of their age. For new brokers, working in the office environment, surrounded by others doing the same work, was important for gaining needed knowledge. For more experienced brokers, the concern was much more social in nature. As one older broker said, "It would simply be lonely to be at home all day; . . . sure, I could function without help but why bother if I have nothing to look forward to. . . . I enjoy the walk to work; . . . the view from the 20th floor of the Merrill Lynch home office is worth coming to work for. . . . If I was in the Staten Island office I would want to stay at home and work" (Reichle, 1980, pp. 21–22).

These kinds of comments suggest that work decentralization needs to be assessed as a function of the stage in the person's career. A new employee may need to work in a conventional office setting to learn how things are done, what is the acceptable quality and quantity of work—in other words, for socialization into the work role. For an older worker, the role of work in the office may be quite different. These persons may be important as teachers for younger and less experienced workers, and benefit from the social contact and sense of change the office environment provides as compared to working at home.

It is worth noting, in this regard, that the younger employee spends more time working both in the office and at home than the older worker. For the younger worker, particularly those who were single, working late at the office was done because: "I might as well stay at work. I really have nothing special to go home for and I have all the facilities I need right here." For those with families, although staying later at the office was often considered more efficient, there was a sense that it was "worth the distractions" to see their spouse and children and then work a few more hours at home.

The adaptations to these distractions from family (rather than the notion that work detracted from family time) took several forms. Interestingly, several of the brokers felt as one person did who, when asked whether he made any adaptations in interactions with family members, said, "no adaptations. I either move to another room or stop what I am doing" (Reichle, 1980, p. 37). Typically, individuals saved their "quiet work" for home and remained separated from family members while doing it, in order to concentrate. The implication is that they sacrifice the efficiency of working late at the office for the distractions of family, and then neither work terribly efficiently nor interact very much with the family.

Most of the brokers had available environmental-support systems in the form of a desk in a room set aside for office work at night, but used for other purposes during the day. They worked alone in this room, in contrast to computer programmers who, we found in another pilot study, often carried on their work with others present and interacting. While several brokers noted that they used music as a constant background sound to mask other noises, "family-associated-function noises," such as children and TV, were distracting. Office sounds, such as voices or telephone, were considered routine and not distracting, in contrast to a baby crying.

As one would expect, there was a direct relationship between the number of children at home and the feeling that the home was a distraction. However, even for those who did not have children, the office often presented a better working environment, at least for completing the entire job function. As noted already, several brokers felt the office environment was necessary for providing stimulation and useful learning experiences, irrespective of the nature of the home setting. Fifty percent of the respondents stated emphatically that office transactions could not be carried out at home. It seems clear that the office versus home as workplace is not an either-or choice.

Every broker stated that the office environment was necessary to share ideas, trends, and knowledge. Those who felt these experiences were essential were least satisfied with the home as a work environment. In general, the primary advantage of physically working in an office, surrounded by other account executives, was the interaction: comparing information and ideas, socializing, and being aided by support services. The absence of these kinds of interactions, and the ability of the physical presence of others to spur competition and motivation, were the primary disadvantages of working at home.

The overwhelming sentiment of the respondents, in summary, was satisfaction with their present work environment and the opinion that the physical presence of coworkers was essential to their individual success and performance. Yet almost all the respondents in fact use their home as a work environment a part of the time. To do so even moderately effectively, they have devised environmental-support systems in the form of specially designated desks and rooms for their work, and social support in the form of spouses who act to control and regulate children's behavior. The responses suggest, in particular, the need to focus on different functions the office environment serves for persons at different stages of their career, and, possibly, with different motivation levels. The personal interviews made it clear that an important function of being in the office was getting motivated and maintaining one's competitive spirit. This was more difficult at home, and, from the respondent's perspective, stemmed from the absence of physically seeing others hard at work, taking orders.

Yet it is easy to imagine a home-based computer terminal in which every person's sales activity is continuously recorded for all to see, presumably acting as a motivator. Interactive systems can easily be set up so information is shared in a manner similar to what occurs in the office. The question is whether these kinds of electronic solutions will serve the same motivating function. Will they create stress by presenting others' sales activities without simultaneously facilitating social interaction that helps structure the competition in more socially interesting and stimulating ways? What about the pattern of home/office work? What is an appropriate ratio? Who decides? And then what about the effects on the family? Do children have the opportunity to learn adult roles by seeing their parents work at home? How does the physical location of work at home contribute to these learning opportunities, to social conflict among family members? Reichle's pilot study is the first in a series we are now getting underway to assess these kinds of questions. It is clear that organizations that view electronic portable terminals for use in the home or other settings, such as motels, as a nifty way of increasing work output at little cost to themselves may be creating other kinds of problems. The impact of home-based work, particularly with telematics, will also vary with the kind of work and the people who typically do it. In another aspect of our pilot work, we have begun to explore the effects of telematics work in the home on another special group, computer programmers working in a university setting.

In this study (Bowlus, 1980), a very small sample of four computer programmers—three of whom routinely work in the home using portable terminals, and a fourth who does not—were interviewed in depth about the physical- and social-support systems they use and have evolved in the home to support home-based work, as well as the role relationships and activity patterns that have developed. In particular, we were interested in where people worked at home, whether this was a specially designated space, whether physical modifications had been made to accommodate the work activity or other family activities that may have been displaced by work activities, and the cost of such modifications. With respect to social-support systems, we asked about the effect of working in the home on levels and type of interaction with friends and relatives, as well as other family members. It was as conceivable that more friends would be invited over to provide company for one spouse while the other worked, for example, as it was for less visiting to occur because it detracted from the work activity. We expected that the nature of either the social- or physical-support systems might mediate these kinds of relationships.

The data are very sketchy, of course, but some of the following kinds of issues were suggested by it. The location of work in the home, when involving electronic equipment, is often dictated by the location of the telephone. Since in most cases, the decision about the telephone's location preceded the use of a portable terminal hooked to a telephone, work often takes place in fairly public family areas, such as the kitchen, or in private areas like the bedroom, on a desk placed there for that purpose.

The presence of children creates problems when the work location is one used for joint purposes by other family members. One respondent, for example, reported working in a room adjacent to the master bedroom prior to the birth of a first child. Although this room was located so that traffic had to flow through it to get to other areas of the house from the master bedroom, the space was adequate. Now, however, the baby has been placed in this room. Initially there were no problems, as the baby slept through the noise generated by the terminal. Over a period of months, the sounds began to awaken the baby, and so the baby was moved to the guest room. This was not terribly satisfactory for his wife, so a decision is pending about moving to the basement. Since the basement is unfinished, this would require some modification to make it comfortable, as well as the installation of another telephone. The potential costs of such a move include isolation from family and the family response to this isolation, as well as building and telephone expenses.

The need for appropriate environmental supports that allow separation of work and family life was suggested by another respondent who commented about a desk in the master bedroom that served as the "home office." Computer work generates and requires a large number of printouts. Storage is crucial and typically requires much more space than is needed for the equipment itself. This respondent indicated a strong preference for a separate workspace as a means of coping with his wife's dislike of the ever-present "mess" created by inadequate storage. Another problem was that his typical pattern of working late at night interfered with his wife, who was trying to sleep in the same room. The respondent felt that he placed chores and family plans ahead of work, as indicated by his working after others were asleep.

These kinds of adaptations may be tolerable to the worker but annoying or intolerable to other family members. Homemakers are often concerned about controlling "messiness" (Becker 1974), for example, because they associate it directly with their own competence as a homemaker. They are concerned about the image they project to friends and relatives. In this case, a particular coping strategy affects other family members' behavior in ways that directly contribute to stress—they had less sleep and greater fatigue, as well as more work (to control the mess).

In relation to family-activity patterns, a distinct advantage of the portable terminal is that it allows one to work at home and help with child care while one's spouse runs errands or meets appointments. In part, this is the case because the kind of work done at home is more routine and less inspirational. Respondents did not need quiet and interruptions were not disruptive since they had to wait for information to appear between inputs, in any case. It was possible to relax and talk with the wife while working, but more difficult to do so with children, presumably because children had a more difficult time accommodating their interaction to the rhythms of the machine. One of the respondents also talked about the benefit of working at home in terms of the opportunity it provided for a child to understand what the parents do at work.

The mixed blessings of working at home (for those who work at home and have others adapt largely to their needs, the opportunity to work at home is almost entirely positive, particularly when one's hobby is work) also extend to relationships and behaviors in the office. Unlike the case with the stockbrokers, where the physical presence of others is considered an important motivator and where self-interruption at home is often an issue, computer programmers are typically computer freaks or jockeys. Their greatest difficulty is doing something besides work. Conflict among coworkers may occur when this value system is not shared, regardless of where work is done, because one will always feel at a competitive disadvantage with those who work all the time, and feel guilty about and torn between career aspirations, family responsibilities, and personal hobbies. The availability of home terminals may exacerbate this kind of tension by implicitly suggesting that work should be done at home (over and above that done during the normal working day) and that one who does not work at home is not sufficiently dedicated.

The evidence for this kind of situation, and for the kinds of tensions one would expect to build up both at home and with coworkers in the office is almost entirely speculative, based on our pilot data. It is worth noting as an issue for continued exploration. When everyone works in the same office, one's sense of how much others work is based on a rough visual assessing of their presence or absence and activity patterns. The opportunity to work at home creates a situation in which one may be less sure about how much coworkers are working. Ambiguity is increased, and it may be unpleasant. If the impression is that coworkers always work, the potential for tension and hostility may be exacerbated between employees who have a spouse and/or children, compared with those who do not. Conversely, the opportunity to work at home on a portable terminal may relieve tension by allowing the family person to put in a similar number of hours compared to the single person, without remaining out of the house for all but sleep.

As with the stockbrokers, social contact and face-to-face communication were considered important reasons for continuing to work in the office. In part, this was because some information was poorly communicated electronically, both in terms of time taken and subtlety of meaning. It is likely that other benefits from working in the office include making contacts, or developing an understanding of the politics of a situation that may enable one to more effectively implement ideas.

In a third pilot study in this series, looking at the effects of paid work in residential settings, McLaughlin (1980) assessed the nature of social- and enviornmental-support systems used by persons working for pay at home, and some of the kinds of role relationships and activity patterns that evolved in response to the use of the home as a work setting. McLaughlin focused on a group of Tupperware dealers who sell plastic kitchen products.

Sales is common part-time work in general, and in 1978 there were 76,000 Tupperware dealers in the United States. Almost all of these dealers are women, and in 1978 they combined to sell approximately $584 million worth of products (Anreder, 1978, cited by McLaughlin [1980]). These dealers do not currently use computers per se, but they make extensive use of telephones and calculators and are a potential market for telematics applications. The bulky nature of the products also places increased pressures on environmental-support systems, and thus helps focus on their contribution to the effects of paid work in the home on family members. Tupperware dealers provide a useful comparison to the better-educated, male-dominated groups working at home who were the focus of the other pilot studies.

McLaughlin's sample consisted of 11 families in which the wife/mother was engaged in direct home sales. Eight of the women were between 25 and 35, two were over 35, and one was under 25. The respondents' children varied in age, but most were either preschoolers or of school age. Four persons had a high school education, and the remainder either had done some college work, or had a college degree, including two persons who had completed some graduate study.

Six of the women estimated that they spent less than 20 hours per week working, with the remainder estimating they spent more than 20 hours per week working. This estimate includes work at home, such as taking orders, packing the products, and doing bookkeeping, as well as work outside the home, including parties (the primary selling situation) which the dealer arranges at someone else's house. Friends of the person giving the party come to the hostess's home and chat, look at samples of kitchen products, and place their orders for those they want. Each party takes a minimum of two hours, and the company mandates a minimum number of parties for each month. In the seven days prior to responding to the questionnaire, the 11 respondents gave an average of slightly more than two parties each.

For all of the women in McLaughlin's study, the prime benefit of their job was the flexibility it gave them to maintain a high level of involvement in their roles as family homemaker and mother. Not having to leave their children with a babysitter was a prime advantage. A second major advantage was the time and flexibility their job gave them to keep up with household tasks. With the exception of one family, the predominant pattern was for the wife/mother to perform household chores herself. For these women, then, taking on a part-time job simply added to their existing workload as homemaker and mother. Other family members were more likely to help out with the paid-work than with common-household and child-rearing tasks. Of the paid-work tasks, six respondents reported that family members often helped out by taking telephone messages, and the same number indicated that family members occasionally helped make deliveries.

The minimal help these women received from family members on common-household and child-rearing tasks, and the greater, but still small, involvement in aspects of the job itself, may account, at least in part, for the high turnover among Tupperware dealers. Only two of the 11 women had worked at the job for more than two years, and seven had worked at it for less than one year. Whether it is aspects of support systems that contribute to this high turnover, or aspects of the job or nature of the organization, cannot be determined from McLaughlin's data.

Although all the respondents valued the flexibility their jobs permitted in maintaining a high level of involvement with their families, McLaughlin found that only three of her families reported spending more time together. Three reported spending about the same time together, and five said they spent less time together since beginning their work. The reasons for spending less time together appear to be related to the nature of the job itself. The job requires frequent packing of products, keeping track of individual orders, and arranging and attending parties at other people's homes. While two mothers indicated that they schedule their work activities around their children's schedules and interests, several others indicated that they expected their children to entertain themselves elsewhere while they were working. Children were often left with husbands or babysitters during visits to other homes.

The work entered into the life of the family in additional ways. Use of the home as a work setting for this type of sales work led to customers' occasional visits to the home on business. Several people reported feeling they must keep their home particularly clean and orderly in case a customer drops in. Several persons reported feeling embarrassed and tense when people drop in and the house is a "wreck." To control for such eventualities, children were required to maintain their rooms at a level considered appropriate for critical visitors rather than at a level the parents themselves considered appropriate, and in one case a dishwasher was bought primarily as a device for hiding dirty dishes from unexpected visitors.

These kinds of adaptations to the home as a work setting are not extreme in themselves, but taken together they contribute to a climate that transforms the more relaxed backstage behavior associated with the privacy of the home setting into the more regulated behavior associated with the traditional workplace. While the potential for children learning adult roles and accepting responsibility for contributing to the family's overall economic resources may be enhanced, at the same time, children may find the quality of interaction with their parents more formalized and tense and the nature of the activities they are allowed to engage in at home restricted. For example, several respondents reported leaving family outings early or missing them entirely when they conflict with their work activities.

Few of the respondents were able to physically separate their work and family activities. Work activities, such as packing, were done on the kitchen table, the kitchen floor, living-room rug, family-room table, and family-room floor. The telephone was a major tool for these workers. It was used where it had been placed for non-work-life patterns, often in the kitchen. The need for storage of order forms and other notes, as well as interruptions from family members engaging in nonwork activities in the same room as the telephone, were sources of irritation.

The lack of specially designated workspace may have implications for motivation and productivity as well. Several women reported liking the absence of a supervisor looking over their shoulder, but they were concerned about a lack of motivation and self-interruption. Three of the women talked about feeling disorganized and unprofessional because makeshift and inadequate storage made it difficult to find things. It may be that the lack of a specific space reserved for work contributes to a conception of the job as temporary and makeshift, undermining a sense of commitment to the job on the part of both the worker and the spouse.

Several women mentioned the positive contribution of the environment to their motivation, but in ways entirely unrelated to task efficiency. Prizes for sales competitions took the form of household objects, furniture, and appliances, including color televisions, bedroom sets, and swings. Family members, including children, generally knew what their mother or spouse could win by meeting certain sales competitions. They urged her to meet these goals in order to win prizes they wanted. The environment of the home serves as a constant reminder of the benefits of hard work, and creates expectations for all family members about the mother's work performance.

The findings from these pilot studies identify the beginning of a journey rather than an arrival at some clearly focused destination. The findings suggest several issues which need to be addressed further:

- How do adaptations to the world of work, when located in the home, affect the work itself, family members, and the relations between work and family? Success at work may trigger family conflict and tension that leads to abandonment of the job itself, or to a reduced commitment to it.
- Does the nature of ther environmental-support systems, including storage and specifically defined work spaces, contribute to levels of motivation and commitment as well as to effective performance in terms of task efficiency.
- If environmental-support systems, in the form of telephone lines, micro-computers, storage facilities are important to work, as they are recognized to be in the office and as our data indicate they are in the home, does the organization's responsibility for providing necessary support services extend to providing such supports in the home. Does the organization have a responsibility to help the home-based worker manage these facilities, so they work effectively, and can this be done without becoming involved in

family living patterns in ways that violate some of the formal separation between work and the home that we generally take for granted?

The question is not whether work at home, with or without telematics, has benefits. It certainly does. The meaningful question is who benefits, how, and at what costs to whom.

BIBLIOGRAPHY

Adams, R. Location as a feature of instructional interaction. *Merrill Palmer Quarterly*, 1969, *15*, 4, 309–322.

Aldous, J. Occupational characteristics and male's role performance in the family. *Journal of Marriage and the Family*, 1969, *31*, 707–712.

Aldrich, H. *Organizations and Environments*. Englewood Cliffs, N.J.: Prentice-Hall, 1979.

Altman, I. *The Environment and Social Behavior*. Monterey, Calif.: Brooks/Cole, 1975.

Altman, I. Personal communication, September, 1976.

Anifant, D.C. Risk-taking behavior in children experiencing open space and traditional school environments. Unpublished Ph.D. dissertation, University of Maryland, 1972. (*Dissertation Abstracts International*, 1972, 33, 2491A).

Armstrong, D.G. Open space vs. self-contained. *Educational Leadership*, 1975, *32*, 291–295.

Ashby, W.R. Self-regulation and requisite variety. In W.R. Ashby (ed.), *Introduction to Cybernetics*. New York: Wiley, 1956.

Ashworth, S. *The relationships between images of self and home*. Unpublished master's thesis, Cornell University, Ithaca, N.Y. 1979

Babchuck, N., and Goode, W.J. Work incentives in a self-determined group. *American Social Review*, 1951, *16*, 679–687.

Barker, R. *Ecological Psychology*. Palo Alto, Calif.: Stanford University Press, 1968.

Barker, R.G., and Gump, P.V. *Big School, Small School*. Stanford, Calif.: Stanford University Press, 1964.

Barnlund, D., and Harland, C. Propinquity and prestige as determinants of communication networks. *Sociometry*, 1963, *26*, 467–479.

Bass, B.M., and Klubeck, S. Effects of seating arrangement on leaderless group discussions. *Journal of Abnormal Psychology*, 1952, *47*, 724–727.

Bauer, R. *Second-order Consequences*. Cambridge, Mass.: MIT Press, 1966.

Baum, A., and Valins, S. *Architecture and Social Behavior: Psychological Studies of Social Density.* New York: Lawrence Erlbaum Associates, 1979.

Beck, W. Human factors in the health care environment. Paper presented to Department of Design and Environmental Analysis, College of Human Ecology, Cornell University, Ithaca, N.Y., October 1979.

Becker, F.D., Sommer, R., Bee, J., and Oxley, B. College classroom ecology. *Sociometry*, 1973, *36*, 4, 514–525.

Becker, F.D. *Design For Living: The Residents' View of Multifamily Housing.* Ithaca, N.Y.: Center for Urban Development Research, Cornell University, 1974.

Becker, F.D. *Housing Messages.* Stroudsburg, Pa.: Dowden, Hutchinson, and Ross, 1977.

Becker, F.D. Building by design, *Human Ecology Forum*, 1978, *9*, 2, 3–7.

Becker, F.D., Ashworth, S., Poe, D., and Beaver, D. *User Participation, Personalization, and Environmental Meaning.* Ithaca, N.Y.: Program in Urban and Regional Studies, Cornell University, 1978.

Bell, A.E., Switzer, F., and Zipursky, M.A. Open area education: An advantage or disadvantage for beginners? *Perceptual and Motor Skills*, 1974, *39*, 1, 407–416.

Bergermaier, R., Sundstrom, E., and Berg, I. Environmental and biographical factors in the intention to turnover. Talk given at American Psychological Association Annual Convention, Montreal, September 1980.

Berkowitz, L. Group norms among bomber crews: patterns of perceived crew attitudes, actual crew attitude, and crew liking related to air crew effectiveness in Far East combat. *Sociometry*, 1956, *19*, 141–153.

Blauner, R. *Alienation and Freedom.* Chicago: University of Chicago Press, 1964.

Boutourline, S. The concept of environmental space management. In H. Proshansky, W. Ittelson, and L. Rivlin (eds.), *Environmental Psychology.* New York: Holt, Rinehart and Winston, 1970.

Bowlus, L. A preliminary study of the physical and social support systems and role relationships in families operating in-home computers. Unpublished manuscript, Cornell University, 1980.

Boyce, P.R. User's assessments of a landscaped office. *Journal of Architectural Research,* 1974, *3*, 44–62.

Braverman, H. *Labor and Monopoly Capital: The Degradation of Work in the Twentieth Century*. New York: Monthly Review Press, 1974.

Brill, M. Evaluating buildings on a performance basis. In J. Lang, C. Burnette, W. Moleski, and D. Vachon (eds.), *Designing for Human Behavior: Architecture and the Behavioral Sciences*. Stroudsburg, Pa.: Dowden, Hutchinson, and Ross, 1974.

Brookes, M.J., and Kaplan, A. The office environment: space planning and effective behavior. *Human Factors*, 1972, *14*, 5, 373–391.

Brunetti, F.A. Noise, distraction and privacy in conventional and open school environments. *Proceedings of the EDRA Conference*. Los Angeles: University of California, 1972.

Burleigh, K. The computer and the facility manager. Presentation at Herman Miller Facility Management Institute, Ann Arbor, Mich., May 22, 1980.

Bush-Brown, L. *Garden Blocks for Urban America*. New York: Charles Scribner's and Sons, 1969.

Byrne, D. Attitudes and attraction. In L. Berkowitz (ed.), *Advances in Experimental Social Psychology*, vol, 4. New York: Academic Press, 1969.

Canty, D. Evaluation of an open office landscape: Weyerhaeuser Co. *American Institute of Architects Journal*, 1977, *66*, 40–45.

Chapman, L., and Campbell, D. An attempt to predict the performance of three-man teams from attitude measurements. *Journal of Social Psychology*, 1957, *46*, 277–286.

Chu, C.C. The wetting properties of textile fibers. Talk given at Cornell University, Ithaca, May 9, 1980.

Clearwater, Y. Comparison of effects of open and closed office design on job satisfaction and productivity. Unpublished Ph.D. dissertation, University of California, Davis, 1980.

Cohen, E.G. Open-space schools: The opportunity to become ambitious. *Sociology of Education*, 1973, *46*, 1–8.

Coniglio, C. The meaning of personalization and freedom of choice within residential interiors. Unpublished Master's Thesis, Cornell University, Ithaca, 1974.

Contract 1980a. Astounding technology portends erratic office changes in the '80's. *Contract*, January 1980, 127–138.

Contract 1980b. 10,000-office-worker study measures job satisfaction and productivity. *Contract*, January 1980, 139–143.

Cooper, C. Adventure playgrounds. In G. Coates (ed.), *Alternative Learning Environments*. Stroudsburg, Pa.: Dowden, Hutchinson, and Ross, 1974.

Cooper, H. Life in a space station: I. *New Yorker*, August 30, 1976, pp. 34–66.

Cooper, R., and Foster, M. Sociotechnical systems. *American Psychologist*, 1971, *26*, 5, 467–474.

Cooper, C.L., and Payne, R. *Stress at Work*. New York: John Wiley and Sons, 1978.

Crookston, B. Milieu management. *National Association of Student Personnel Administrators Journal*, 1975, *13*, 1, 45–55.

Davitz, J., and Davitz, L. The communication of feelings by content-free speech. In S. Wertz (ed.), *Nonverbal Communication*. New York: Oxford University Press, 1974.

Dean, A.O. Evaluation of an open office landscape: AIA headquarters. *American Institute of Architects Journal*, 1977, *66*, 8, 32–39.

Dordick, H.S., Bradley, H.G., Nanus, B., and Martin, T.H. *The Emerging Network Marketplace*. Center for Future Research, University of Southern California, Los Angeles, 1978.

Dubin, R. Work in modern society. In R. Dubin (ed.), *Handbook of Work, Organization, and Society*. Chicago: Rand McNally, 1976.

Duffy, F., Cave, C., and Wothington, J. (eds.). *Planning Office Space*. London: Architectural Press, 1976.

Dunnette, M. (ed.). *Handbook of Industrial and Organizational Psychology*. Chicago: Rand McNally, 1976.

Dutton, W., Danziger, J., and Kramer, K. Did the policy fail? The selective use of automated information in the policy making process. Policy Research Organization and School of Social Sciences, University of California, Irvine, 1978.

Edelman, M. *Politics as Symbolic Action: Mass Arousal and Quiescence*. Chicago: Markham, 1971.

Eigenbrod, F. The effects of territory and personality compatibility on identity and security. Unpublished Ph.D. dissertation, University of Michigan, Ann Arbor, 1969.

Ellison, M., Gilbert, L.L., and Ratsoy, E.W. Teacher behavior in open-area classrooms. *The Canadian Administrator*, 1969, *8*, 5, 17–21.

Freedman, J.L., Klevansky, S., and Ehrlich, P. The effects of crowding on human task performance. *Journal of Applied Social Psychology*, 1971, *1*, 7–25.

Freidson, E. (ed.). *The professions and their prospects*. Beverly Hills, Calif.: Sage Publications, 1973.

Friedman, L. *Government and Slum Housing: A Century of Frustration*. Chicago: Rand McNally and Co., 1968.

Gans, H. *People and Plans*. New York: Basic Books, 1972.

George, P.S. Ten years of open space schools: A review of the research. Gainesville: Florida Educational Research and Development Council, University of Florida, 1975.

Gibson, J.J. *The Perception of the Visual World.* Boston: Houghton Mifflin, 1950.

Glass, D., and Singer, J. *Urban Stress: Experiments on Noise and Social Stressors*. New York: Academic Press, 1972.

Goffman, I. *The Presentation of Self in Everyday Life*. New York: Anchor/ Doubleday, 1961.

Gomez, T. The relationship between the organizational goals and the physical design of a multi-service center. Unpublished master's thesis, Cornell University, Ithaca, 1979.

Gostinian, L. An investigation of the effects of word processing. Unpublished manuscript, Department of Design and Environmental Analysis, Cornell University, Ithaca, 1980.

Grapko, M.F. A comparison of open space and traditional classroom structures according to independence measures in children, teachers' awareness of children's personality variables, and children's academic progress. Final report. Toronto: Ontario Department of Education, 1972 (ERIC Document Reproduction Service, No. ED088 180).

Greenberg, C. Toward an integration of ecological psychology and industrial psychology: undermanning theory, organizational size, and job enrichment. *Environmental Psychology and Nonverbal Behavior*, 1979, *3*, 4, 228–242.

Griffitt, W. Environmental effects on interpersonal affective behavior: ambient-effective temperature and attraction. *Journal of Personality and Social Psychology*, 1970, *15*, 3, 240–244.

Griffitt, W. and Veitch, R. Hot and crowded: influences of population density and temperature on interpersonal affective behavior. *Journal of Personality and Social Psychology*, 1971, *17*, 92–98.

Guest, R. Quality of worklife: learning from Tarrytown. *Harvard Business Review*, 1979 (July-August), 76–87.

Gullahorn, J.T. Distance and friendship as factors in the gross interaction matrix. *Sociometry*, 1952, *15*, 123–134.

Hackman, J.R., and Lawler, E. Employer reactions to job characteristics. *Journal of Applied Psychology*, 1971, 55, 259–286.

Hall, E.T. *The Hidden Dimension*. New York: Doubleday, 1966.

Hare, P., and Bales, R. Seating position and small-group interaction. *Sociometry*, 1963, *20*, 480–486.

Harris, L. The open plan is scrutinized in a pioneering survey on offices. *Architectural Record*, January 1979, 141–144.

Hearn, G. Leadership and the spatial factor in small groups. *Journal of Abnormal and Social Psychology*, 1957, *54*, 269–272.

Herzberg, F. *Work and the Nature of Man*. Cleveland: World, 1966.

Homans, G. *The Human Group*. New York: Harcourt Brace and World, 1950.

Horowitz, P., and Otto, D. The teaching effectiveness of an alternative teaching facility. Alberta, Canada: University of Alberta, 1973 (ERIC Document Reproduction Service, No. ED 083 242).

Howells, L. and Becker, S. Seating arrangements and leadership emergence. *Journal of Abnormal and Social Psychology*, 1962, *64*, 148–150.

Hundert, A.T. and Greenfield, N. Physical space and organizational behavior: a study of an office landscape. Talk given at American Psychological Association, Washington, D.C., September 1969.

Hunt, R.G., Lichtman, C.M., and McClintock, C.C. Psycho-social aspects of health in the work organization. *Journal Supplement Abstract Service*, 1972, *2*, 84.

Hutt, C., and Vaizey, J. Differential effects of group density on social behavior. *Nature*, 1966, *209*, 1371–1372.

Indik, B. Organization size and member participation. *Human Relations*, 1965, *18*, 339–350.

Ittelson, W., Rivlin, L., and Proshansky, H. The use of behavioral maps in environmental psychology. In H. Proshansky, W. Ittelson, and L. Rivlin (eds.), *Environmental Psychology*. New York: Holt, Rinehart and Winston, 1970.

Ives, R., and Ferdinands, R. Working in a landscape office. *Personnel Practice Bulletin*, 1974, *30*, 126–141.

Johansen, R., Vallee, J., and Spangler, K. Electronic meetings: Utopian dreams and complex realities. *Futurist*, 1978, *XII*, 5, 313–320.

Justa, F.C., and Golan, M.B. Office design: Is privacy still a problem? *Journal of Architectural Research*, 1977, *6*, 2, 5–12.

Kaiser, L. The eco-system model: designing organizational environments. Paper presented at Annual Meeting of the Society of General Systems Research, New York, January 1975.

Kanter, R.M. *Work and Family in the United States: A Critical Review and Agenda for Research and Policy*. New York: Russell Sage, 1977.

Kaplan, A. Human needs in the work environment. *Modern Office Procedures*, Sept. 1977, 132–133.

Katzell, R., Bienstock, P., and Faerstein, P. *A Guide to Worker Productivity Experiments in the United States, 1971–1975*. New York: New York University Press, 1977.

Koffka, K. *Principles of Gestalt Psychology*. New York: Harcourt Brace, 1935.

Kohn, M.L., and Schooler, C. Occupational experience and psychological functions: an assessment of reciprocal effects. *American Sociological Review*, 1973, *38*, 97–118.

Koneya, M. Location and interaction in row and column seating arrangements. *Environment and Behavior*, 1976, *8*, 2, 265–282.

Krantz, P., and Risley, T. The organization of group care environments: behavioral ecology in the classroom. Lawrence: Kansas University, 1972 (ERIC Document Reproduction Service, No. ED 078 915).

Kuhn, T. *The Structure of Scientific Revolutions*. Chicago: University of Chicago Press, 1962.

Kuriloff, A. *Reality in Management*. New York: McGraw-Hill, 1966.

Landau, J. Clerical workers in three different office settings. Unpublished manuscript. Department of Design and Environmental Analysis, Cornell University, Ithaca, May 1980.

Lawler, E. Job design and employee motivation. *Personnel Psychology*, 1969, *22*, 426–435.

Lawler, E. *Motivation in Work Organizations*. Monterey, Calif.: Brooks/Cole, 1973.

Lawler, E., and Porter, L. The effect of performance on job satisfaction. *Industrial Relations*, 1967, *7*, 20–28.

Liebow, E. Work and mental health. Washington, D.C.: National Advisory Mental Health Council, National Institute of Mental Health, 1976.

Lipman, A., Cooper, I., Harris, R., and Tranter, R. Power, a neglected concept in office design. *Journal of Architectural Research*, 1978, *6*, 3, 28–37.

Loo, C. The effects of spatial density on the social behavior of children. *Journal of Applied Social Psychology*, 1972, *2*, 4, 372–381.

Loo, C. Important issues in researching the effects of crowding on humans. *Representative Research in Social Psychology*, 1973, *4*, 1, 219–226.

Lynch, K. *Image of the City*. Cambridge, Mass.: MIT Press, 1960.

Lynch, K. *What Time is this Place?* Cambridge, Mass.: MIT Press, 1972.

Machlowitz, M. *Workaholics: How to Live with Them, How to Work With Them.* Reading, Mass.: Addison-Wesley, 1980.

Manning, P. Office design: a study of environment. In H. Proshansky, W. Ittelson, and L. Rivlin (eds.), *Environmental Psychology*. New York: Holt, Rinehart and Winston, 1970.

Marien, M. Toward a devolution of services. *Social Policy*, November/December 1978, 26–35.

Maslow, A., and Mintz, M. Effects of aesthetic surroundings: I. Initial effects of three aesthetic conditions uppon perceiving "energy" and "well-being" in faces. *Journal of Psychology*, 1956, *41*, 247–254.

McClintock, C.C. Patterns of uncertainty and organizational learning. Unpublished manuscript, Department of Human Service Studies, Cornell University, Ithaca, 1979.

McCormick, E.J. *Human Factors in Engineering and Design*. New York: McGraw-Hill, 1976.

McLaughlin, M. Some effects of increased spatial density on family interaction and activities. Unpublished manuscript, Cornell University, Ithaca, 1978.

McLaughlin, M. Home as work place: a study of Tupperware dealers. Unpublished manuscript, Cornell University, Ithaca, 1980.

Meyer, J. The impact of the open space school upon teacher influence and autonomy: the effects of an organizational innovation. Stanford University, 1971 (ERIC Document Reproduction Service, No. ED 062 291).

Michelson, W. *Man and His Urban Environment*. Reading, Mass.: Addison-Wesley, 1970.

Milmoe, S., Novey, M., Kagan, J., and Rosenthal, R. The mother's voice: postdictor of aspects in her baby's behavior. In S. Wertz (ed.), *Nonverbal Communication*. New York: Oxford University Press, 1974.

Mintz, H. Effects of aesthetic surroundings: II. Prolonged and repeated experience in a "beautiful" and an "ugly" room. *Journal of Psychology*, 1956, *41*, 459–466.

Myers, R.E. A comparison of the perceptions of elementary school children in open area and self-contained classrooms in British Columbia. *Journal of Research and Development in Teaching*, 1971, *9*, 100–106.

Nahemow, L., and Lawton, P. Toward an ecological theory of adaptation and aging. In H. Proshansky, W. Ittelson, and L. Rivlin (eds.), *Environmental Psychology: People and their Physical Settings*. New York: Holt, Rinehart and Winston, 1976.

Neff, W.A. *Work and Human Behavior*. New York: Atherton, 1968.

Nelkin, D. (ed.). *Controversy: Politics of Technical Decisions*. Beverly Hills, Calif.: Sage Publications, 1979.

New York Times. Office 80's. Special Advertising Supplement, October 28, 1979.

Oldham, G., and Brass, D. Employee reaction to an open-plan office: a naturally occurring quasi-experiment. *Administrative Science Quarterly*, 1979, *24*, 267–284.

Perin, C. *With Man in Mind: An Interdisciplinary Prospectus for Environmental Design*. Cambridge, Mass.: MIT Press, 1970.

Perry, J. *The Story of Standards*. New York: Funk and Wagnalls, 1955.

Pfeffer, J. Management as symbolic action: the creation and maintenance of organizational paradigms. In L. Cummings and B. Staw (eds.), *Research in Organizational Behavior*, vol. 3. Greenwich, Conn.: JAI Press, 1980.

Pile, J. *Open Office Planning*. New York: Whitney Library of Design, 1978.

Piotrkowski, C.S. *Work and the Family System: A Naturalistic Study of Working Class and Lower-Middle-Class Families*. New York: Free Press, 1979.

Porter, T.B. Human and organizational factors in the office of tomorrow. Paper presented at Annual Meeting of American Psychological Association, Montreal, September 1980.

Porter, L., and Lawler, E. Properties of organization structure in relation to job attitudes and job behavior. *Psychological Bulletin*, 1965, *64*, 1, 23–51.

Porter, L., Lawler E., and Hackman, J. *Behavior in Organizations*. New York: McGraw-Hill, 1975.

Porter, L., and Steers, R. Organizational, work, and personal factors in employee turnover and absenteeism. *Psychological Bulletin*, 1973, *80*, 151–176.

Preiser, W. (ed.). *Facility Programming*. Stroudsburg, Pa.: Dowden, Hutchinson, and Ross, 1978.

Prescott, E., Jones, E., and Kritchevsky, S. Group day care as a child rearing environment: An observational study of day care programs. Pasadena, Calif.: Pacific Oaks College, 1967 (ERIC Document Reproduction Service, No. ED 024 453).

Propst, R. *Action Office: The System That Works For You*. Ann Arbor, Michigan, Herman Miller Research Corp., 1978.

Proshansky, H., Ittelson, W., and Rivlin, L. The influence of the physical environment on behavior: some basic assumptions. In H. Proshansky, W. Ittelson, and L. Rivlin (eds.), *Environmental Psychology*. New York: Holt, Rinehart and Winston, 1970.

Pye, R., and Williams, E. Teleconferencing: Is video valuable or is audio adequate? *Telecommunications Policy*, 1977, 230–241.

Rapoport, A. Symbolism and environmental design. *International Journal of Symbology*, 1970, *1*, 1–9.

Rapoport, R., and Rapoport, R. *Dual-Career Families*. Baltimore: Penguin, 1971.

Reichle, J. The effect of technology on the possible decentralization of the office environment: home vs. office. Unpublished manuscript, Department of Design and Environmental Analysis, Cornell University, Ithaca, 1980.

Reiss, W., and Dydhalo, N. Persistence, achievement, and open space environments. *Journal of Educational Psychology*, 1975, *67*, 506–513.

Riland, L.H., and Falk, J.Z. Employee reactions to office landscaping environment. Unpublished manuscript, Psychological Research and Services, Personnel Relations Department, Eastman Kodak Company, 1971.

Rist, R. Student social class and teacher expectations: the self-fulfilling prophecy in ghetto education. *Harvard Educational Review*, 1970, *40*, 411–451.

Robichaud, B. *Selecting, Planning, and Managing Office Space*. New York: McGraw-Hill, 1958.

Roethlisberger, J., and Dickson, W. *Management and the Worker*. Cambridge, Mass.: Harvard University Press, 1939.

Rohe, W., and Patterson, A.H. The effects of varied levels of resources and density on behavior in a day care center. In R.C. Moore (ed.), *Man-Environment Interactions: Evaluations and Applications, Volume 12: Childhood City*. Washington, D.C.: Environmental Design Research Association, 1974.

Ruesch, J., and Kees, W., *Nonverbal Communication*. Berkeley, Calif.: University of California Press, 1964.

Salancik, G., and Pfeffer, J. A social information processing approach to job attitudes and task design. *Administrative Science Quarterly*, 1978, *23*, 224–253.

San Francisco Chronicle, May 7, 1979, p. 10.

Sanoff, H. *Methods of Architectural Programming*. Stroudsburg, Pa.: Dowden, Hutchinson, and Ross, 1977.

Saroson, S.B., Carrol, C., Maton, K., Cohen, S., and Lorentz, E. *Human Services and Resource Networks*. San Francisco: Jossey-Bass, 1977.

Sauser, W., Arauz, C., and Chambers, R. Exploring the relationship between level of office noise and salary recommendations: a preliminary research note. *Journal of Management*, 1978, *4*, 1, 57–63.

Schlitt, M. Facility management in practice. Presentation at Herman Miller Facility Management Institute, Ann Arbor, Mich., May 1980.

Schopler, J., and Stockdale, J. An interference analysis of crowding. *Environmental Psychology and Nonverbal Behavior*, 1977, *1*, 2, 81–88.

Schwebel, A., and Cherlin, D. Physical and social distancing in teacher-pupil relationships. *Journal of Educational Psychology*, 1972, *63*, 543–550.

Shapiro, S. Preschool ecology: a study of three environmental variables. *Reading Improvement*, 1975, *12*, 4, 236–241.

Sharp, L. Steel axes for stone age Australians. In E. Spicer (ed.), *Human Problems in Technological Change*. New York: Russell Sage, 1952.

Sherrod, D. Crowding, perceived control, and behavioral aftereffects. *Journal of Applied Social Psychology*, 1974, *4*, 2, 171–186.

Silverstein, M., and Jacobson, M. Restructuring the hidden program: toward an architecture of social change. In W. Preiser (ed.), *Facility Programming*. Stroudsburg, Pa.: Dowden, Hutchinson, and Ross, 1978.

Sloan, S. Translating psycho-social criteria into design determinants. In W. Mitchell (ed.), *Proceedings of Environmental Design Research Association*. Los Angeles, U.C.L.A., 1972.

Sommer, R. *Design Awareness*. San Francisco: Rinehart Press, 1972.

Sommer, R. Further studies in small group ecology. *Sociometry*, 1965, *28*, 4, 337–348.

Sommer, R. Hawthorne dogma. *Psychological Bulletin*, 1968, *70*, 592–598.

Sommer, R. Leadership and group geography. *Sociometry*, 1961, *24*, 1, 99–110.

Sommer, R. Participatory design. *Herman Miller Research Ideas*, 1979, *3*, 4, 4–5.

Sommer, R. *Personal Space: The Behavioral Basis of Design*. Englewood Cliffs, N.J.: Prentice-Hall, 1969.

Sommer, R. Classroom ecology. *Journal of Applied Behavioral Science*, 1967a, *3*, 489–503.

Sommer, R. Small group ecology. *Psychological Bulletin*, 1967b, *67*, 2, 145–152.

Sommer, R. *Tight Spaces: Hard Architecture and How to Humanize It*. Englewood Cliffs, N.J.: Prentice-Hall, 1974.

Spaulding, W. Undiscovered values in meetings. *Journal of Systems Management*, 1978, *29*, 6, 24–27.

Spivak, M. The political collapse of a playground. In G. Coates (ed.), *Alternative Learning Environments*. Stroudsburg, Pa.: Dowden, Hutchinson, and Ross, 1974.

Stanford University Proceedings of International Symposium on Office Automation, Palo Alto, California, March 26–28, 1980.

Starbuck, W. Organizations and their environments. In M. Dunnette (ed.), *Handbook of Industrial and Organizational Psychology*. Chicago: Rand McNally, 1976.

Steele, F. *Physical Settings and Organizational Development*. Reading, Mass.: Addison-Wesley, 1973.

Steers, S. When is an organization effective? *Organizational Dynamics*, 1976, 5, 2, 50–63.

Steinzor, B. The spatial factor in face-to-face discussion groups. *Journal of Abnormal and Social Psychology*, 1950, 45, 552–555.

Stokols, D., Rall, M., Pinner, B., and Schopler, J. Physical, social, and personal determinants of the perception of crowding. *Environment and Behavior*, 1973, 5, 1, 87–116.

Stokols, D., and Shumaker, S. People in places: a transactional view of settings. In T. Harvey (ed.), *Cognition, Social Behavior, and the Environment*. Hillsdale, N.J.: Lawrence Erlbaum, 1980.

Strodbeck, F.L., and Hook, L.H. The social dimensions of a twelve man jury table. *Sociometry*, 1961, 24, 397–415.

Sundstrom, E., Burt, R., and Kamp, D. Privacy at work: architectural correlates of job satisfaction and job performance. *Academy of Management Journal*, 1980, 23,1, 101–117.

Swain, A. Design of industrial jobs a worker can and will do. *Human Factors*, 1973, 15, 2, 129–136.

Szilagyi, A., and Holland, W. Changes in social density: relationships with functional interaction and perceptions of job characteristics, role stress, and work satisfaction. *Journal of Applied Psychology*, 1980, 65, 1, 28–33.

Taylor, F. *Principles of Scientific Management*. New York: Harper and Row, 1911.

Theodorson, G. (ed.). *Studies in Human Ecology*. New York: Harper and Row, 1961.

Thompson, J. *Organizations in Action*. New York: McGraw-Hill, 1967.

Trist, E., and Bamforth, K. Some social and psychological consequences of the Longwall methods of coal-getting. *Human Relations*, 1951, *4*, 3–38.

Tyler, M. Productivity and telecommunications. Presentation at Conference on Telecommunications and Productivity, Center for Science and Technology Policy, New York University, January 1980, 29–30.

Tyler, M. Transportation, energy, and information: some opportunities for conservation policy. In R.S. Fazzolare and C.B. Smith (eds.), *Energy Use Management*. London: Pergammon Press, 1977.

Vail, H. The automated office. *The Futurist*, 1978, *XII*, 2, 73–78.

Van der Ryn, S., and Silverstein, M. *Dorms at Berkeley*. Berkeley: University of California Center for Planning and Development Research, 1967.

Vollmer, H. and Mills, D. *Professionalization*. Englewood Cliffs, N.J.: Prentice-Hall, 1966.

Walker, C., and Guest, R. *The Man On the Assembly Line*. Cambridge, Mass.: Harvard University Press, 1952.

Weick, K. *The Social Psychology of Organizing*. Reading, Mass.: Addison-Wesley, 1969.

Weinstein, C. The physical environment of the school: a review of the research. *Review of Educational Research*, 1979, *49*, 4, 577–610.

Weiss, C. Research for policy's sake: the enlightenment function of social research. *Policy Analysis*, 1977, *3*, 531–545.

Weitz, S. (ed.). *Nonverbal Communication*. New York: Oxford University Press, 1974.

Wells, B. Individual differences in environmental response. In H. Proshansky, W. Ittelson, and L. Rivlin (eds.), *Environmental Psychology*, New York: Holt, Rinehart and Winston, 1970.

Whyte, W. F. *Human Relations in the Restaurant Industry*. New York: McGraw-Hill, 1948.

Whyte, W.F. *Money and Motivation*. New York: Harper and Row, 1955.

Wicker, A. *An Introduction to Ecological Psychology*. Monterey, Calif.: Brooks/Cole, 1979.

Wicker, A. Ecological psychology: some recent and prospective developments. *American Psychologist*, 1979, *34*, 9, 755–764.

Williams, E.P. Forces toward participation in behavior settings. In R.G. Barker and P.V. Gump (eds.), *Big School, Small School: High School Size and Student Behavior*. Stanford, Calif.: Stanford University Press, 1964.

Williams, L. Management and personnel issues in office design. Talk given to Department of Design and Environmental Analysis, College of Human Ecology, Cornell University, Ithaca, January 1980.

Work in America. Report of a special task force to the Secretary of Health, Education, and Welfare. Cambridge, Mass.: MIT Press, 1973.

Zeisel, J. Negotiating a shared community image. *Ekistics*, 1976, *42*, 251, 224–227.

Zifferblatt, S.M. Architecture and human behavior: toward increased understanding of a functional relationship. *Educational Technology*, 1972, *12*, 8, 54–57.

Zlutnick, S. and Altman, I. Crowding and human behavior. In J.F. Wohlwill and D.H. Carson (eds.), *Environment and Social Sciences: Perspectives and Applications*. Washington, D.C.: American Psychological Association, 1972.

INDEX

absenteeism, 26, 86; effect of organizational size on, 122

activities: affected by work in the home, 191, 193–195, 196–197, 199–200, framework for assessing, 102–103

Adams, R., 113

administrators: as space managers, 168–170 (*see also* programming, planning, design process)

Aldous, J., 180

alienation, 69

Altman, I., 110, 154

ambiguity, 25–26; definition of, 41; in design of physical settings, 40; in design process, 41–45; and environmental scale, 52–55, and informations, 40, 41–45, and personal resources, 46–48; in relation to stability and flexibility, 40–41, 51–52; rules governing use, 44–45; social and organizational constraints on, 48–49; under what conditions, 49–52

Anifant, D. C., 114

Arauz, C., 118

architects: orientation to built environment, 8 (*see also* design process, programming, planning)

Ashby, W.R., 26, 53

Ashworth, S., 179

assumption mapping, 163

attention processes: in design process, 24–25, 32, and the experienced environment, 36–37; and information transformations, 57; as management responsibility, 37, and perception of the environment, 41, and personal characteristics, 32–34; and predicting outcomes, 90–91; and social context, 34–36; as social process, 32, and time/use patterns, 27–32 (*see also* design process)

authority function (*see* ordering principles)

Babchuk, N., 82

Bales, R., 113

Bamforth, K., 75

Barker, R., 90, 122, 125, 127, 128

Bateson, G., 99

Bauer, R., 22, 31, 184

Beck, W., 77

Becker, F. D., 8, 16, 23, 24, 35, 48, 56, 83, 85, 99, 101, 154, 165, 179, 197

Becker, S., 87

behavior setting, 126–127

behavioral environment, 18

Bell, A.E., 120

Bell, D., 77

Berg, I., 86, 120

Bergermaier, R., 86, 120

Berkowitz, L., 105

Bienstock, P., 51, 153

Blauner, R., 31, 61, 69, 70

bounded predictability, 92–93

Boutourline, 2

Bowlus, L., 196

Boyce, P.R., 106, 108

Brass, D., 56, 85, 100, 104, 105, 106, 139, 150

Braverman, H., 61, 62, 63, 64, 65, 66, 80

Brookes, M.J., 59, 85, 106, 111, 146

Brunetti, F.A., 114

building codes: (*see* standards)

built environment: (*see* environment)

Burt, R., 56

Bush-Brown, L., 154

Byrne, D., 118

Campbell, D., 105

Canty, D., 23, 67, 68

Cave, C., 58

change: response to environmental change, 172–173 (*see also* design process, planning, programming)

Chapman, L., 105

Cherlin, D., 115

ABOUT THE AUTHOR

FRANKLIN D. BECKER is Associate Professor of Human-Environment Relations in the College of Human Ecology, Cornell University. He has taught previously at the Graduate School of Design at Harvard University as a Visiting Associate Professor.

Dr. Becker has published widely in the area of environmental psychology. His articles have appeared in the *Journal of Personality and Social Psychology*, *Environment and Behavior*, and the *Journal of Nonverbal Behavior*. He is the author of a number of monographs and a book, *Housing Messages*.

Dr. Becker holds a B.A. from the University of California at Davis, a M.A. from Boston University, and a Ph.D. in environmental and social psychology from the University of California, Davis, California.